Chemical Product Law and Supply Chain Stewardship

A GUIDE TO NEW TSCA

LYNN L. BERGESON, EDITOR

ABA
AMERICAN BAR ASSOCIATION
Environment, Energy, and Resources Section

Cover design by Mary Anne Kulchawik/ABA Design

Printed in the United States of America.

29 28 27 26 25 5 4 3 2 1

ISBN 978-1-63905-559-3

Contents

Note to Readers

This book was tendered to the American Bar Association for processing for publication on July 1, 2024. The U.S. Environmental Protection Agency's (EPA's) implementation of TSCA as amended by the Frank R. Lautenberg Chemical Safety for the 21st Century Act is ongoing and will be for years to come. We have included EPA implementing actions as of this date but, of course, rulemakings and other initiatives occurring after this date are not included.

Acknowledgement

The authors wish to thank Allison MacDougall Davidson and Paula M. Bérard for their relentless pursuit of perfection and tireless efforts in preparing this book for publication.

About the Editor

Lynn L. Bergeson is managing partner of Bergeson & Campbell, P.C. (B&C®), a law firm based in Washington, D.C., that concentrates on conventional, nanoscale, and biobased industrial, agricultural, product approval and regulation, product defense, and associated business issues. Ms. Bergeson is also president of The Acta Group (Acta®), B&C's scientific and regulatory consulting arm, with offices in the United States, the United Kingdom, and China, and president of B&C® Consortia Management, L.L.C. (BCCM), which helps the chemical industry achieve shared research, testing, regulatory, and access goals. Ms. Bergeson is one of the most experienced and admired attorneys practicing in chemical and pesticide regulatory work today. Ms. Bergeson served as chair of the American Bar Association Section of Environment, Energy, and Resources; was president of the Product Stewardship Society Board of Directors; is a regent and fellow of the American College of Environmental Lawyers (ACOEL); and is chair of the International Bar Association, Agriculture and Food Section, among many other leadership roles. She graduated magna cum laude from Michigan State University (B.A.), and the Columbus School of Law, Catholic University of America, where she was a member of the Law Review. She is admitted to the bar of the District of Columbia, the U.S. District Court for the District of Columbia, and the U.S. Courts of Appeals for the Ninth Circuit and the District of Columbia Circuit.

About the Authors

Lisa R. Burchi is of counsel with Bergeson & Campbell, P.C. (B&C®). Ms. Burchi delivers more than 25 years of experience assisting companies with Toxic Substances Control Act (TSCA) regulatory compliance, including import and export requirements; TSCA audits, including training and development of standard operating procedures; and representing companies responding to enforcement matters. Ms. Burchi also counsels on matters related to California law, including Proposition 65 (Prop 65) and Safer Consumer Products Regulations. She graduated cum laude from Tufts University (B.A.) and received her J.D. from George Washington University's National Law Center. Ms. Burchi is admitted to the bars of the District of Columbia and California.

Richard E. Engler, Ph.D. is B&C's director of chemistry. Dr. Engler is a 17-year veteran of the U.S. Environmental Protection Agency (EPA) and is one of the most widely recognized experts in the field of green chemistry, having served as senior staff scientist in EPA's Office of Pollution Prevention and Toxics and leader of EPA's Green Chemistry Program. Dr. Engler's expansive understanding of the TSCA review process is invaluable to companies wishing to develop and commercialize sustainable, renewable, and other novel chemistries. He graduated with honors from Haverford College (B.S., chemistry) and received his Ph.D. in physical organic chemistry from the University of California, San Diego.

Kelly N. Garson is a senior associate with B&C. Ms. Garson developed her skills in handling regulatory matters at the local, state, and federal levels through an impressive track record of clerkships and internships, including positions with the EPA Office of Enforcement and Compliance Assurance; the U.S. Department of Justice, Environment and Natural Resources Division; and the New York State Department of Environmental Conservation. Ms. Garson holds a J.D. from the George Washington University Law School and degrees in history and environmental studies from Binghamton University,

State University of New York. Ms. Garson is admitted to the bars of the District of Columbia and New York state, and the U.S. Courts of Appeals for the Ninth Circuit and the District of Columbia Circuit.

Carla N. Hutton is a regulatory analyst with B&C. Ms. Hutton brings a wealth of experience and judgment to her work in federal, state, and international chemical regulatory and legislative issues, and has for more than 25 years monitored, researched, and written about regulatory and legislative issues that may affect chemical industry stakeholders. Ms. Hutton's areas of expertise include industrial chemicals, agricultural chemicals, metals, nanotechnology, and biobased and other emerging chemical technologies. She graduated with honors from the University of Pennsylvania (B.A.) and received her J.D. from Washington College of Law.

Todd J. Stedeford, Ph.D. is of counsel with B&C. He delivers exceptional legal acumen and scientific experience developed over a 20-year career spanning international laboratory research; corporate and federal legal appointments; industry health, safety, and environment (HS&E) positions; and scientific leadership of U.S. federal agencies. Dr. Stedeford is a Diplomate of the American Board of Toxicology (DABT®), a European Registered Toxicologist (ERT), a fellow of the Academy of Toxicological Sciences (ATS), and a member of the bars of the District of Columbia and the state of New York. He holds a Ph.D. in toxicology and risk assessment from the University of South Florida and a J.D. from the Levin College of Law, University of Florida.

Introduction

Lynn L. Bergeson

Products of all sorts—electronics, consumer goods, textiles and apparel, furniture, sporting equipment, appliances, and many more—are all derivative of chemicals. Everything we like, use, cannot live without, purchase, and rely upon started as a new chemical innovation and ended as the sum of dozens or thousands of chemical components in the form of a finished good. Most people understandably do not think of chemicals when using their iPhones, but this ubiquitous product started as a chemical creation. Like many finished products, several steps along the way of its development and distribution are subject to federal regulation under the Toxic Substances Control Act (TSCA).

Long thought of as a quirky, obscure federal law with limited application to entities beyond manufacturers of pure or "neat" chemicals, TSCA has jurisdictional reach and relevance to the business community that are anything but "limited"—and are only expanding. TSCA's metamorphosis from idiosyncratic and discrete to game-changing and extensive is profoundly important and must be understood by product innovators, investors, insurers, manufacturers, importers and exporters, and businesspeople of all stripes in the United States and beyond. Failure to do so could result in catastrophic business decisions and failed businesses.

The linchpin of this amazing metamorphosis is the 2016 collection of amendments to TSCA brought about by enactment of the Frank R. Lautenberg Chemical Safety for the 21st Century Act (Lautenberg) and the U.S. Environmental Protection Agency's (EPA's) implementation of this sweeping federal law. As this book describes, Lautenberg greatly enhanced EPA's authority under TSCA to regulate chemicals, and EPA's expansive implementation of Lautenberg has insinuated TSCA's reach into commercial transactions in fundamentally new, unexpected, and transformative ways.

Based on our many years of TSCA practice, we decided to write this book to ensure that, regardless of legal training, stakeholders in the business community—whether a start-up or a mature business, an investor or insurer, a chief executive officer (CEO), board member, compliance officer, or employee of a product manufacturer—understand exactly how TSCA's expanding jurisdictional relevance applies to a growing number of what we refer to as "nontraditional" TSCA stakeholders. You and your business may well be part of this community, and failure to know how TSCA impacts your business can invite significant adverse and business-derailing legal consequences.

The goal of this book is to provide those in the business community with an understanding of TSCA so they can make informed business decisions. Businesspeople throughout today's supply chain—not merely lawyers and compliance advisors—need to understand TSCA's growing commercial relevance and application over chemicals and manufactured goods produced both domestically and abroad. TSCA affects business decisions from choice of raw materials to whether a manufacturing operation should be located domestically or abroad, what materials and/or products can or should be imported, how to assess the compositional elements of a product, and much more. We seek to answer these questions from a business transactions perspective rather than an academic or overly legalistic perspective. In other words, this book does not assume the readers understand what TSCA is and how it applies; it assumes the readers know the complexities of their own businesses but may not be aware that TSCA applies or could apply to their business decisions.

We start by providing a history of "old" TSCA, which, remarkably, remained largely unchanged from its enactment in 1976 until 2016. This history is needed to contextualize "new" TSCA (post-Lautenberg) and how the complex social, scientific, and legal cross-currents then in play converged in 2016 and facilitated Lautenberg's enactment. This review includes a brief synopsis of the European Union's (EU's) enactment of the Registration, Evaluation, Authorisation and Restriction of Chemicals (REACH) regulation, Europe's equivalent of TSCA, and how its approach to chemical management differs from TSCA. REACH regulates chemicals based on their inherent hazard, and not the risk they pose; "risk" is the result of exposure plus hazard. The proliferation of REACH-like statutes globally, the ascendance of state chemical initiatives, the maturation of "product" laws, and the explosive growth of consumer interest in chemical exposures all contributed to a growing consensus by stakeholders that TSCA was not able to ensure chemical safety.

We next provide a broad overview of how TSCA works. This overview is geared toward the law's application to businesspeople and business transactions. As we note above, this once-discrete federal law now applies to an extremely diverse and growing range of businesses and business transactions in the manufacturing sector and beyond. Unless you know, or have reason to believe, your business transactions are exempt from TSCA, your commercial operation may be noncompliant, exposing it to fines and significant commercial disruption. A key goal of this book is to provide readers with the knowledge necessary to avoid this result.

Next, we explain how entities that are deemed "importers of record" of finished commercial goods are, under TSCA, considered de facto manufacturers of the chemicals, and how EPA has targeted certain chemicals for TSCA restriction, even in finished commercial goods. Importers of record are the entities that pay the custom duty and manage the imports. To many unfamiliar with TSCA, it is bewildering to learn that import of a finished good that contains a chemical component, often regardless of how much of that chemical is present, can result in the importer's change of status under TSCA from that of an "importer" of a finished good (or "article," in the vernacular of TSCA) to that of a "chemical manufacturer" of the chemical component embedded in the product. To many businesspeople, it is counterintuitive to consider an importer of computers (an article), for example, as a chemical manufacturer merely because EPA has targeted for restriction a chemical component embedded in the computer. Yet, under TSCA, the importer of the computer is considered a manufacturer of the targeted chemical, and the importer is responsible for TSCA compliance for the chemical components that their imported articles contain.

We next explore the processes EPA employs to evaluate "new" chemical innovations, which are newly commercialized and altogether new uses of "existing" chemicals that have been in commercial use for decades. This explanation is followed by an overview of EPA's risk evaluation and assessment processes. A general understanding of the concept of "unreasonable risk" as defined by TSCA is essential to make informed business decisions. An EPA determination that your chemical or a critical product on which your business depends is found by EPA to pose unreasonable risk invites serious legal, commercial, and optical challenges. We explain these concepts through the lens of business transactions, avoiding the scientific and legal jargon that may not successfully convey to everyone TSCA's application in the business world.

If, for example, you work for an investment firm and are preparing to make a sizable Series A investment in a promising chemical technology, you should have a general understanding of the factors that EPA will be required by TSCA to consider in evaluating that chemical technology's potential to pose an unreasonable risk. If the anticipated uses of that new chemical technology are determined to pose what EPA defines as an "unreasonable risk," EPA is required under TSCA to implement restrictions that abate those risks. These restrictions can diminish or erase entirely the commercial potential of that new chemical innovation. EPA's protracted reviews and lengthy regulatory processes are likely to delay the opportunity for generating revenue, and factoring these realities into the planning process is essential from a business perspective. Failure to know, and thus engineer around, these potentially catastrophic commercial limitations can make or break a business, and thus dictate the wisdom of an investment in that business.

An important and often overlooked area of the law is the role TSCA plays in the due diligence that accompanies business transactions like divestitures, acquisitions, and related commercial transactions. Despite the outsized importance TSCA compliance has in any transactions involving an entity in the manufacturing sector, TSCA is often either overlooked completely or given inadequate attention. TSCA fines may not be as substantial as other potential financial liabilities, but if, for example, an acquisition target is operating out of compliance with TSCA, an acquiring company may find itself in a position to have to cease entirely the commercial activity while the acquisition target company completes the actions necessary to achieve compliance. In this book, we identify commonly overlooked areas of transactions in the TSCA realm and offer checklists and other tools to assist in the due diligence process.

We next discuss the growing number of limitations on chemicals defined as per- and polyfluoroalkyl substances (PFAS). We appreciate that some PFAS are appropriately regulated and deserving of careful review and restriction. Not all PFAS are harmful, however, and EPA recognizes that the properties and functionalities of PFAS meeting TSCA's stringent standards can be commercialized. Our focus in this book is on the regulation of PFAS under TSCA, the limitations that EPA applies to PFAS, and business strategies that might be considered in supporting existing and commercializing new PFAS substances, despite the widespread demonization to which this class of substances is subject.

We conclude with a review of what EPA is authorized to do in cases of noncompliance. EPA's authority under TSCA is considerable. EPA can shut down a business, deny approval of a critically essential component of a product (thus preventing commercial production), impose massive multimillion-dollar penalties, assert violations that can irreparably damage a company's brand and reputation, throw you in jail (for willful violations), and much, much more. Chemicals are risky business, and when it comes to enforcement, EPA means business and takes its enforcement responsibilities seriously in this realm.

In addition to these chapters, we offer a useful glossary of TSCA terms, checklists to help your business comply with TSCA and be successful, and various templates of business documents involved in TSCA compliance to help make the journey easier.

1

Old TSCA and the Forces That Led to Its Revitalization

Lynn L. Bergeson

Key Messages

- TSCA was part of a new wave of environmental legislation that arose in the 1970s.
- By the 1990s, TSCA was widely believed by all stakeholders to be ineffective and broken.
- The lack of a viable federal law regulating chemicals invited state laws and chemical product initiatives that increasingly interfered with interstate commerce.
- Public health activists and NGOs successfully weaponized TSCA's weaknesses and galvanized the consumer community to be increasingly distrustful of TSCA's ability to ensure chemical safety.
- The EU's new and precautionary REACH regulation offered a sharp contrast to TSCA, further eroding the public's confidence in the federal government's ability to assure chemical safety.

- All of these forces coalesced to enable Lautenberg's enactment in 2016, ushering in a new and more formidable federal chemical law.

The Toxic Substances Control Act (TSCA)[1] is not top of mind for most businesspeople, or even their lawyers. It has a long tradition of being thought of as a quirky federal law with relatively specialized applications, chiefly to large companies that manufacture chemicals, and limited relevance beyond. Some explanation is needed to understand TSCA's origins, its culture, and why the business community has been challenged to accept TSCA's ubiquitous relevance to commercial transactions today.

The Frank R. Lautenberg Chemical Safety for the 21st Century Act (Lautenberg),[2] or "new TSCA," as it is often called, emerged from the coalescence of several forces that had been gaining momentum over the decades before 2016, the year of Lautenberg's enactment. These include a shared recognition by diverse chemical stakeholders that "old TSCA" was structurally flawed and incapable of commanding the public's confidence that it could ensure chemical safety, a federal appellate ruling that eviscerated the U.S. Environmental Protection Agency's (EPA's) ability to ban uses of chemicals deemed to pose unreasonable risk, the European Union's (EU's) modernization of its chemicals management law and the unflattering comparison with old TSCA that the new EU law created, a proliferation of state chemical initiatives threatening to undermine interstate commercial transactions, and a growing and vocal coalition of states, public health activists, and nongovernmental organizations (NGOs) demanding change. The convergence of these potent domestic forces, coupled with an emerging global regulatory dynamic favoring enhanced chemical "product" regulation, helped get new TSCA over the legislative goal line.

1. 15 U.S.C. §§ 2601–2697. (References to the act in this book are based on U.S. Code (U.S.C.) version of the act, https://uscode.house.gov/browse/prelim@title15/chapter53&edition=prelim.)
2. Frank R. Lautenberg Chemical Safety for the 21st Century Act, Pub. L. No. 114-182, 130 Stat. 448 (2016), https://www.congress.gov/114/plaws/publ182/PLAW-114publ182.pdf.

1.1 TSCA's Beginning

TSCA was first enacted in 1976 after growing congressional concern with multiple high-profile incidents involving chemicals and a keen congressional awareness that existing and emerging federal law regulated chemicals only after they become pollutants.[3] Chemical manufacturing had increased significantly after World War II,[4] and by the 1970s, the United States was experiencing an extraordinarily active period of legislation focusing on environmental protection. The Clean Air Act (CAA) was adopted in 1970,[5] the Clean Water Act (CWA) in 1972,[6] and the Resource Conservation and Recovery Act (RCRA) in 1976,[7] the same year as TSCA.

Select U.S. Chemical Regulatory Laws: Timeline of Enactment

1938	**Federal Food, Drug, and Cosmetic Act (FFDCA)**
1947	**Federal Insecticide, Fungicide, and Rodenticide Act (FIFRA)**
1970	**Clean Air Act**
1972	**Clean Water Act**
1976	**Resource Conservation and Recovery Act (RCRA)**
1976	**Toxic Substances Control**

Figure 1.1. Timeline of enactment of select U.S. chemical regulatory laws

3. David L. Markell, *An Overview of TSCA, Its History and Key Underlying Assumptions, and Its Place in Environmental Regulation*, 32, Wash. U. J. L. & Pol'y 333 (2010).
4. *See WWII and the Rise of Petrochemicals (1941–1959)*, DOW, https://corporate.dow.com/en-us/about/company/history/timeline/wwii-and-the-rise-of-petrochemicals.html (last visited Sept. 27, 2024); Hillary S. Kativa, *It's a Mad, Mad World: Dow and the Age of Consumption*, Distillations Mag. (Sept. 23, 2015), https://www.sciencehistory.org/stories/magazine/its-a-mad-mad-world-dow-and-the-age-of-consumption/.
5. 42 U.S.C. §§ 7401–7675.
6. 33 U.S.C. §§ 1251–1389.
7. 42 U.S.C. §§ 6901–6992k.

Debate about "toxic substances" had begun years earlier. The Council on Environmental Quality (CEQ), for example, issued a report in 1971[8] outlining the country's societal challenges posed by chemicals, including their introduction into the environment, their capacity to cause adverse human health and environmental effects, the limitations of existing legal authorities addressing injury posed by chemical exposure, and the need for new legal authority.[9] The idea of TSCA was premised in part on Congress's intention to empower the federal government to control the production, processing, distribution, and export of chemical substances and to ensure a new federal mandate worked in tandem with other federal environmental laws to protect human health and the environment.[10] Enactment and implementation of the CWA and the CAA increasingly revealed that these laws were deployed late in the life cycle of manufactured chemicals. These laws applied only after chemicals had been released into the environment in the form of stack or fugitive air emissions, pollutants in direct and indirect water discharges, and solid and hazardous wastes at the point of discard. These regulatory measures, referred to as end-of-pipe controls, were necessary but insufficient if, as Congress desired, the federal government were successful at assessing chemicals earlier in their life cycles to prevent harm to human health and the environment.[11] Congress intended TSCA to fill this regulatory gap and assess chemicals upstream of their distribution, use, and discharge as pollutants.[12]

TSCA's legislative history confirms that Congress intended TSCA's reach to be exceedingly broad. Under TSCA, EPA is authorized to regulate the import, manufacture, and processing of "chemical substances."[13] Congress intentionally defined "chemical substances"

8. CEQ, Toxic Substances (Apr. 1971), *reprinted in* Environmental and Natural Resources Policy Division, Legislative History of the Toxic Substances Control Act 757 (1976).
9. *Id.* at 759–60.
10. TSCA § 2, 15 U.S.C. § 2601.
11. *See* Markell, *supra* note 3, at 344 (citing testimony of John Quarles, then-EPA deputy administrator, in testimony before Congress, that most existing federal authorities are designed to prevent harmful exposures only after the substances have been introduced into production).
12. TSCA §§ 2(b)(1), 4–13, 15 U.S.C. §§ 2601(b)(1), 2603–2612.
13. TSCA §§ 2(c), 3(1)–(2), 15 U.S.C. §§ 2601(c), 2602(1)–(2) (defining "chemical substance" as "any organic or inorganic substance of a particular molecular identity, including—(i) any combination of such substances occurring in whole or in part as a result of a chemical reaction or occurring in nature, and (ii) any element or uncombined radical").

expansively to include *any* "organic or inorganic substance of a particular molecular identity."[14] Given the breadth of the definition, it is reasonable to assume that all chemical substances are regulated under TSCA unless specifically excluded. Congress intended TSCA to apply to chemicals not regulated under another federal law.[15] Chemicals used for pesticidal purposes, for example, are regulated by EPA under the Federal Insecticide, Fungicide, and Rodenticide Act (FIFRA), a law dating back to the 1940s.[16] Similarly, chemicals used as drugs, food, food additives, or cosmetics are regulated by the U.S. Food and Drug Administration (FDA) under the Federal Food, Drug, and Cosmetic Act (FFDCA), which dates back to 1938.[17] Other chemicals not subject to TSCA include nuclear materials regulated by the Nuclear Regulatory Commission under the Atomic Energy Act,[18] and tobacco or tobacco products.[19] In short, if a company makes chemicals, imports chemicals or products that contain chemicals, distributes chemicals, or uses chemicals to produce products, TSCA likely applies. Only if any of these other federal laws apply instead will TSCA not be applicable. This has always been the case, but as we will explain, new TSCA and EPA's expansive policies under it are directly applicable to many more businesses and business transactions than ever before.

1.2 Shortcomings in Old TSCA

Despite Congress's good intentions in enacting TSCA in 1976, the law was hampered from the start by its lack of a clear legislative mandate requiring EPA to prioritize, evaluate, and regulate the then 62,000-plus existing chemicals in commerce that were "grandfathered" in under TSCA. While the law was crystal clear that Congress intended EPA to regulate new and existing chemicals, have sufficient information about chemicals to inform its judgment in assessing them, and

14. TSCA § 3(2)(A), 15 U.S.C. § 2602(2)(A).
15. *See generally* TSCA § 9, 15 U.S.C. § 2608.
16. *See generally* 7 U.S.C. §§ 136–136y.
17. *See generally* 21 U.S.C. §§ 301–392.
18. *See generally* 42 U.S.C. §§ 2011–2296b-7.
19. A chemical substance is regulated under any number of federal laws, the relevance of which are determined by use. A chemical can be regulated by TSCA, FIFRA, and/or the FFDCA, depending upon the use, but not at the same time.

regulate chemicals found to pose unreasonable risk of injury to human health and the environment, TSCA was silent as to how to achieve these goals. The aspirational goal of chemical safety has always been clear; the how-to-do-it part, not so much.

TSCA's more well-documented and much publicized shortcomings were identified by the U.S. Government Accountability Office (GAO) in 2013.[20] Among the most debilitating limitations were EPA's limited ability to compel chemical testing and EPA's truncated authority to regulate existing chemicals because of the "least burdensome" language in TSCA section 6(a)[21] and its judicial construction under *Corrosion Proof Fittings*.[22]

Congress intended TSCA to apply to both "existing" chemicals—those actively used and distributed in commerce in the late 1970s—and to "new" chemicals, meaning those introduced into commerce after the original TSCA Chemical Substance Inventory (TSCA Inventory) was created in 1978.[23] As noted, the 62,000-plus existing chemicals in commerce were grandfathered in, meaning the chemicals were "covered" under TSCA, but were not subject to any EPA review or risk evaluation as a condition of continued commercialization. The law required no such review, nor did EPA provide any regulatory mechanism to undertake even a cursory assessment. This status of "existing" chemicals unfortunately gave rise to the misperception that existing chemicals listed on the TSCA Inventory were somehow "approved" by EPA. Rather, it simply meant these chemicals were in commerce when TSCA was enacted, regardless of the risk they posed, and grandfathered in to permit their continued production and use. This allowed manufacturing processes to develop and complicated chemical supply chains to evolve over the decades since 1976, largely unfettered by EPA inquiry into whether these "existing" chemical substances might pose risks to human health or the environment.

---

20. *See, e.g.*, GAO, GAO-13-696T, Chemical Regulation: Observations on the Toxic Substances Control Act and EPA Implementation (2013), https://www.gao.gov/products/gao-13-696t.
21. 15 U.S.C. § 2605(a).
22. Corrosion Proof Fittings v. EPA, 947 F.2d 1201 (5th Cir. 1991), https://law.justia.com/cases/federal/appellate-courts/F2/947/1201/153685/.
23. EPA, 740R78103, Toxic Substances Control Act (TSCA), PL 94-469: Candidate List of Chemical Substances—Addendum III, Chemical Substances of Unknown or Variable Composition, Complex Reaction Products, and Biological Materials (1978), https://www.epa.gov/nscep (search by using "740R78103").

In the early days of TSCA implementation, back in the late 1970s, EPA's focus was elsewhere and not on assessing and regulating existing chemicals in commerce. EPA had much to do in creating the administrative scaffolding of the TSCA regulatory program. It focused on setting up the TSCA Inventory, developing the "new" chemical review program, writing new rules to develop TSCA's many recordkeeping and data reporting provisions under section 8, developing import and export requirements, and addressing related provisions to implement the then-new law. New chemicals, unlike existing chemicals, were subject to premarket review by EPA and could not be manufactured. Under TSCA, "manufacturing" is defined to include import or processing for commercial purpose without prior EPA approval. "New" is defined under both iterations of TSCA as any chemical not listed on the TSCA Inventory being manufactured for a commercial purpose and not otherwise exempt.[24] EPA had plenty to keep it busy, and the regulation of existing chemicals was not a priority.

EPA's most high-profile foray into reviewing an existing chemical involved asbestos, identified as an extremely toxic chemical long before 1976.[25] In 1989, EPA issued a final rule under TSCA section 6 (the provision of the law authorizing EPA to regulate and even ban uses of a chemical substance found to pose unreasonable risk) seeking to ban the manufacture, import, and processing of nearly all asbestos-containing products manufactured in the United States.[26] The rule was judicially challenged in the U.S. Court of Appeals for the Fifth Circuit in *Corrosion Proof Fittings* and set aside. The court determined that EPA failed to consider adequately potential regulatory measures less burdensome than a ban to abate the unreasonable risks EPA determined asbestos posed. The court concluded that EPA must consider substitute products and must support the claimed benefits of the proposed rule by evaluating the toxicity of these substitute products. The court let stand only those narrow portions of the final rule that banned manufacture or importation of asbestos for new uses.

24. TSCA § 3(10)–(11), 15 U.S.C. § 2602(10)–(11).
25. P.W.J. Bartrip, *History of Asbestos Related Disease*, 80 Postgraduate Med. J. 72, 72–76 (2004), https://www.ncbi.nlm.nih.gov/pmc/articles/PMC1742940/pdf/v080p00072.pdf; *EPA Actions to Protect the Public from Exposure to Asbestos*, EPA, https://www.epa.gov/asbestos/epa-actions-protect-public-exposure-asbestos (last updated Mar. 18, 2024).
26. Asbestos; Manufacture, Importation, Processing, and Distribution in Commerce Prohibitions, 54 Fed. Reg. 29,460 (July 12, 1989).

The legal impact of *Corrosion Proof Fittings* was devastating to EPA's authority to regulate asbestos and other existing chemicals. The ruling also delivered a near-fatal blow to TSCA's ability to ban uses of chemicals EPA identified as posing unreasonable risks. The court's judicial determination that EPA must find and evaluate the "least burdensome" alternative to control an unreasonable risk imposed an impossibly heavy burden on EPA. Many believed that EPA could never meet this legal standard.[27] The decision effectively ended EPA's administrative efforts to ban existing chemicals.[28] EPA unsuccessfully tried to ban under TSCA section 6 acrylamide and N-methylolacrylamide grout. The ban would have been precedent-setting in that it relied entirely on occupational exposures to support a TSCA section 6 ban. The rule was never issued in final.

The optical and public relations impacts of the decision were even more profound. The thought rampant in the court of public opinion was if EPA could not ban uses of asbestos—a chemical notorious for causing well-recognized adverse health effects—what could it ban? TSCA was widely perceived[29] after *Corrosion Proof Fittings* as being critically flawed and ineffective in controlling unreasonable risks from existing chemicals. The decision also dealt a terrible blow to the public's confidence in TSCA as an effective tool to ensure chemical safety. To many in the chemical industry, the decision marked the beginning of the end of TSCA as a federal law that could be taken seriously.

1.3 International Initiatives

While in the United States EPA was struggling with implementing TSCA and fighting a losing battle in convincing the public that chemicals were safe, the EU was busy updating and strengthening its chemical control programs. Concern with chemical exposures has long been at the forefront of EU regulatory focus. The "precautionary

27. *See, e.g.*, *Oversight of EPA Authorities and Actions to Control Exposures to Toxic Chemicals: Hearing before S. Comm. on Env't and Pub. Works*, 112th Cong. (2012) (testimony of William K. Rawson, Partner, Latham & Watkins) [hereinafter Rawson Testimony] ("I will first address the failed effort to ban uses of asbestos, which has been cited as evidence that the evidentiary burden EPA must meet under section 6 is too high.").
28. *See* Proposed Ban on Acrylamide and N-methylolacrylamide Grouts, 56 Fed. Reg. 49,863 (Oct. 2, 1991).
29. *See* Rawson Testimony, *supra* note 27, at 4 ("Nevertheless, I acknowledge that there has been an erosion of public confidence in TSCA . . . .").

principle" is a foundational concept underlying the EU's approach to governing policies relating to environmental health and food safety. It first emerged in the 1970s and has since been incorporated in several international treaties on the environment, in the Treaty on the Functioning of the European Union,[30] and the national legislation of certain member states. Article 191(2) of the Treaty on the Functioning of the European Union provides that all EU policy on the environment shall be based on the precautionary principle, which aims to ensure a higher level of environmental protection through preventive decision-making in the case of risk. The principle's application was extended to health and safety policy in 2000.

Core to the precautionary principle is the belief that risk prevention is essential in the face of scientific uncertainty. The principle is controversial. To some, it is a logical response to the absence of scientific certainty. To others, particularly to the non-EU community, it lacks grounding in science and discourages innovation.

The EU had been considering its approach to chemical management for years before the European Parliament and the Council enacted a groundbreaking new law on December 18, 2006. The law, titled the Registration, Evaluation, Authorisation and Restriction of Chemicals (REACH), came into force on June 1, 2007.[31] REACH is the functional equivalent in the EU to TSCA. Under REACH, the chemical manufacturer and/or importer bears the responsibility for evaluating the use-specific risks posed by a chemical, new or existing, and producing data to support the determination that a chemical is safe for its intended uses. Under old TSCA, the reverse was true. EPA had the burden of proving an existing chemical posed an unreasonable risk, and *Corrosion Proof Fittings* made that burden impossibly difficult for EPA to support.

REACH is premised on the precautionary principle and is hazard-based, unlike TSCA, which is risk-based. Under REACH, new and existing chemicals require registration if they are manufactured or imported into the EU in quantities of one ton per year or more, unless the substance is exempt.[32] The registration requirements apply to neat

30. *See* Consolidated Version of the Treaty on the Functioning of the European Union, 2016 O.J. (C 202) 47, https://eur-lex.europa.eu/legal-content/EN/TXT/?uri=CELEX:12016E/TXT.
31. Regulation (EC) No. 1907/2006 of the European Parliament and of the Council of 18 December 2006 concerning the Registration, Evaluation, Authorisation and Restriction of Chemicals (REACH), 2006 O.J. (L 396) 1.
32. *Id.*

(pure) chemicals, chemicals in mixtures, and chemicals in articles when the chemicals are intended to be released under normal or reasonably foreseeable conditions of use. Registration requires data, and data requirements increase with the volume of chemical produced or imported each year. In other words, higher volumes of chemical substances (substances manufactured or imported in quantities of ten metric tons per year or more) require more data (regardless of exposure) and the preparation of a chemical safety report, among other requirements, as a predicate to registration.

Since REACH was enacted in 2006, other countries have opted to adopt chemical control laws based on it—and notably *not* based on TSCA. Versions of REACH are in effect in Turkey,[33] South Korea,[34] China,[35] and India.[36] REACH's enactment in the EU, and the "REACH-creep" that has occurred since, was a major impetus for calls for chemical reform in the United States. The EU's REACH program quickly became the default gold standard for chemical control legislation and, in comparison, TSCA was increasingly thought to be substandard, especially after *Corrosion Proof Fittings*.

TSCA and TSCA-like risk-based regulations	**REACH** and REACH-like hazard-based regulations
United States	European Union United Kingdom Turkey South Korea China India

Figure 1.2. Risk-based and hazard-based regulatory systems

33. Kimyasalların Kaydı, Değerlendirilmesi, İzni ve Kısıtlanması (referred to as KKDIK). *See Turkish REACH: KKDIK Registration*, Intertek Grp., https://www.intertek.com/assuris/chemicals/regulatory/turkish-reach-kkdik/ (last visited Sept. 27, 2024).
34. Act on the Registration and Evaluation of Chemicals (referred to as K-REACH). *See K-REACH Registration*, CIRS, https://www.cirs-group.com/en/chemicals/k-reach-registration#:~:text=The%20purpose%20of%20K%2DREACH,or%20Notification%20of%20Chemical%20Substances (last visited Sept. 27, 2024).
35. Measures for the Environmental Management Registration of New Chemical Substances (referred to as China REACH). *See New Chemical Substance Registration (China REACH)*, CIRS, https://www.cirs-group.com/en/chemicals/new-chemical-substance-registration-china-reach-mee-order-12(last visited Sept. 27, 2024).
36. Chemicals Management and Safety Rules (referred to as India REACH). *See India REACH Services*, REACHLaw, https://www.reachlaw.fi/india-reach/ (last visited Sept. 27, 2024).

1.4 The Emergence of State Chemical Initiatives

Given the disarray with TSCA and the body blow *Corrosion Proof Fittings* dealt to its ability to ensure chemical safety, public confidence in TSCA was tanking by 2010. Public health professionals, NGOs, and state legislatures were growing increasingly concerned with chemical exposures, their effect on human health, and TSCA's well-documented shortcomings. Scientific developments were also emerging that were capable of detecting chemicals in human bodily fluids.[37] The internet was making information on chemicals and chemical exposures widely and relatively easily available, and its utility fueled the growing interest in knowing more about the chemicals in food, cosmetics, clothing, and other everyday items.[38] The influence of NGOs and public health activism was growing rapidly as early as the 1990s, and state chemical initiatives were emerging at a rapid pace. These developments were fueled by a perception that TSCA was ineffective in ensuring chemical safety.

Several states stand out in enacting game-changing chemical control measures. Disclosure measures came first. California's Proposition 65 (Prop 65), the Safe Drinking Water and Toxic Enforcement Act of 1986, raised consumer chemical awareness to a whole new level. Voted into law by Californians in 1986, Prop 65 requires businesses in that state to provide warnings to Californians about exposures to chemicals that are believed to cause cancer, birth defects, or other reproductive harm. Aside from the legal and commercial implications of the law on businesses in California and others wishing to offer products for sale in California, Prop 65 catalyzed consumer awareness of the prevalence of chemicals in everyday life and in consumer products.

Later, California pioneered adoption of "green chemistry" laws, largely patterned after REACH. In 2008, California enacted legislation that laid the foundation for its "Green Chemistry Initiative," a program intended to identify toxic chemicals in products and replace

---

37. Yoav Y. Broza et al., *Disease Detection with Molecular Biomarkers: From Chemistry of Body Fluids to Nature-Inspired Chemical Sensors*, 119 Chem. Revs. 11761, 11761–817 (2019), https://pubs.acs.org/doi/10.1021/acs.chemrev.9b00437.

38. Sabrina Hartmann & Ursula Klaschka, *Interested Consumers' Awareness of Harmful Chemicals in Everyday Products*, 29 Env't Scis. Eur. 29 (2017), https://www.ncbi.nlm.nih.gov/pmc/articles/PMC5698398/; Tom Neltner, *Consumer Concern about Chemicals in Food Continues to Grow*, Env't Def. Fund (June 6, 2016), https://business.edf.org/insights/consumer-concern-about-chemicals-in-food-continues-to-grow/.

them with chemicals believed to be safer.[39] The statute directs the California Department of Toxic Substances Control (DTSC) to adopt regulations establishing "a process for evaluating chemicals of concern in consumer products, and their potential alternatives, to determine how best to limit exposure or to reduce the level of hazard posed by a chemical of concern."[40] A few years later in 2011, DTSC released a draft of its Safer Consumer Products Regulations, which outline how DTSC intends to implement key mandates contained in the state's Green Chemistry Initiative. DTSC has been identifying chemicals of concern and their replacement for years now.

Washington state has also been a leader in this area. In 2008, it adopted its Children's Safe Products Act.[41] The law requires the state to develop a list of chemicals of "high concern for children" and to identify products or product categories that may contain chemicals of high concern for children. Manufacturers of children's products must provide annual notice to the Washington Department of Ecology disclosing that a product contains a chemical of high concern. Manufacturers must also provide notice to sellers and distributors of these products. Maine adopted a similar law in 2007, seeking to reduce exposure of "chemicals of high concern" in products marketed for children and replace them with safer alternatives.[42]

The diversity and scope of these state measures are too numerous to note here. According to one account, between 2004 and 2010, regulations addressing product manufacturing restrictions, product marketing or distribution measures, end-of-pipe restrictions, and product design requirements grew significantly.[43] All stakeholders appreciated the confounding impact these chemical- and product-specific state initiatives were having on interstate commerce. This trend, perhaps more than any other, was responsible for growing alarm in the industrial chemical sector and incentivized the business community to consider TSCA "modernization" opportunities.

---

39. Hazardous Materials and Toxic Substances Evaluation and Regulation, A.B. 1879 ch. 559, 2007-2008 Leg. (Cal. 2008).
40. *Id.* § 25253.
41. Wash. Rev. Code § 70.240.010 *et seq.*
42. *See* Toxic Chemicals in Children's Products, Me. Rev. Stat. tit. 38, § 1691 *et seq.*
43. *See, e.g.*, Congressional Research Service, R45149, Title I of the Toxic Substances Control Act (TSCA): A Summary of the Statute (2018), https://crsreports.congress.gov/product/pdf/R/R45149/5#:~:text=If%20EPA%20finds%20that%20a,risks%20in%20an%20expedited%20manner; Safer States, 2024 Analysis of State Legislation Addressing Toxic Chemicals and Plastics (2024), https://saferstates.org/wp-content/uploads/Safer-States-2024-Multistate-Analysis.pdf.

1.5 New TSCA

A smattering of legislative initiatives had been introduced over TSCA's decades-long existence. It was not until 2005, when Senator Frank Lautenberg (D-N.J.) introduced the Kid Safe Chemicals Act, that TSCA reform seemed headed for serious consideration.[44] New TSCA had its most significant legislative origins in 2010, when far-reaching measures to fix TSCA were introduced in both houses of Congress.[45] It was not until several years later when Senator David Vitter (R-La.), a strong advocate for the chemical industry and an unexpected champion of chemical reform, joined with Senator Lautenberg shortly before his death in June 2013 that bipartisan legislation was able to emerge. Although it took three years, legislation passed on June 7, 2016, and President Obama signed on June 22, 2016, the Frank R. Lautenberg Chemical Safety for the 21st Century Act.

Lautenberg fundamentally revises TSCA, greatly expands EPA's authority, and addresses many of the shortcomings old TSCA possessed. New TSCA shifts the burden of demonstrating chemical safety—all chemicals, old and new—to chemical manufacturers, processors, and manufacturers of the finished goods that contain them, away from EPA proving the opposite. A quick rundown of key legislative provisions includes:

- Mandating safety reviews for chemicals in commerce
- Eliminating the challenging "least burdensome" requirement for assessment of chemicals in commerce, which for years prevented EPA from taking meaningful action on chemicals in commerce
- Establishing a health-based safety standard and authorizing the consideration of cost in developing risk abatement measures
- Requiring the protection of vulnerable populations, including children and pregnant women
- Limiting the ability of entities to claim information as confidential, thus preventing disclosure, and authorizing the

44. Press Release, Environmental Working Group, Lautenberg Advances Bill to Protect Kids from Toxic Chemicals (Apr. 14, 2011), https://www.ewg.org/news-insights/news-release/lautenberg-advances-bill-protect-kids-toxic-chemicals.

45. Safe Chemicals Act of 2010, S. 3209, 111th Cong. (introduced Apr. 15, 2010); Toxic Safe Chemicals Act of 2010, H.R. 5820, 111th Cong. (introduced July 22, 2010).

sharing of needed confidential information with states and first responders, as necessary, to fulfill their duties

- Establishing judicially enforceable deadlines by which EPA must act to implement the law
- Preserving the role of states to regulate chemicals as balanced against the need for a clear and centralized federal chemical management law
- Requiring EPA to prioritize its review of chemicals that are persistent and bioaccumulative and that are known carcinogens and highly toxic

In the almost nine years since new TSCA was enacted, much has changed. In addition to significant changes in the law, EPA has dramatically modified its interpretation of underlying policies and interpretations of the law. The fact that three different administrations have been in office since 2016 has complicated matters for TSCA stakeholders, given shifting and often confusing policies and different interpretations of key terms. The remainder of this book will explain how new TSCA and EPA's evolving interpretations of the law directly impact businesspeople and the commercial transactions in which they are engaged.

Takeaways

- Original TSCA's structural limitations ultimately led to the perception that it was ineffective.
- Lautenberg's enactment in 2016 was fueled by this perception, aided by growing NGO and public health activists' discontent with TSCA and a federal appellate decision that gutted EPA's ability to control risks from existing chemicals.
- New TSCA goes a long way in addressing TSCA's structural deficits and provides EPA with new and broad authority to control chemical risks.

2

In a Nutshell: TSCA Overview

Lynn L. Bergeson

Key Messages

- TSCA's jurisdiction is vast, and businesses should assume it applies to some aspects of their production unless another federal chemical law is known to apply.
- The 2016 amendments to TSCA greatly expanded EPA's authority to regulate existing chemicals and manufactured products containing chemicals that are regulated by EPA under TSCA.
- EPA is required to prioritize "high priority" chemicals for risk evaluation and, to the extent necessary, eliminate any risk deemed to be unreasonable.
- EPA's focus on potential risk to health and the environment from chemicals regulated under TSCA has made business entities throughout the supply chain as well as the end users of products containing chemicals more aware.

Signed into law by President Gerald R. Ford in October 1976, the Toxic Substances Control Act (TSCA)[1] is intended to protect human

1. 15 U.S.C. §§ 2601–2697.

health and the environment from "unreasonable risks" of chemical substances and mixtures. TSCA focuses on industrial chemicals used and distributed in commerce. TSCA contains six titles. This book focuses on Title I: Control of Toxic Substances. Other TSCA titles focus on other chemical substances and topics, including asbestos in schools, indoor air radon, lead-based paint, state grants to improve environmental health in schools, and formaldehyde standards for composite wood products.

2.1 Congressional Findings and National Policy

Major federal laws are often prefaced with a summary of congressional findings, policy, and intent for the statute. TSCA is no exception. Section 2 of Title I of TSCA identifies Congress's findings regarding TSCA. They include that humans and the environment are exposed to many chemical substances and mixtures, and that some may present an "unreasonable risk" of injury to human health or the environment when manufactured, processed, distributed in commerce, used, or disposed of.[2] What constitutes "unreasonable risk" and how the U.S. Environmental Protection Agency (EPA) manages such risks are critically important concepts that practitioners and businesspeople alike need to understand and anticipate to manage actual and perceived legal and commercial risk under TSCA.

Based on its findings, Congress declared it the policy of the United States that EPA should have adequate information, developed by chemical manufacturers and processors, on the health and the environmental effects of chemical substances and mixtures, and that EPA should have sufficient authority to regulate chemical substances and mixtures that EPA identifies as presenting an unreasonable risk of injury to health or the environment. Importantly, Congress also declared it the policy of the United States that EPA would exercise its TSCA authority so as "not to impede unduly or create unnecessary economic barriers to technological innovation."[3]

These findings remained unchanged with the enactment in 2016 of the Frank R. Lautenberg Chemical Safety for the 21st Century

2. *See generally* TSCA § 2(a)(2), 15 U.S.C. § 2601(a)(2) (finding that there are "some whose manufacture, processing, distribution in commerce, use, or disposal may present an unreasonable risk of injury to health or the environment").
3. TSCA § 2(b), (c), 15 U.S.C. § 2601(b), (c).

Act (Lautenberg; "new TSCA"). As we will discuss, the balancing between these noted U.S. policies of regulating chemicals and not unduly encumbering chemical innovation has proven challenging. Some argue that EPA's new chemical review program impedes technological innovation in violation of domestic policy and point to the dramatic drop in research and development (R&D)[4] and new chemical notification submissions despite the crucial need for new chemicals to replace more aggressive existing ones. Others claim robust regulation of new chemicals is needed to prevent potentially dangerous chemicals from entering the market and repeating the sins of the past.

TSCA is not an especially straightforward law, and basic TSCA concepts are sometimes counterintuitive to practitioners and businesspeople unfamiliar with the law, history, and practice of TSCA. We describe key basic TSCA concepts and then describe in general terms how TSCA is intended to work. This summary is abbreviated and is not a comprehensive overview of TSCA and its structure and operation.[5]

2.2 Scope of Persons Subject to TSCA

A foundational question for any practitioner or businessperson is determining whether TSCA applies at all to a business operation. Many chemicals have multiple functionalities, and the fact that a chemical is used in a particular manufacturing operation is not dispositive of TSCA's jurisdictional relevance.

For example, phenol is an organic compound used to synthesize plastics and other materials. In this use capacity, phenol is regulated under TSCA. Phenol is also used in a variety of pesticide products and is a core ingredient in several over-the-counter drug products, such as throat lozenges. Phenol thus can be subject to TSCA when used in

---

4. *See* Coal. for Chem. Innovations, https://chemicalinnovations.org/ (under "Our Research and Analysis" section of the website, discussing FTI Consulting's Presentation to the Coalition for Chemical Innovations (CCI): Economic and Societal Impacts of EPA's Implementation of Section 5 of the Lautenberg Chemical Safety Act: Context, Methodology and Approach, Survey Results, and Findings (2022)) (last visited Sept. 27, 2024) ("R&D investment at CCI member companies has dropped from $324 million annually to $65 million annually, *a stunning 80 percent reduction*[.]").

5. For more information, see Swati D.G. Rayasam et al., *Toxic Substances Control Act (TSCA) Implementation: How the Amended Law Has Failed to Protect Vulnerable Populations from Toxic Chemicals in the United States*, 56 Env't Sci. & Tech. 11969 (2022).

an industrial manufacturing application, subject to the Federal Food, Drug, and Cosmetic Act (FFDCA) and subject to U.S. Food and Drug Administration (FDA) regulation when used in a drug, and subject to the Federal Insecticide, Fungicide, and Rodenticide Act (FIFRA) and regulated by EPA when used in a pesticide product formulation.

It is important to know which law among the three U.S. chemical product law "buckets" applies to the business operations in question—TSCA, FIFRA, or FFDCA. Many chemicals are used in ways that make it entirely possible all three could apply depending upon the chemical and the commercial intent behind its use, and at what point jurisdictional relevance is being assessed.

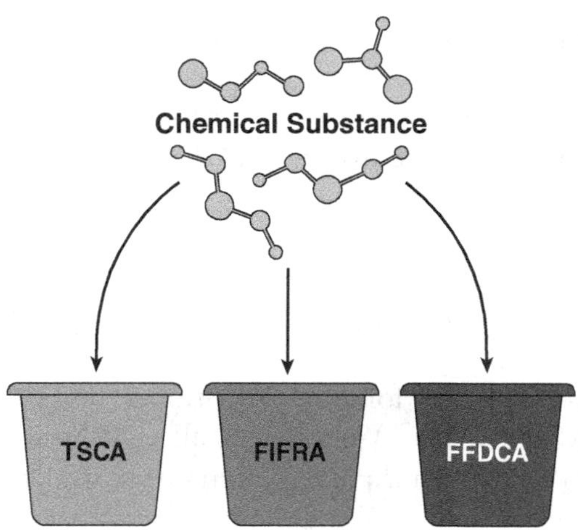

Figure 2.1. One chemical substance can be subject to different chemical product laws depending on use

TSCA explicitly excludes "chemical substances" that are:

- Mixtures
- Pesticides as defined under FIFRA when manufactured, processed, or distributed in commerce for use as a pesticide
- Tobacco and tobacco products
- Certain materials regulated under the Atomic Energy Act
- Firearms and ammunition
- Foods, food additives, drugs, cosmetics, and devices regulated under FFDCA[6]

6. TSCA § 3(2)(B), 15 U.S.C. § 2602(2)(B).

Some substances that meet the definition of an "excluded substance" in certain circumstances may be subject to TSCA requirements in others. This fact makes intent and the specific commercial application of a chemical critically important elements in determining the relevant law that applies. Once it has been confirmed that a business operation is in the TSCA bucket, assessing *how* TSCA applies may commence. As we will discuss, the law and EPA's implementing regulations apply to stakeholders in the supply chain—chemical producers, processors, distributors, and users—in vastly different and rapidly evolving ways.

In enacting the original TSCA, Congress intended it to cover a broad spectrum of commercial activities and intentionally defined TSCA's jurisdictional reach with a wide aperture. While the 2016 amendments did not amend TSCA's jurisdictional reach, EPA's implementation of TSCA since Lautenberg has greatly expanded the act's scope to include many more commercial entities, business interests, and commercial operations, often in ways that are poorly understood, if they are even known.

TSCA applies most broadly to "persons," defined broadly as "any individual, firm, company, corporation, joint venture, partnership, sole proprietorship, association, or any other business entity; any State or political subdivision thereof; any municipality; any interstate body; and any department, agency, or instrumentality of the Federal Government."[7] As noted, TSCA subjects different persons to applicable requirements depending on the type of activity in which a person is engaged (e.g., manufacturing, importing, processing, distributing, using).

TSCA imposes most of its requirements on manufacturers of chemicals. Terminology is unique and specialized under TSCA, and "manufacture" is defined to mean "to import into the customs territory of the United States (as defined in general note 2 of the Harmonized Tariff Schedule of the United States), produce, or manufacture."[8] Critically important is the understanding that this broad definition of "manufacture" includes importers, specifically the importer of record of chemical substances. This term is ill-defined under TSCA and typically is defined to include the entity that acts as the importer for Customs transactions (i.e., the importer of record). This fact is often

7. 40 C.F.R. §§ 704.3, 710.3(d), 716.3, 717.3(f), 720.3(x) (2023).
8. TSCA § 3(9), 15 U.S.C. § 2602(9). *See, e.g.*, 40 C.F.R. § 710.3(d) (2023) ("Manufacture means to manufacture, produce, or import for commercial purposes.").

overlooked or misunderstood by businesspeople and practitioners, an oversight that is the source of considerable business risk and enforcement liability. The importer of record may not necessarily be the entity that actually imports the chemical product or ever takes ownership of the product.[9] Customs stated:

> The language of section 13 refers to liability of the owner and consignee. These are two of the possible importers who may sign the certification statement. The rule uses the broader Customs definition of importer for several reasons. (1) As a practical matter, since the rule involves entering goods through Customs, allowing the person who normally acts as the importer for Customs transactions (i.e., importer of record) to sign the certification statement is least disruptive, confusing, and burdensome for industry and Customs. (2) The section 13 language encompasses all rules under TSCA, therefore the section 13 definition of importer must be broad enough to cover any TSCA definition of importer. Under other sections of TSCA the importer is defined as a manufacturer, and in some cases this importer-manufacturer may be a person other than the consignee. Thus, section 13 should not limit the importer definition to only the consignee. (3) The importer who signs the certification statement, unlike the importer responsible for other TSCA requirements such as premanufacture notification, need not be the "most" knowledgeable person about the chemical shipment, as long as he is assured that the shipment meets the requirements of TSCA. Thus, any authorized person who meets the information requirements may sign the certification statement, at the convenience of the parties to the importation.[10]

The important point to remember is that all the entities in the supply chain need to know which entity is responsible for discharging the various obligations that arise under TSCA. Who is the importer of record? Who signs the TSCA section 13 import certification? These issues should be addressed in agreements among the entities involved in the supply chain.

---

9. *See* Customs Regulations Amendments Relating to Special Classes of Merchandise, 48 Fed. Reg. 34,734 (Aug. 1, 1983).
10. *Id.* at 34,735.

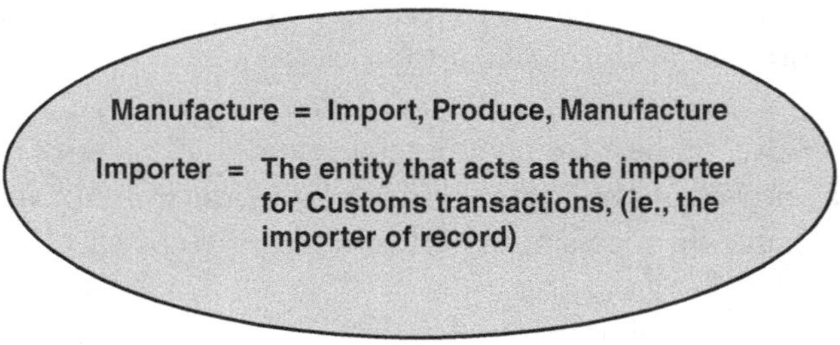

Figure 2.2. Terminology is unique and specialized under TSCA

TSCA applies both to bulk, imported "neat" (pure) chemicals and increasingly to manufactured products, often referred to as "articles," if the imported product contains a chemical component regulated by EPA under TSCA. An importer of a smart television probably does not think of itself as a chemical manufacturer. Under TSCA, however, the importer of record is deemed a chemical manufacturer if EPA regulates, as it has, a chemical contained in the smart television that EPA has identified as posing unreasonable risk to health and the environment.

Under TSCA, "manufacture" is also defined to mean "to manufacture for commercial purposes."[11] In EPA implementing regulations, the meaning of "manufacture for commercial purposes" has been clarified to mean "[t]o import, produce, or manufacture with the purpose of obtaining an immediate or eventual commercial advantage for the manufacturer."[12] EPA also states, "Manufacturer means a person who produces or manufactures a chemical substance."[13] A person that contracts with a toll manufacturer to manufacture a chemical may also be a manufacturer under TSCA.

Under TSCA, "processors" of chemical substances may be also regulated.[14] TSCA defines "process" as

> the preparation of a chemical substance or mixture, after its manufacture, for distribution in commerce—(A) in the same form or physical state as, or in a different form or physical state from, that in which it

11. TSCA §§ 5(i)(1), 8(f), 15 U.S.C. §§ 2604(i)(1), 2607(f).
12. 40 C.F.R. §§ 704.3, 710.3(d), 716.3, 717.3(e), 720.3(r) (2023).
13. *Id.* §§ 704.3, 716.3, 720.3(t).
14. *See id.* §§ 704.1, 710.1, 712.1, 716.5(c), 717.1, 720.3(bb), 721.1.

was received by the person so preparing such substance or mixture, or (B) as part of an article containing the chemical substance or mixture.[15]

Under TSCA, "process for commercial purposes"[16] means processing "with the purpose of obtaining an immediate or eventual commercial advantage" and "[p]rocessing of any amount of a chemical substance or mixture . . . ."[17]

Chemical "distributors" and "users" are not explicitly defined under TSCA or under EPA implementing regulations. In guidance, EPA states, "If a company controls all distribution of a substance manufactured by another firm, and that company does not prepare, repackage, or otherwise process the substance prior to distribution, the firm is a distributor but not a processor of the substance."[18]

2.3 Chemical Substances

Key to understanding how TSCA applies to business operations is how TSCA regulates "chemical substances." TSCA defines this term broadly to include "any organic or inorganic substance of a particular molecular identity, including (i) any combination of such substances occurring in whole or in part as a result of a chemical reaction or occurring in nature, and (ii) any element or uncombined radical."[19] EPA has interpreted this term to include items people may not typically associate with or identify as traditional chemicals. Microorganisms are, for example, considered chemical substances under TSCA.[20]

---

15. TSCA § 3(13), 15 U.S.C. § 2602(13); 40 C.F.R. § 720.3(aa) (2023). "Processor" is defined as "any person who processes a chemical substance or mixture." TSCA § 3(14), 15 U.S.C. § 2602(14); 40 C.F.R. § 720.3(bb) (2023). *See also* EPA, Question and Answer Summary: EPA Seminar on Industry Obligations under TSCA 1–2 (1986) [hereinafter Q&A Summary].
16. TSCA §§ 5(i)(1), 8(f), 15 U.S.C. §§ 2604(i)(1), 2607(f).
17. 40 C.F.R. § 704.3 (2023).
18. Q&A Summary, *supra* note 15, at 2.
19. TSCA § 3(2)(A), 15 U.S.C. § 2602(2)(A).
20. EPA, Microbial Products of Biotechnology: Summary of Regulations under the Toxic Substances Control Act (2012), https://www.epa.gov/sites/production/files/2015-08/documents/biotech_fact_sheet.pdf.

2.4 Chemical Mixtures

"Mixtures" as defined under TSCA are excluded from the definition of a "chemical substance." A mixture of Chemical X and Chemical Y is not subject to notification under TSCA section 5 if both Chemical X and Chemical Y components are listed on the TSCA Chemical Substance Inventory (TSCA Inventory), discussed in the following section. Some mixtures are, however, subject to certain TSCA authorities.[21] TSCA defines "mixture" as

> any combination of two or more chemical substances if the combination does not occur in nature and is not, in whole or in part, the result of a chemical reaction; except that such term does include any combination which occurs, in whole or in part, as a result of a chemical reaction if none of the chemical substances comprising the combination is a new chemical substance and if the combination could have been manufactured for commercial purposes without a chemical reaction at the time the chemical substances comprising the combination were combined.[22]

EPA provides as examples of mixtures alloys, inorganic glasses, ceramics, frits, and cements, including Portland cement.[23]

A chemical substance or mixture that is a component of an article (e.g., electrical cable, tire, cell phone, automobile) does not lose its character as a chemical substance or mixture when part of the article and, as noted previously, increasingly is subject to TSCA regulation.[24] For example, for a person that imports or processes an electronic appliance that is an article as defined under TSCA, a constituent of

---

21. *See, e.g.*, 40 C.F.R. pt. 799 (2023) (mixtures may be subject to TSCA § 4 testing requirements); *id.* pt. 717 (TSCA § 8(c) recording of significant adverse reactions applies to mixtures).
22. TSCA § 3(10), 15 U.S.C. § 2602(10). *See also* 40 C.F.R. § 720.3(u) (2023).
23. 40 C.F.R. § 710.4(c)(2) note (2023).
24. "Article" is defined at 40 C.F.R. § 704.3 and substantially similarly elsewhere in TSCA regulations as

> a manufactured item (1) which is formed to a specific shape or design during manufacture, (2) which has end use function(s) dependent in whole or in part upon its shape or design during end use, and (3) which has either no change of chemical composition during its end use or only those changes of composition which have no commercial purpose separate from that of the article, and that result from a chemical reaction that occurs upon end use of other chemical substances, mixtures, or articles; except that fluids and particles are not considered articles regardless of shape or design.

which is Chemical X, that importer is considered an importer and hence manufacturer of Chemical X. Although certain TSCA regulations exempt chemical substances when part of an article or the persons that manufacture or process them, EPA is increasingly regulating chemical substances as part of articles and persons that manufacture or process them in its implementation of TSCA. This expansive interpretation of TSCA has greatly expanded TSCA's jurisdictional reach over commercial entities in ways the business community can ill afford to ignore.

2.5 Chemical Inventory

Congress directed EPA under TSCA section 8(b) to "compile, keep current, and publish a list of each chemical substance which is manufactured or processed in the United States."[25] This list is known as the "TSCA Chemical Substance Inventory." EPA compiled the initial TSCA Inventory in 1977. Certain naturally occurring substances are automatically included on the TSCA Inventory, whether they are explicitly listed or not.[26]

Under TSCA, chemical substances that are listed on the TSCA Inventory are considered "existing" chemical substances. Chemical substances that are not listed on the TSCA Inventory are considered "new" chemical substances.[27] Whether a chemical substance is listed on the TSCA Inventory and, if not, whether it is required to be listed is the source of significant business and legal interest. The TSCA Inventory is continually updated by the addition of chemical substances for which a premanufacture notice (PMN) and subsequent notice of commencement (NOC) have been submitted.

The TSCA Inventory has two portions: one public and one confidential. The public portion includes all existing chemical substances whose identities have not been claimed as confidential business information (CBI). The confidential portion of the TSCA Inventory is not publicly accessible and includes all existing chemical substances whose identity has been claimed as CBI.[28] In 2016 when Lautenberg

25. TSCA § 8(b)(1), 15 U.S.C. § 2607(b)(1).
26. Naturally occurring substances are automatically included on the TSCA Inventory only if they meet certain criteria.
27. 40 C.F.R. § 720.3(v) (2023).
28. *Id.* § 720.25(b)(1).

was enacted, there were 85,346 entries listed on the TSCA Inventory—67,673 nonconfidential chemical substances and 17,673 confidential chemical identities.[29]

Chemical substances on the public portion of the TSCA Inventory are listed by a specific name and a Chemical Abstracts Service Registry Number® (CAS RN®)—a unique number assigned by the Chemical Abstracts Service (CAS) to a specific chemical substance.[30] Chemical substances whose identities are claimed as confidential, however, are listed in the TSCA Inventory but by an Accession Number (AN), assigned by EPA, and a generic chemical name that masks the specific chemical identity of the substance. The identity of the chemical substance remains confidential by use of these masking tools. Keeping proprietary chemical formulations confidential is an important bedrock principle under TSCA, and it is essential to protect proprietary commercial interests that are so much a part of a competitive business environment. This business interest competes, however, with the right-to know sentiment now so much a part of chemical product regulation and citizen activism. Amendments to TSCA in 2016 and EPA implementing regulations have made it significantly more challenging to assert and maintain CBI claims.

Under the Lautenberg amendments, Congress directed EPA to denote which substances listed on the TSCA Inventory are "active" and which are "inactive." This process was colloquially called the "Inventory reset" when it was undertaken in 2018.[31] The process did not remove any substances from the TSCA Inventory; it merely reclassified them. The statute obligates companies that have manufactured or imported substances in the ten years prior to enactment to send active notices for those substances.[32]

Companies wishing to maintain CBI identities are required to reassert and substantiate each CBI claim.[33] Substances listed on the confidential portion of the TSCA Inventory that have received no substantiated CBI claims are moved to the public portion of the

29. A single substance may have more than one entry on the confidential portion of the TSCA Inventory.
30. 40 C.F.R. § 720.25(b)(1) (2023).
31. EPA proposed the rule to reset the TSCA Inventory on January 13, 2017. *See* Bergeson & Campbell, P.C., TSCA: EPA Proposes Requirements for TSCA Inventory Notification (Active-Inactive) (Jan. 17, 2017), http://www.lawbc.com/regulatory-developments/entry/epa-proposes-requirements-for-tsca-inventory-notification-active-inactive.
32. TSCA § 8(b)(4)(A)(i), 15 U.S.C. § 2607(b)(4)(A)(i).
33. TSCA § 8(b)(4)(B)(ii), 15 U.S.C. § 2607(b)(4)(B)(ii).

TSCA Inventory.[34] Substances that have received no active notices are now deemed to be "inactive."[35] CBI substances that have received no active notices remain listed as CBI on the TSCA Inventory.[36] Prior to manufacturing or importing an inactive chemical, however, a company must submit an active notice.[37] As with the initial Inventory reset, CBI claims must be substantiated in subsequent active notices.[38]

EPA released on February 19, 2019, an update of the TSCA Inventory, listing chemicals that are "active" versus "inactive" in commerce within the United States. The update confirmed what many suspected, namely that thousands of chemicals listed on the TSCA Inventory are no longer in commercial use. EPA reported that a "key result of the update is that less than half of the total number of chemicals on the current TSCA Inventory (47 percent or 40,655 of the 86,228 chemicals) are currently in commerce."[39] According to EPA, more than 80 percent (32,898) of the chemicals in commerce have identities that are not CBI, increasing public access, according to EPA, to additional information about them.

2.6 Chemical Substances Exempt from TSCA Reporting

Some chemical substances that are exempt from reporting under TSCA are excluded from being listed on the TSCA Inventory.[40] This is a confusing concept to many and means that just because a chemical substance is not listed on the TSCA Inventory does not necessarily mean that its manufacture, distribution, and use are unlawful. A substance is exempt from reporting and listing on the TSCA Inventory if it is:

- An impurity[41]—defined as a substance "unintentionally present with another chemical substance"[42]

34. TSCA § 8(b)(4)(B)(iv), 15 U.S.C. § 2607(b)(4)(B)(iv).
35. TSCA § 8(b)(4)(A)(iii), 15 U.S.C. § 2607(b)(4)(A)(iii).
36. TSCA § 8(b)(5)(B)(ii), 15 U.S.C. § 2607(b)(5)(B)(ii).
37. TSCA § 8(b)(5)(B)(i), 15 U.S.C. § 2607(b)(5)(B)(i).
38. TSCA § 8(b)(5)(B)(ii), 15 U.S.C. § 2607(b)(5)(B)(ii).
39. Press Release, EPA, EPA Releases First Major Update to Chemicals List in 40 Years (Feb. 19, 2019), https://www.epa.gov/newsreleases/epa-releases-first-major-update-chemicals-list-40-years#:~:text=A%20key%20result%20of%20the,chemicals)%20are%20currently%20in%20commerce.
40. 40 C.F.R. § 710.4(d) (2023).
41. *Id.* § 710.4(d)(1).
42. *Id.* § 710.3(d).

- A byproduct[43]—defined as a substance produced "without a separate commercial intent during the manufacture, processing, use, or disposal of another chemical substance(s) or mixture(s)"[44] (Note that a byproduct may lose this exemption if used for a separate commercial purpose (e.g., as feedstock for another chemical reaction).)[45]
- A substance that is the result of a chemical reaction that occurs incidental to exposure of another chemical substance, mixture, or article to an environmental factor such as air, moisture, microbial organisms, or sunlight[46]
- A substance that results from a chemical reaction that occurs incidental to storage of another chemical substance, mixture, or article[47]
- A substance that results from a chemical reaction that occurs upon end use of other chemical substances, mixtures, or articles, but that is not itself manufactured for distribution in commerce or used as an intermediate (e.g., cured paints or adhesives, or fuel or fuel additive combustion byproducts)[48]
- A substance that results from a chemical reaction that occurs upon use of curable plastic, rubber molding compounds, inks, drying oils, adhesives, paints, and so on[49]
- A substance that results from a chemical reaction that occurs when a stabilizer, colorant, odorant, antioxidant, filler, solvent, carrier, surfactant, plasticizer, corrosion inhibitor, antifoamer or defoamer, and the like, functions as intended[50]
- A substance that is not intentionally removed from the equipment in which it is manufactured[51]
- A nonisolated intermediate—a substance formed during a chemical reaction that is reacted further without being isolated from the reaction vessel or ancillary equipment,

43. *Id.* § 710.4(d)(2).
44. *Id.* § 710.3(d).
45. *Id.* § 720.30(g); *see also* EPA, TSCA Chemical Data Reporting Fact Sheet: Byproducts Reporting for the Printed Circuit Board Industry (2016), https://www.epa.gov/sites/production/files/2016-02/documents/final_cdr_fact_sheet_printed_circuit_board_2_22_16.pdf.
46. 40 C.F.R. § 710.4(d)(3) (2023).
47. *Id.* § 710.4(d)(4).
48. *Id.* § 710.4(d)(5).
49. *Id.* § 710.4(d)(6).
50. *Id.* § 710.4(d)(7).
51. *Id.* § 710.4(d)(8).

including continuous flow reactors—a nonisolated intermediate may not be stored after manufacture[52]
- A substance manufactured for export only, subject to labeling requirements[53]
- A mixture, as defined in 40 C.F.R. § 710.3(d) (although individual components of a mixture must be listed)[54]
- A substance manufactured or imported in small quantities solely for R&D, subject to labeling requirements[55]
- A polymer that meets the polymer exemption criterion, subject to certain polymer exemption reporting and recordkeeping

Whether a chemical substance can properly be considered exempt from reporting and thus excluded from the requirement to be listed on the TSCA Inventory requires a thorough understanding of the substance's chemical identity and its intended uses. This generally requires the assistance of an experienced TSCA chemist and TSCA regulatory experts.

2.7 Small Business Interests

Small manufacturers, importers, and processors maintain a special status under TSCA. They are exempt from select section 8 reporting requirements.[56] The 2016 TSCA amendments direct EPA to consult with the Small Business Administration within 180 days of enactment and then at least once every ten years to assess the eligibility criteria for determining whether manufacturers/importers and processors qualify as small manufacturers/importers and processors and, following public notice and comment, update them as warranted.[57] Section 26 also directs EPA to set lower fees for "small business concerns" when developing the TSCA administrative fee structure.[58] These provisions reflect Congress's acknowledgment that TSCA, like

52. *Id.* §§ 710.4(d)(8), 720.3(w).
53. *Id.* § 720.30(e).
54. *Id.* § 710.4(c)(2).
55. *Id.* §§ 710.4(c)(3), 720.36(a).
56. TSCA § 8(a)(1), 15 U.S.C. § 2607(a)(1); *see also* 40 C.F.R. §§ 704.3, 711.9, 712.25(c) (2023).
57. TSCA § 8(a)(3)(C), 15 U.S.C. § 2607(a)(3)(C).
58. TSCA § 26(b)(4)(A), 15 U.S.C. § 2625(b)(4)(A).

other federal environmental regulatory requirements, can impose disproportionately heavy burdens on small business interests.

2.8 Administration of the Act

Congress amended extensively section 26 (Administration of the Act) to be more explicit about EPA's responsibilities. Newly added TSCA section 26(*l*) (Policies, Procedures, and Guidance) requires that EPA develop any policies, procedures, and guidance needed to carry out the changes in new TSCA[59] and that it review and, as needed, revise them at five-year intervals. EPA is required to review the adequacy of animal, nonanimal, and epidemiological test methods and procedures for assessing and determining risk, and to revise such policies, procedures, and guidance as EPA determines necessary to "reflect new scientific developments or understandings."[60]

Newly added section 26(o) requires EPA to establish an advisory committee to be known as the Science Advisory Committee on Chemicals (SACC).[61] The purpose of the SACC is to provide independent advice and expert consultation with respect to the scientific and technical aspects of issues relating to the implementation of new TSCA. It must include representatives of such science, government, labor, public health, public interest, animal protection, industry, and other groups as EPA determines to be advisable, including representatives that have specific scientific expertise in the relationship of chemical exposures to women, children, and other potentially exposed or susceptible subpopulations.[62]

According to EPA, the SACC will be composed of 14 members and will be managed under the Federal Advisory Committee Act.[63] EPA has suggested that as many as nine of the proposed 14 members will be selected from interested and available members of the existing EPA Chemical Safety Advisory Committee. The latter has been

59. TSCA § 26(*l*)(1), 15 U.S.C. § 2625(*l*)(1).
60. TSCA § 26(*l*)(2), 15 U.S.C. § 2625(*l*)(2).
61. TSCA § 26(o), 15 U.S.C. § 2625(o).
62. TSCA § 26(o), 15 U.S.C. § 2625(o).
63. SACC; Establishment of a Federal Advisory Committee; Request for Nominations, 81 Fed. Reg. 58,925 (Aug. 26, 2016).

primarily engaged in the review of risk assessments for the TSCA Work Plan Chemicals.[64]

2.9 How TSCA Works

Despite the harsh criticism that has been directed at TSCA as originally enacted, the original statute was logically organized and, on paper anyway, thoughtfully crafted. We start with section 8 information gathering authority. TSCA authorizes EPA to obtain all kinds of information and documents from regulated entities. As Figure 2.3 illustrates, EPA can obtain chemical use, exposure, health and safety, risk, and other information from chemical manufacturers, processors, and distributors under several section 8 provisions.

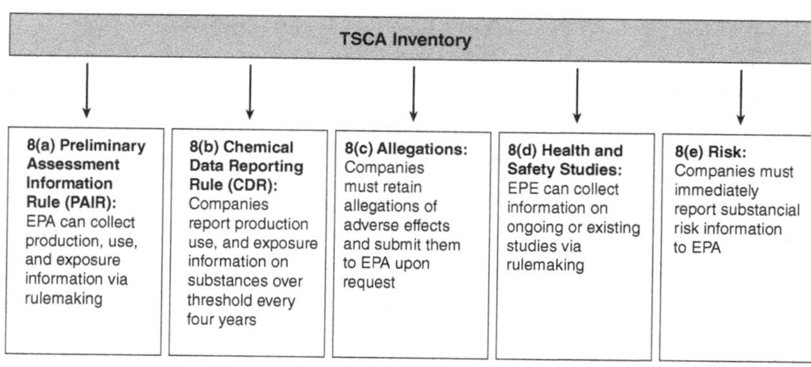

Figure 2.3. TSCA section 8 provisions authorizing EPA to gather information

If, based on the information collected, or potentially a lack of available information, EPA determines under section 6 that a chemical may pose unreasonable risk to health or the environment, EPA is authorized to compel testing under TSCA section 4 to elicit more information to assist EPA in regulating the chemical.

The 2016 TSCA amendments authorize EPA to issue unilaterally testing orders, authority it lacked previously. This means that EPA may now issue an order compelling recipients to initiate testing to generate data EPA believes are essential to determine whether

64. *See id.* at 58,926; *TSCA Scientific Peer Review Committees*, EPA, https://www.epa.gov/tsca-peer-review (last updated Sept. 17, 2024).

a chemical substance poses unreasonable risk to health or the environment. If, after testing and information collection, EPA identifies concerns, EPA is authorized under TSCA section 6 to assess whether a chemical poses an unreasonable risk and, if so, to require means to abate to the greatest extent possible such risk.

It is in this area that Congress made sweeping changes to TSCA that significantly bolster EPA's authority to identify and address the risk posed by existing chemicals. Under "old TSCA," EPA was required to demonstrate that any regulatory measure EPA imposed on a chemical to address unreasonable risk considered costs and benefits and that EPA selected the "least burdensome" option. The *Corrosion Proof Fittings* case[65] held that EPA failed to meet that burden in seeking to ban certain asbestos applications, a decision broadly viewed as the death knell of EPA's ability to regulate existing chemicals and a major driver of TSCA modernization. Lautenberg strikes the "least burdensome" requirements and forbids EPA to consider cost and other nonrisk factors when making unreasonable risk determinations. EPA's authority is not unlimited. EPA is required "to the extent practicable" and "based on reasonably available information" to consider costs and other nonrisk factors, provided the regulation EPA wishes to impose is necessary to eliminate the unreasonable risk.

We summarize broadly in Section 2.9.1 and subsections the new and still very much evolving chemical prioritization, risk evaluation, and risk management process.

2.9.1 Chemical Prioritization, Risk Evaluation, and Risk Management

As originally enacted, TSCA did not explicitly address chemical prioritization or risk evaluation/risk assessment steps, an omission that contributed greatly to the perception that TSCA was irretrievably broken. After all, with tens of thousands of existing chemicals in commerce, the lack of a process to prioritize chemicals for review was debilitating. Section 6 now includes requirements that EPA establish a staged scientific evaluation procedure beginning with a chemical prioritization process, followed, as necessary, by a risk evaluation process. These stages precede and serve to tee up chemicals for regulatory

65. Corrosion Proof Fittings v. EPA, 947 F.2d 1201 (5th Cir. 1991), https://law.justia.com/cases/federal/appellate-courts/F2/947/1201/153685/.

action if certain exposure conditions and hazard determinations regarding "unreasonable risk" can be met.

2.9.1.1 Chemical Prioritization

After Lautenberg's enactment, EPA established by rule a risk-based screening process, including criteria for designating chemicals as being "high-priority" cases for risk evaluation or "low-priority" cases for which risk evaluations are not warranted at the time.[66] Conditions to be considered in determining whether a chemical is high or low priority include consideration of persistence and bioaccumulation; identification of potentially exposed or susceptible subpopulations; storage near significant sources of drinking water; conditions of use (COUs) of a chemical or significant changes in the COU;[67] and the volume or significant changes in the volume of the chemical substance manufactured or processed.

A designation of high priority requires a conclusion, without consideration of costs or other nonrisk factors, that a chemical "may present an unreasonable risk of injury to health or the environment because of a potential hazard and a potential route of exposure under the [COU], including an unreasonable risk to a potentially exposed or susceptible subpopulation identified as relevant by [EPA]."[68] A designation of low priority requires a conclusion "based on information sufficient to establish, without consideration of costs or other nonrisk factors, that such substance does not meet the standard" for designating a chemical substance a high-priority substance.[69]

2.9.1.2 Risk Evaluation

TSCA specifies a series of requirements that EPA must meet in conducting risk evaluations. TSCA now requires that the risk evaluation integrate and assess available information on hazards and exposures. The risk evaluation includes an EPA determination of the COUs that serve as an implicit initial stage that focuses on the exposure component of the risk evaluation.

66. TSCA § 6(b)(1)(A), 15 U.S.C. § 2605(b)(1)(A).
67. The term "conditions of use" is defined in TSCA § 3(4) as "the circumstances, as determined by [EPA], under which a chemical substance is intended, known, or reasonably foreseen to be manufactured, processed, distributed in commerce, used, or disposed of." 15 U.S.C. § 2602(4).
68. TSCA § 6(b)(1)(B)(i), 15 U.S.C. § 2605(b)(1)(B)(i).
69. TSCA § 6(b)(1)(B)(ii), 15 U.S.C. § 2605(b)(1)(B)(ii).

2.9.1.3 Risk Management

Once EPA makes a finding of unreasonable risk, it is required to manage that risk. On March 28, 2024, EPA issued its long-awaited first final TSCA risk management rule banning the import and eventual use of chrysotile asbestos, the only asbestos form known to be used in the United States. EPA's approach to the risk management of chrysotile asbestos has much broader implications, and the rule and the litigation it inspired are being closely watched.[70]

Chrysotile asbestos has been imported and used by the chlor-alkali industry for the fabrication of semipermeable diaphragms used in the production of chlorine and sodium hydroxide. EPA approached the regulation of chrysotile asbestos used at the handful of sites processing and using asbestos on a site-by-site basis. As of May 28, 2024, the effective date of the final rule, all persons in the chlor-alkali industry are prohibited from the manufacture, including import, of chrysotile asbestos, including any chrysotile asbestos-containing products or articles. Beginning five years after the effective date of the final rule, entities are prohibited from processing, distributing in commerce, and commercially using chrysotile asbestos for diaphragms in the chlor-alkali industry, except as provided in the rule. Entities may process, distribute in commerce, and commercially use chrysotile asbestos for diaphragms in the chlor-alkali industry at no more than two facilities until eight years after May 28, 2024, if they meet certain conditions, and at not more than one facility until 12 years after the effective date of the final rule, if they meet certain conditions specified under the rule. On the whole, the phaseout periods are considerably longer than EPA proposed, and they reflect a careful balancing of interests as required under TSCA.

In addition to the chemical bans noted previously, many other prohibitions, restrictions, and recordkeeping obligations apply. Central to this discussion is what EPA decided to require regarding workplace controls during the phaseout period. For most of the COUs where the prohibition on processing and industrial use will take effect in five or more years, EPA requires owners or operators to comply with an eight-hour existing chemical exposure limit (ECEL) beginning six

70. Am. Chemistry Council v. EPA, No. 24-11206 (11th Cir. filed Apr. 18, 2024); Tex. Chemistry Council v. EPA, No. 24-60193 (5th Cir. filed Apr. 19, 2024); United Steel, Paper & Forestry v. EPA, No. 24-01089 (D.C. Cir. filed Apr. 19, 2024); Asbestos Disease Awareness Org. v. EPA, No. 24-01090 (D.C. Cir. filed Apr. 19, 2024). On May 7, 2024, these four suits were consolidated in the Fifth Circuit under the *Texas Chemistry Council* case.

months after the effective date of the final rule. EPA identified the specific COUs to which this requirement applies.

EPA's stated goal is to require compliance with these interim workplace controls as set forth in the final rule. Adherence to these interim workplace controls adequately addresses, in EPA's view, the unreasonable risk from chrysotile asbestos to workers directly handling the chemical or in the area where it is used until the relevant ban goes into effect. This is a critically important concept, as EPA's authority under TSCA section 6(a) to impose restrictions is explicitly limited "to the extent necessary so that the chemical substance or mixture no longer presents such risk."

The TSCA risk management requirements incorporate and reinforce requirements in Occupational Safety and Health Administration (OSHA) standards. For chrysotile asbestos, EPA's approach for interim controls seeks to align with certain elements of the existing OSHA standard[71] for regulating asbestos. EPA acknowledges, however, that it is applying a lower, more protective ECEL derived from EPA's TSCA risk evaluation.

Why is this important, and what are the key takeaway points? First, the rule's scope is significant. It applies to the few, limited ongoing uses of chrysotile asbestos that were not banned in the 1980s. In addition to the chlor-alkali industry uses outlined earlier, the rule also bans the use of chrysotile asbestos to make industrial gaskets, oilfield brake blocks, aftermarket brakes, and other automotive industry products. The rule does not apply to the asbestos types that may already be in place, such as in old buildings. These will be addressed in a separate rulemaking including legacy uses and associated issues related to asbestos disposal.

Second, EPA concluded that the use of chrysotile asbestos in chlor-alkali production does not present an unreasonable risk if protective measures are used, such as engineering controls, glove boxes, and personal protective equipment (PPE). In the final risk management rule, EPA nevertheless asserts that chrysotile asbestos must be banned because "EPA believes that an ECEL cannot ensure that chrysotile asbestos does not present unreasonable risk to workers and, therefore, it is not a substitute for a ban as a long-term risk management solution."[72] In other words, the necessary PPE *may* not be used

71. 29 C.F.R. §§ 1910.1001 (2021), 1926.1101 (2023).

72. Asbestos Part 1; Chrysotile Asbestos; Regulation of Certain Conditions of Use under the Toxic Substances Control Act (TSCA), 89 Fed. Reg. 21,970, 21,983 (Mar. 28, 2024).

correctly, or monitoring to or below the ECEL "*may* at times be problematic," or owners "*may* be unable to reliably ensure with sufficient confidence" that workers are protected.[73] To some, this reflects a whole lot of unsupported anticipatory speculation that looks more like the precautionary principle than it does a reasoned cost-benefit risk analysis, as required under TSCA.

Taken to its logical extreme, this means that EPA will be compelled to ban all or nearly every substance it reviews under TSCA section 6, at least for the foreseeable future, because it is entirely likely that the substances EPA reviews over the next several decades will be sufficiently hazardous for EPA to conclude that the chemical substances present an unreasonable risk from routine, unprotected inhalation and/or dermal exposures. This logical inference alone raises alarm bells for chemical stakeholders, and businesspeople need to be aware of the commercial implications of EPA's regulatory decisions.

Finally, the final rule raises novel legal and science policy issues that are equally likely to arise in other risk management rules EPA is issuing, including the promulgated final risk management rule on methylene chloride issued on May 8, 2024.[74] EPA's use in the asbestos rule of the rescinded 2018 *Application of Systematic Review in TSCA Risk Evaluations*[75] invites significant controversy and reflects a disturbing departure from EPA's commitment to use best available science as required under TSCA section 26(h).

Whether EPA met its legal burden in the chrysotile asbestos rule will be decided by the court. EPA in May 2024 issued a final risk management rule on methylene chloride that reflects many of the same legal and science policy deficiencies. It too has already been judicially challenged.[76]

EPA's new risk prioritization, risk evaluation, and risk management processes are depicted in Figure 2.4.

---

73. *Id.* at 21,982 (emphasis added).
74. Methylene Chloride; Regulations under the Toxic Substances Control Act (TSCA), 89 Fed. Reg. 39,254 (May 8, 2024).
75. EPA, Application of Systematic Review in TSCA Risk Evaluations (2018), https://www.epa.gov/sites/default/files/2018-06/documents/final_application_of_sr_in_tsca_05-31-18.pdf.
76. Two small businesses filed a joint petition in the Fifth Circuit Court of Appeals. East Fork Enters., Inc. & EPIC Paint Co. v. EPA, No. 24-60227 (5th Cir. filed May 10, 2024). The Sierra Club has also filed in the Ninth Circuit. Sierra Club v. EPA, No. 24-03550 (9th Cir. filed May 28, 2024).

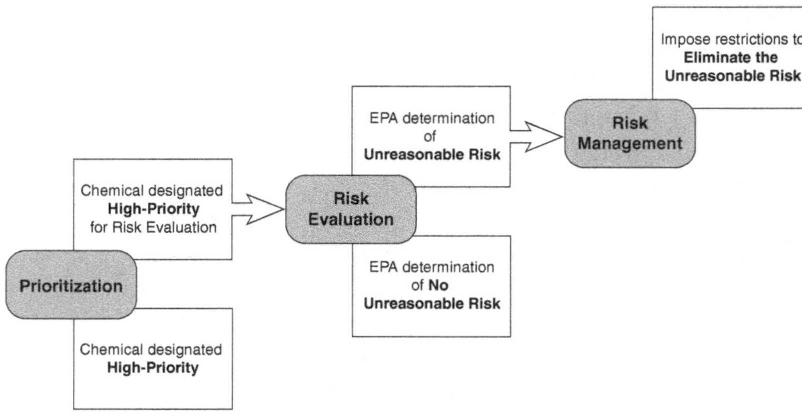

Figure 2.4. EPA's new risk prioritization, risk evaluation, and risk management process

Source: *Risk Evaluations for Existing Chemicals under TSCA*, EPA, https://www.epa.gov/assessing-and-managing-chemicals-under-tsca/risk-evaluations-existing-chemicals-under-tsca (last updated May 6, 2024).

2.9.2 Chemical Import

TSCA also regulates the import of chemicals into the United States. As noted, import is considered manufacture for TSCA purposes. We discuss these TSCA provisions in detail in Chapter 3. The key takeaway message for businesspeople is the extraordinary relevance of chemical components in products imported into the United States and TSCA's growing jurisdictional reach over importers of articles that contain chemicals regulated under TSCA.

Takeaways

- New TSCA significantly expands EPA's authority to regulate chemicals and the businesses that produce, import, process, distribute, and use them.
- Heightened awareness of chemical exposures has revolutionized supply chain relationships, making TSCA awareness in business transactions essential.
- The 2016 TSCA amendments offer some degree of predictability regarding the imposition of chemical restrictions, allowing businesses to plan more effectively to prevent restrictions to market access.

3

Importing Chemicals and Other Goods into the United States

Kelly N. Garson

Key Messages

- Importing neat chemicals and products containing chemicals of interest to EPA is increasingly complicated and requires a thorough understanding of TSCA.
- Increasingly, imports of products not subject to TSCA are subject, and TSCA noncompliance can result in market entry challenges, significant business disruption, and penalties.
- EPA and CBP work closely together and employ sophisticated tools to monitor imports to detect TSCA noncompliance.

3.1 Introduction to Imports under TSCA

U.S. companies import a vast array of products into the United States, ranging from textiles, electronics, pharmaceuticals, musical instruments, perfumes, inks, pesticides, petrochemicals, and plastic materials to organic chemicals. On a typical day, U.S. Customs and Border Protection (CBP) may oversee an average of 82,823 truck, rail, and sea containers and an average of $7.49 billion worth of imported products.[1] Many federal agencies work closely with CBP to facilitate lawful trade and compliance with U.S. environmental and consumer protection laws, including the U.S. Department of the Treasury, U.S. Consumer Product Safety Commission, U.S. Department of Agriculture, U.S. Food and Drug Administration (FDA), and U.S. Environmental Protection Agency (EPA). Many companies, however, may not be aware of the applicability and scope of requirements under the Toxic Substances Control Act (TSCA) that pertain to their goods before, at the time of, and after import into the United States. The commercial consequences of market entry and/or delay are significant, and TSCA import restrictions increasingly are posing challenges for businesses.

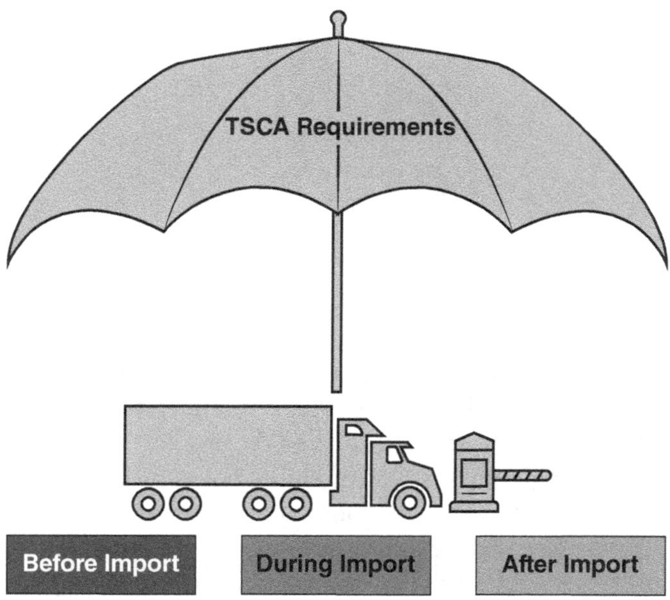

Figure 3.1. Requirements under TSCA may apply before, during, and after import of goods into the United States

1. *See On a Typical Day in Fiscal Year 2022, CBP . . .*, CBP, https://www.cbp.gov/newsroom/stats/typical-day-fy2022 (last modified June 21, 2024).

Given this potential scope, any company that has imported chemical substances, mixtures, or finished goods (articles under TSCA) must evaluate whether its import activities are regulated under TSCA, for several reasons. First and foremost, the preeminent requirement that applies to imports into the United States are "import certification requirements" under TSCA section 13. The only section dedicated entirely to imports, TSCA section 13 mandates that the U.S. Secretary of the Treasury must refuse entry into the customs territory of the United States of any chemical substance regulated under TSCA, including chemical substances contained in mixtures or in articles that are designed to be used or released from articles unless the importer certifies that the product complies with TSCA. Awareness of and compliance with TSCA section 13 requirements *before* importing a TSCA-regulated chemical or product ensure that companies have the information needed to prepare any requisite import certifications, and not only avoid the risk of CBP detaining or denying entry of a shipment, but also circumvent the risk of civil or criminal penalties under TSCA.

Import requirements under TSCA, however, are not limited to TSCA section 13. Though the term "import" appears only five times throughout the statutory text, companies that import products into the United States, whether import experts or newcomers to TSCA, must be aware that this scarcity of references does not mean that imports are not a regulatory priority under other sections of TSCA. On the contrary, TSCA defines "manufacture" as including "import into the customs territory of the United States." As a result of this key definition, companies that have never handled a chemical substance on their premises, such as companies that deal solely in finished goods, may be surprised that they are considered "manufacturers" under TSCA.

It may seem counterintuitive that both a domestic producer that manufactures a chemical at its facility and an importer that has never physically handled the substance are both considered "manufacturers" of that substance. The inclusion of "import," however, within the scope of TSCA's definition of "manufacture" enables EPA to catalog all chemical substances present in U.S. commerce, whether introduced via domestic manufacture or via import. EPA uses information gathered under TSCA reporting and notification requirements from manufacturers (including importers) to track, prioritize, evaluate, and regulate chemical substances in U.S. commerce. Accordingly, as crucial as it is for EPA to understand what, where, and how much of a chemical substance is currently in U.S. commerce, it is similarly crucial for current or prospective importers of covered substances or products to be aware of what, where, and how much of a chemical substance is in its supply chain and what regulatory requirements may apply.

As EPA's regulatory landscape continues to evolve under amended TSCA, importers, and predominantly importers of articles, may find that their import activities are subject to additional or new requirements. As a result, importers of finished products that may have previously wondered "What's a TSCA?" must begin evaluating their supply chains and identify product categories that may now fall within TSCA's orbit, including articles that may contain polychlorinated biphenyls (PCB) or per- and polyfluoroalkyl substances (PFAS).

Whether your company is well familiar with its importer-manufacturer status or just discovered that it can check "manufacture a chemical substance" off its bucket list, all companies that import products should be aware of several key definitions and both long-standing and emerging requirements under TSCA that are outlined in this chapter. First, this chapter will address the scope of import activities regulated under TSCA and the applicability of TSCA section 13 import certification requirements. Next, this chapter will address what importers need to know when preparing for compliance with other requirements under TSCA. This includes how importers can develop standard operating procedures (SOPs) or other protocols to review their supply chains and ensure compliance with TSCA.

3.2 The Scope of Regulated Import Activities under TSCA

The first step importers should take in assessing compliance with TSCA is to determine whether their import activities fall under TSCA's jurisdiction. All companies that import finished goods should have a baseline working knowledge of key TSCA definitions that apply to imports. For all importers, training on the requirements and key definitions that apply to importers is vital in navigating the many new and constantly evolving TSCA requirements.

3.2.1 Key TSCA Definitions All Importers Should Know

TSCA section 3(9) defines "manufacture" as including "import into the customs territory of the United States (as defined in general note

2 of the Harmonized Tariff Schedules of the United States), produce, or manufacture."[2] Accordingly, "manufacturers" under TSCA include chemical manufacturers and distributors that import chemical substances as a cornerstone of their businesses, companies that imported one-time samples for research and development (R&D) purposes, and companies that solely import finished goods containing chemical substances specifically regulated under TSCA (subject to a few exclusions).

TSCA regulates imports of three broad categories of products: chemical substances, chemical substances imported as part of mixtures, and chemical substances and mixtures imported as part of articles. Companies that exclusively import chemical substances and mixtures will have differing (and more) responsibilities under TSCA than companies that exclusively import finished goods (or articles). The definitions of these terms are key.

A "chemical substance" under TSCA includes

> [a]ny organic or inorganic substance of a particular molecular identity, including—
>
> (i) any combination of such substances occurring in whole or in part as a result of a chemical reaction or occurring in nature, and
>
> (ii) any element or uncombined radical.[3]

An example of an imported "chemical substance" includes the import of neat ethanol for use as a gasoline additive. A "mixture" is defined, generally, as any combination of two or more chemical substances.[4] Accordingly, the import of ethanol blended with gasoline is considered import of a mixture under TSCA. The importers of finished goods reading this may harken back to the last time they studied chemistry and picture chemical substances in various physical forms (i.e., dry powder, pellets or large crystals, water- or solvent-wet solids, other solids, gas or vapor, or liquids). Subject to a few exceptions and exemptions, imports of those substances and mixtures are likely regulated under TSCA.

---

2. 15 U.S.C. § 2602(9). General headnote 2 of the Tariff Schedules of the United States defines "customs territory of the United States" as including "only the States, the District of Columbia, and Puerto Rico." *See* U.S. International Trade Commission, Harmonized Tariff Schedule of the United States Revision 9, at GN2 (2024), https://hts.usitc.gov/.
3. TSCA § 3(2)(A), 15 U.S.C. § 2602(2)(A).
4. TSCA § 3(10), 15 U.S.C. § 2602(10).

TSCA also regulates the import of "articles." "Articles," in essence, are "finished goods" and encompass a wide range of products, including but not limited to consumer and industrial products such as clothing, furniture, cookware, electronics, transformers, and automobiles. Though TSCA does not legislatively define "article," EPA regulations implementing TSCA define "article" as a manufactured item formed to a specific shape or design whose end use function is dependent in whole or in part upon that shape or design during end use, and whose chemical composition does not change during use.[5] Though chemical substances that are imported as part of articles are generally exempt from certification or reporting requirements under TSCA, EPA is increasingly regulating articles and has issued a handful of TSCA rules that apply explicitly to chemicals as components of articles when imported and/or processed. This includes PFAS, which, as discussed in later chapters, are subject to reporting requirements under TSCA section 8(a)(7), and it includes PFAS imported as part of an article. Given the complexity of supply chains, importers, and, especially, importers of articles, importers may not have knowledge of the chemicals imported as part of articles they import.

In the case of PFAS, in addition to reviewing product materials such as any safety data sheets (SDSs), other product specifications, or supplier certifications (addressed later in this chapter), companies that import articles that are generally known to contain a chemical substance should be on high alert for potentially applicable requirements. In the case of PFAS, this includes products including but not limited to coatings for clothes and furniture (such as water-resistant fabrics or stain-resistant coatings), electronics, pipes, sports articles, toys, automotive products (e.g., lubricants (oils and grease)), transportation equipment, carpets, and keyboard cleaners (i.e., canned "air" dusters).

3.2.2 Exclusions from the Definition of "Chemical Substance"

Just as important as understanding *what is covered* under these definitions is understanding *what is not covered*. In addition to the definition provided earlier, TSCA section 3 also defines "chemical substance" as *excluding* the following categories:

5. 40 C.F.R. §§ 704.3, 710.3(d), 720.3(c) (2023).

- Any mixture
- Tobacco or tobacco products
- Any source material, special nuclear material, or byproduct materials as defined under the Atomic Energy Act of 1954 and its implementing regulations
- Articles such as firearms and ammunition[6]
- Any "pesticide," as defined under the Federal Insecticide, Fungicide, and Rodenticide Act (FIFRA)
- Any "food, food additive, drug, cosmetic, or device" regulated by FDA and as defined under section 201 of the Federal Food, Drug, and Cosmetic Act (FFDCA)

Because TSCA does not define "mixture" within the definition of "chemical substance," TSCA and EPA's implementing regulations specifically identify instances where a requirement applies to chemical substances, mixtures, or both.

While imports of tobacco products, nuclear materials, and firearms and ammunition are categorically excluded from regulation under TSCA, imports of pesticides and FDA-regulated products (any food, food additive, drug, cosmetic, or device, and components thereof) are also excluded from regulation under TSCA depending on the intended use of the chemical substance (including as part of a mixture or article) at the time of import.[7]

The import of these products "would not be subject to regulation under TSCA insofar as it is actually manufactured, processed, or distributed in commerce for use as a pesticide, food, food additive, drug, cosmetic or device."[8]

Returning to the example of imports of ethanol, a company could import ethanol in any number of ways that fall under FIFRA or FFDCA jurisdiction, such as use as a component in hand sanitizers (drugs) and in antimicrobial hard surface cleaners (pesticides). If ethanol is imported for *exclusive use* in hand sanitizer at the time of

---

6. This exclusion includes articles such as pistols, revolvers, and firearms (other than pistols and revolvers), the sale of which is subject to section 4181 of the Internal Revenue Code of 1986 (determined without regard to any exemptions from such tax provided by section 4182 or section 4221 or any other provision of such code) and any components of such articles (limited to shot shells, cartridges, and components of shot shells and cartridges). *See* TSCA § 3(2)(B)(v), 15 U.S.C. § 2602(2)(B)(v).
7. TSCA § 3(2)(B), 15 U.S.C. § 2602(2)(B).
8. *See* Part 710—Inventory Reporting Regulations, 42 Fed. Reg. 64,572, 64,585–86 (Dec. 23, 1977), https://www.govinfo.gov/content/pkg/FR-1977-12-23/pdf/FR-1977-12-23.pdf.

import, or imported as part of a formulated, antimicrobial hard surface cleaner, such imports would be considered imports of drugs or pesticides regulated under FFDCA and FIFRA, respectively, and not subject to TSCA. If a company imports ethanol for multiple uses or for undifferentiated uses, such as a company that imports neat ethanol for ultimate use in a fuel *and/or* in hand sanitizers, such imports are still subject to TSCA or fall under the dual jurisdiction of both TSCA and FFDCA. Accordingly, companies that import these types of products should maintain careful documentation, such as separate records, of imports intended for use under the exclusive jurisdiction of FFDCA or FIFRA and monitor activities that may be subject to regulation under TSCA.

Once a company determines that it imports chemical substances, mixtures, or articles that fall within the scope of TSCA, its attention must then turn to TSCA section 13 and whether potential import requirements apply. As discussed in the next section, even though TSCA excludes certain products from the definition of "chemical substances," TSCA section 13 establishes import certification requirements for imports of products that are not clearly identifiable as "excluded" to confirm that TSCA does not apply to the shipment.

3.3 TSCA Section 13 Import Requirements

TSCA section 13 governs the entry of chemical substances, mixtures, and articles containing chemical substances or mixtures, including R&D samples, into the customs territory of the United States. The CBP, via authority delegated by the Secretary of the Treasury, must refuse entry into the United States any shipment that fails to comply with TSCA or that is offered for entry in violation of TSCA section 5 or 6 or Subchapter IV (Lead Exposure Reduction).[9] In carrying out TSCA section 13, CBP regulations[10] and EPA's chemical substance import policy require that importers file signed statements, or import certificates, that certify a shipment is compliant at the time of import.[11] Import certificates are written statements wherein an importer certifies that imported chemicals comply with TSCA (a

9. 15 U.S.C. § 2612.
10. 19 C.F.R. §§ 12.118–.127, 127.28 (2024).
11. 40 C.F.R. § 707.20 (2023).

positive certification) or, if not clearly identified as excluded from TSCA, are not subject to TSCA (a negative certification). Compliance with Federal Express, DHL, and other companies' import clearance procedures may not guarantee that shipments comply with TSCA importation requirements.

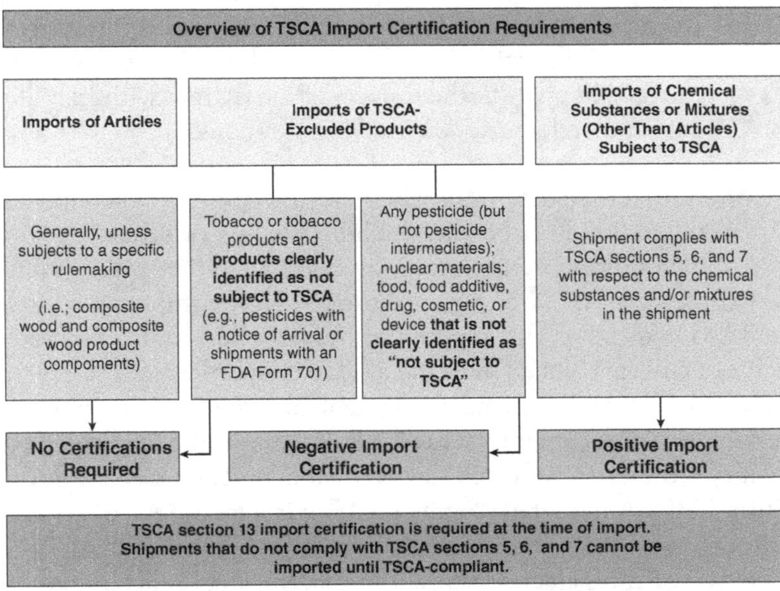

Figure 3.2. Chart summarizing requirements for TSCA import certification process

Whether companies handle imports directly or through customs brokers or other authorized agents, this section outlines the important definitions that apply under CBP regulations and steps that importers can take to help ensure compliance with TSCA section 13.

3.3.1 Positive Import Certification Requirements

In determining whether import certification requirements apply, importers should first look to CBP's implementing regulations for applicable definitions and requirements.

Of note, CBP defines "importer," or the "person primarily liable for the payment of any duties on the merchandise, or an authorized agent acting on his behalf," as including the following:[12]

12. 19 C.F.R. § 101.1 (2024).

- The consignee
- The importer of record
- The actual owner of the merchandise, if an actual owner's declaration and superseding bond has been filed in accordance with 19 C.F.R. § 141.20
- The transferee of the merchandise, if the right to withdraw the merchandise in a bonded warehouse has been transferred in accordance with 19 C.F.R. Part 144, Subpart C (requirements that apply to the transfer of the right to withdraw all or part of merchandise "entered for warehouse")[13]

Importers must then determine whether the shipment, which includes "the merchandise described on the bill of lading or other document used to file or support entry, or in the oral declaration when applicable," contains a TSCA-covered substance.[14] If the shipment contains regulated items, then the importer or the importer's authorized agent, such as a customs broker, must file a signed import certification on an appropriate entry document or commercial invoice, or as an attachment to either document, to the CBP director at the applicable port of entry.[15] Import certificates may be filed in writing or electronically within CBP's Automated Commercial Environment (ACE) system.[16] CBP issued a final rule requiring the use of ACE when filing TSCA import certificates electronically. Of note, this final rule eliminated a previous option for importers or their agents to submit a paper-based "blanket certification" that qualified for TSCA compliance recurring shipments of the same chemicals to the same port for a one-year duration.

CBP identifies four categories of merchandise that are subject to import certification requirements: chemical substances imported in bulk form, mixtures, specified articles that require positive certifications affirming the shipment is "TSCA-compliant," and TSCA-excluded

13. "Entered for warehouse" is defined as meaning that a warehouse entry summary, or documentation or electronic submission of data necessary for CBP to assess duties, collects statistics on imported merchandise and determines compliance with applicable laws or regulations. The summary has been filed with CBP in proper form through CBP's Automated Commercial Environment (ACE) system or any other CBP-authorized electronic data interchange system. *Id.* § 141.0a(g).
14. *Id.* § 101.1.
15. *Id.* § 12.121(a); 40 C.F.R. § 707.20(b)(2) (2023).
16. Toxic Substance [sic] Control Act Chemical Substance Import Certification Process Revisions, 81 Fed. Reg. 94,980 (Dec. 27, 2016) (codified at 19 C.F.R. pts. 12 & 127).

products, which may require a negative certification affirming that TSCA does not apply to the shipment.[17] CBP defines these categories as follows: "Chemical substances imported in bulk form" are chemical substances imported in containers.[18] Imports of neat ethanol, for example, for use as a gasoline additive would require positive certification. CBP defines "chemical substance as part of a mixture" as "a chemical substance . . . that is part of a combination of two or more chemical substances as set forth in section 3(10) of TSCA."[19] Imports of ethanol blended with gasoline also would require a positive certification. Articles containing a chemical substance or mixture, if so required by EPA by a specific rule or order issued under TSCA, also require a "positive" certification.[20] CBP regulations define "article" as a manufactured item that:

> (i) Is formed to a specific shape or design during manufacture,
> (ii) Has end use functions dependent in whole or in part upon its shape or design during the end use, and
> (iii) Has either no change of chemical composition during its end use or only those changes of composition which have no commercial purpose separate from that of the article [such as changes that occur upon end use for products including, but not limited to, matches, batteries, fuels and fuel additives, and other specified products,] except that fluids and particles are not considered articles regardless of shape or design.[21]

A chemical substance or mixture that is intended to be released from an article or that has an end use or commercial purpose separate from the article is not considered an article. For example, a pen is an article, but the ink in the pen is a substance (or a mixture of substances) and therefore is not a component of the article. For imports of articles, an article that is imported and then subsequently undergoes a phase change, such as plastic or metallic sheeting that is melted or extruded, or crayons, or soldering wires, is not considered an article at the time of import. Imported articles may undergo subsequent

17. 19 C.F.R. §§ 12.119, 12.121 (2024).
18. *Id.* § 12.120(b). CBP further specifies that this definition does not include the import of chemical substances as part of an article, and the chemical substance is intended to be removed from the container and has an end use or commercial purpose separate from the container.
19. *Id.* § 12.120(c).
20. *Id.* §§ 12.119(c), 12.120(a), 12.121(b).
21. *Id.* § 12.120(a).

processing if the shape or design of the product is maintained as an essential feature of the product. A copper ingot is not an article; a copper wire that is used to transmit electric signals over a distance is an article. For example, plastic or metallic sheeting cut to a different length, if necessary to make the final product, is still considered an article at the time of import. Similarly, a bolt of fabric that is cut and formed into apparel is still an article.

Chemical substances that are contained within articles for purposes of transportation or containment, such as drums, barrels, or other containers, are considered chemical substances imported "in bulk" and are not considered imported as part of an article, although the container is an article. Waste goods imported to be used to recover constituent chemicals (e.g., importing waste printed circuit boards for the purpose of recovering metals, such as copper) may have been articles when used, but as waste, the form of the good (a circuit board) is no longer related to its use (as a feedstock). EPA's guidance states that such goods are not considered articles.[22]

EPA considers a chemical substance or a mixture to be imported as part of an article only if the substances or mixtures are not intended to be removed or released from the article, in addition to having no end use or commercial purpose separate from the article.[23] For example, ethanol that is contained in a finished product or an article, regardless of whether it is in a cosmetic or other excluded product, would not be subject to TSCA section 13 import certification requirements because EPA has not promulgated a rulemaking to regulate ethanol imported as part of an article.

CBP must detain, at the importer's risk and expense, shipments of a commodity if it is banned by rule or under TSCA section 5 or 6 or if it has been ordered seized because of imminent hazards specified under TSCA section 7.[24] Moreover, CBP must also detain shipments of covered commodities if the CBP port director or EPA have reasonable grounds to believe the shipment does not comply with TSCA or

---

22. EPA, TSCA Chemical Data Reporting Fact Sheet: Imported Articles (2016), https://www.epa.gov/chemical-data-reporting/tsca-chemical-data-reporting-fact-sheet-imported-articles.
23. Office of Enforcement and Compliance Assurance, EPA, Compliance Guide for the Chemical Import Requirements of the Toxic Substances Control Act 4 (2008) [hereinafter Compliance Guide], https://www.epa.gov/sites/default/files/2013-09/documents/importguidejune2008.pdf.
24. 19 C.F.R. § 12.122(a) (2024).

whenever the importer fails to certify compliance.[25] If a shipment is detained, the importer has an opportunity to provide written documentation to show cause why the shipment should not be refused entry; otherwise, if entry is denied, the importer is required to export the noncomplying shipment or waive the right to export the shipment by presenting a notice of abandonment to the port director, and the importer incurs any liabilities for expenses incurred in storing or disposal of the abandoned or unclaimed merchandise.[26]

3.3.2 Negative Import Certification Requirements

Next, TSCA section 13 also requires importers of chemicals for non-TSCA uses to certify that compliance with TSCA is not required.[27] CBP requires negative import certifications for TSCA-excluded chemicals, or chemicals excluded from the definition of "chemical substances" under TSCA section 3(2)(B)(ii)–(vi) (including pesticides, food, food additives, drugs, cosmetics, or devices, nuclear material, tobacco products, and firearms and ammunition) in cases where it is not clear that the shipment is not subject to TSCA.[28] EPA guidance states that products "may be considered clearly identified when they are associated with another relevant agency's entry documentation or electronic entry filing requirements (e.g., notice of arrival for pesticides or applicable entry documentation for FDA regulated products)" or if the product is clearly excluded from TSCA.[29] For example, a shipment of neat ethanol for exclusive use in hand sanitizer is excluded from TSCA as an import of an FDA-regulated drug product, but requires a negative TSCA certification since it could also be imported for a TSCA use. Imports of beer, wine, and liquor that contain ethanol are clearly for human consumption; they fall under FDA jurisdiction and do not require TSCA certification.

25. *Id.* § 12.122(b). CBP procedures for detaining a shipment and procedures after detention, including the decision to permit or refuse entry of the shipment, are specified at 19 C.F.R. §§ 12.122(c)–(d), 12.123–.127.
26. *Id.* §§ 12.123–.127.
27. 40 C.F.R. § 707.20(b)(2)(ii) (2023).
28. 19 C.F.R. §§ 12.119(b), 12.120(d), 12.121(a)(2) (2024); 40 C.F.R. § 707.20(b)(2)(ii) (2023).
29. *TSCA Import-Export Requirements: TSCA Requirements for Importing Chemicals*, EPA, https://www.epa.gov/tsca-import-export-requirements/tsca-requirements-importing-chemicals (last updated July 11, 2024).

A formulated antimicrobial hard surface cleaner that is a pesticide product—labeled clearly as such—also does not require a negative certification. An imported product that has both TSCA and FIFRA uses would require a positive certification and a notice of arrival under FIFRA. In contrast, a fine fragrance perfume with ethanol as a solvent requires a negative TSCA certification.

Though TSCA-excluded chemicals are not considered "covered commodities," shipments must still include the requisite negative certification.

3.3.3 Shipments Where No Certification Is Required

Chemical substances or mixtures that are imported as part of an article generally do not require TSCA import certifications. Shipments of chemical substances, mixtures, or articles that are clearly identified as excluded from TSCA also do not require certification, such as tobacco or any tobacco product, or other excluded products. The import of a toy (or any other finished product) that does not include a chemical substance that requires an import certificate by a specific TSCA rule or order does not require any certification, as described further in this chapter.

3.3.4 Import Certification and Regulated Articles

EPA requires import certification for composite wood products (i.e., panels of hardwood plywood, particleboard, medium density fiberboard, and thin-medium density fiberboard), component parts containing such composite wood products, and finished goods containing such composite wood products that are imported into the United States beginning March 22, 2019, under TSCA Subchapter VI.[30] Finished goods subject to this requirement may include picture frames, furniture, or wooden toys that are made of regulated composite wood. Component parts containing regulated composite wood products may include parts to assemble a desk.

EPA may in the future take action to regulate other chemicals imported as part of articles, including requiring import certifications.

30. TSCA § 601, 15 U.S.C. § 2697; 40 C.F.R. § 770.30(d) (2023).

3.4 Preparing for Compliance with TSCA Section 13

Once a company decides to import a chemical substance, mixture, or covered article that requires a positive import certification, the company must take measures to confirm that the shipment complies with TSCA sections 5, 6, and 7, and Subchapter IV rules and orders. Companies may wish to refer to EPA's "TSCA Section 13 Import Compliance Checklist," which provides a road map for ascertaining the TSCA status of a shipment.[31]

3.4.1 Information Required to Certify TSCA Compliance

A positive import certification requires the importer to affirm that the shipment is TSCA-compliant. This includes confirming each of the following:

- **Whether the shipment is imported for the sole purpose of subsequent export.** TSCA section 12(a) states that TSCA requirements (except those under TSCA section 8) do not apply to any chemical substance that is imported solely for export from the United States and in a container that is stamped or labeled as intended for export only.
- **Whether the chemical substance is listed on the TSCA Chemical Substance Inventory (TSCA Inventory).** Importers should confirm whether the product or components thereof are listed on the TSCA Inventory (on either the public or confidential portions) or otherwise subject to an exemption or exclusion under TSCA. A substance that is a naturally occurring chemical substance is considered automatically included on the TSCA Inventory.[32]
- **If the substance is not on the TSCA Inventory and is a new chemical substance, whether the company submitted a TSCA section 5 notice or if the substance is otherwise exempt from notification requirements.** If the substance is not listed on the TSCA Inventory, the importer must confirm that it has submitted a TSCA section 5 notification and is in

31. Office of Pollution Prevention and Toxics, EPA, TSCA Section 13 Import Compliance Checklist (2008) (EPA 740-B-08-001), https://www.epa.gov/sites/default/files/2015-03/documents/checklist.pdf.
32. 40 C.F.R. § 710.4(b) (2023).

full compliance with any related requirements.[33] If a TSCA section 5 notice has not been submitted, the importer must confirm whether any of the exemptions for new chemicals apply to the substance.[34] This also includes new intergeneric microorganisms subject to TSCA section 5.[35]

- **Whether the chemical substance is subject to a TSCA section 5 order to which the importer is a party or a TSCA section 5 significant new use rule (SNUR).** The importer must confirm that the shipment complies with any requirements applicable under a TSCA section 5 order (including, for example, labeling requirements or import volume restrictions), or any requirements under a SNUR (including confirmation that the substance is not imported for a prohibited use or a use designated as a significant new use).
- **Whether the shipment contains chemical substances or products that are specifically regulated under TSCA section 6.** Importers should determine whether the shipment contains PCBs and articles containing PCBs;[36] asbestos-containing products;[37] chemical substances that may be used in metalworking fluids;[38] hexavalent chromium-based water treatment chemicals; and persistent, bioaccumulative, and toxic chemicals.[39] As EPA continues to issue risk management

33. This includes TSCA § 5 notices such as a premanufacture notice (PMN) pursuant to 40 C.F.R. Part 720; a low volume exemption (LVE) under 40 C.F.R. § 723.50; a low release and low exposures exemption (LoREX) under 40 C.F.R. § 723.50; or a test marketing exemption (TME) under 40 C.F.R. § 720.38. This also includes a microbial commercial activity notice (MCAN) for intergeneric microorganisms under 40 C.F.R. § 725.100 or a TSCA experimental release application (TERA) under 40 C.F.R. § 725.250.
34. This includes the R&D exemption (40 C.F.R. § 720.36); the polymer exemption (40 C.F.R. § 723.250); any exemption listed under 40 C.F.R. § 720.30(a) (such as a product manufactured for export only, import as an impurity, byproduct, or noncommercial R&D); or exempt as part of an article (40 C.F.R. §§ 720.3(c) and 720.22(b)(1), though articles are generally not subject to import certification requirements). This also includes exemptions for intergeneric microorganisms under 40 C.F.R. §§ 725.424, 725.428, and 725.300, or applicable R&D exemptions under 40 C.F.R. §§ 725.200–.239.
35. 40 C.F.R. pt. 725 (2023).
36. The import of PCBs is generally prohibited under TSCA § 6(e), 15 U.S.C. § 2605(e), and 40 C.F.R. Part 761, unless subject to an exemption or excluded from regulation.
37. Imports of some asbestos-containing products are prohibited under TSCA § 6(a), 15 U.S.C. § 2605(a), and 40 C.F.R. Part. 763, Subpart I.
38. Certain chemical substances that may be used in metalworking fluids are regulated under TSCA §§ 5(f) and 6(a), 15 U.S.C. §§ 2604(f) and 2605(a), and regulations at 40 C.F.R. Part 747.
39. 40 C.F.R. pt. 751, subpt. E (2023).

rules for substances undergoing risk evaluation, importers should remain apprised of requirements or prohibitions that may apply to the import of certain substances. This includes, for example, risk management rule requirements that apply to imports of methylene chloride.[40]

- **Whether the substance is subject to an action under TSCA section 7.** EPA has the authority to commence a civil action to seize an imminently hazardous chemical substance or mixture or any article containing the substance or mixture, or for relief against any person that manufactures (including import), processes, distributes in commerce, uses, or disposes of an imminently hazardous chemical or mixture, or article containing the substance or mixture.[41]

An importer must be able to affirm that the substance complies with all applicable requirements under TSCA sections 5, 6, and 7 to complete a positive import certification.

3.4.2 Supplier Certifications and the Standard for Determining Compliance

Importers must make a good-faith effort to comply with TSCA section 13 import certification requirements and, whenever possible, base certifications that a shipment is TSCA-compliant on the importer's actual knowledge. Companies may use SDSs, product specifications, and related commercial documents to make the certification. What if the company does not have actual knowledge of the chemical components of an imported product?

EPA's policy statement on imports acknowledges "importers may not have actual knowledge of the chemical composition of imported mixtures." In those cases, companies should make a good-faith effort to determine whether the shipment complies with TSCA and "attempt to discover the chemical constituents of the shipment by contacting another party to the transaction (e.g., his principal or the foreign manufacturer)."[42] Often, companies develop an SOP for obtaining this information via "supplier certification" letters. The importer may

40. *Id.* subpt. B.
41. TSCA § 7(a)(i), 15 U.S.C. § 2606(a)(i).
42. 40 C.F.R. § 707.20(c)(1)(iii) (2023).

request that the foreign supplier of the imported products identify the product components or "at least state that the substances comply with TSCA."[43]

While EPA's policy is that importers, like domestic manufacturers, must ensure that chemical importation complies with TSCA, EPA will consider the effort by an importer to learn the identities of imported substances and determine their TSCA status in determining whether an importer violated TSCA by importing a noncomplying shipment.[44] The "greater the effort" to obtain this information, the smaller the chances of committing a violation. If a violation does occur, EPA will consider the evidence of an importer's good-faith efforts to verify compliance, such as documentation of supplier certification letters or other efforts to obtain the information, which "may obviate or mitigate the assessment of a civil penalty."[45]

To the extent possible, importers should request detailed information in a supplier certification letter that addresses all products or product components in the shipment. This includes information such as the Chemical Abstracts Service Registry Number (CAS RN) or Accession Number (AN) and whether any product or any component thereof is listed on the public or confidential portions of the TSCA Inventory, subject to any TSCA section 5 notices or exemptions, or regulated under a rule or order issued under TSCA sections 5, 6, and 7.

Though importers are not required to certify compliance with other sections of TSCA, importers should also request information on whether the product or any component thereof is subject to TSCA section 12(b) export notification requirements or actions under TSCA sections 4 and 8. This information will ensure that importers are aware of and comply with applicable requirements after import.

If the foreign supplier considers the identities of a chemical substance or product compositions to be proprietary or confidential business information (CBI), the importer should offer to enter into agreements to ensure that information is protected, such as a nondisclosure agreement (NDA) or confidential disclosure agreement (CDA). Companies should involve, as necessary, their sales departments or management to facilitate discussions regarding sharing

43. *Id.*
44. *Id.*; *id.* § 707.20(b)(1).
45. *Id.* § 707.20(c)(1)(iii).

information. If a supplier still declines to provide detailed information, then the importer should request a written assurance from the supplier that the shipment complies with TSCA. The importer should retain documentation of its efforts to obtain such information and the written supplier certification and may rely on the supplier's good-faith representation to demonstrate its own compliance with TSCA.

If a supplier declines to provide *any* assurance as to a shipment's compliance with TSCA, importers must be aware that they would be strictly liable for noncompliance with TSCA in the event of a violation, such as an import of a new chemical substance in violation of TSCA section 5. Though supply chains may be complex, this behavior may invite unacceptable business or regulatory compliance risks. Accordingly, importers should avoid importing products from suppliers that are unwilling to provide information to ensure TSCA compliance.

3.4.3 Protecting Confidential Information

Though TSCA section 13 does not require importers to include substantive information in an import certificate that may be considered CBI, if information that may be considered confidential *is* included in an import certificate, companies can include a notation stating "confidential," "proprietary," or "trade secret" next to the item or items for which confidentiality is claimed. A substantiation for all information claimed as confidential, other than information exempt from substantiation pursuant to TSCA section 14(c)(2), also must be provided to EPA at the time of submission. With regard to electronic import certificates, CBP has stated that "access to nonpublic data contained in the ACE system will be limited to CBP officers and relevant personnel at CBP headquarters, as well as limited personnel at partner government agencies."[46] CBP also notes that access to ACE data including CBI is "limited to personnel with the appropriate roles and permissions and is managed by various audit controls on a continual basis."[47]

46. Toxic Substance [sic] Control Act Chemical Substance Import Certification Process Revisions, 81 Fed. Reg. 94,980, 94,982–83 (Dec. 27, 2016).
47. *Id.* at 94,983.

3.4.4 Shipments That Do Not Enter through a Customs Port

If a shipment bypasses customs, such as imports via regular mail or courier, EPA requires the submission of an import certificate directly to EPA. The first person receiving the shipment is considered the "importer" of that shipment and is responsible for ensuring that the proper positive or negative certification is made to EPA. The import certification can then be based on documentation from the supplier. A paper copy of the import certificate should then be submitted to EPA pursuant to EPA instructions.[48]

This may occur, for example, when a foreign supplier ships R&D chemicals directly to a U.S. R&D laboratory. Companies that supply R&D laboratories should establish an SOP wherein an individual is responsible for contacting overseas suppliers to obtain the necessary information or supporting documentation.

3.4.5 Recordkeeping

TSCA section 13 and its implementing regulations do not specify how long importers should maintain documents demonstrating compliance. In the event of an EPA inspection, however, importers may wish to retain copies of import certifications for each imported chemical substance, mixture, or article for a period of five years after the date of import.

A best practice is to maintain an import certification file with the following:

- Copies of any import certificate
- Any foreign supplier's invoice concerning the shipment
- Any bills of lading concerning the shipment
- Any supplier certification letters concerning the chemical substance, mixture, or article
- If applicable, all correspondence between the importer, EPA, and CBP concerning a detained shipment

3.4.6 SOPs and Other Best Practices

Importers may memorialize the abovementioned procedures into an SOP, designating an employee who will be responsible for managing

48. Compliance Guide, *supra* note 23, at 20.

imports, conducting outreach to suppliers, and ensuring compliance with any applicable TSCA section 13 requirements. The following best practices may be addressed in an SOP:

- Maintain a copy of a TSCA section 13 compliance checklist and draft import certification letters.
- Maintain awareness of the supply chain and assign an employee or contractor who is trained on TSCA section 13 requirements who will determine the regulatory status of all shipments and maintain TSCA import certification records.
- Obtain necessary supplier certification letters.
- Coordinate with a customer's broker (which may include private individuals and organizational brokerages) that is regulated and empowered by CBP to assist importers in meeting federal requirements governing imports and exports. Brokers submit necessary information and appropriate payments to CBP on behalf of their clients.
- Maintain records of import certificates and good-faith efforts to gather information from suppliers to ensure compliance with TSCA section 13 import certification requirements for a period of five years.
- Maintain important documentation relating to imports, including a foreign supplier's invoice, the bill of lading, ACE cargo release indicating EPA "may proceed" status, and correspondence from EPA and CBP in the event of a detained shipment.
- Prepare filing of import certificates for imports that did not enter through a customs port.

3.5 TSCA Requirements That Apply to Importers as "Manufacturers"

Though "import" only appears a handful of times in the statutory text, EPA's TSCA implementing regulations at 40 C.F.R. Chapter I, Subchapter R are peppered with requirements that apply to "import." These requirements that apply to "manufacturers (including importers)" fall under TSCA sections 4, 5, 6, 7, 8, and 12, in addition to TSCA section 13. While EPA may often exclude chemicals imported as part of articles from regulation, EPA has increasingly exercised its authority to extend regulatory requirements to imported finished goods. Importers or companies that seek to import chemical substances, mixtures, and articles under TSCA should be aware of requirements triggered by such imports and issues to consider before initiating an import. The following requirements apply to manufacturers—"including importers"—under TSCA.

3.5.1 TSCA Section 8 Information Collection and Recordkeeping

Importers of chemical substances and mixtures are subject to TSCA section 8 preliminary assessment information rule (PAIR) rulemakings[49] and other chemical-specific reporting and recordkeeping requirements.[50] Importers are also required to maintain records of allegations by employees or downstream users of significant adverse health or environmental reactions and, upon request, to provide those records to EPA under TSCA section 8(c).[51] TSCA section 8(d) requirements to submit copies or lists of unpublished health and safety studies on specified chemical substances and mixtures upon rulemaking also apply to importers of chemical substances and mixtures.[52]

Under TSCA section 8(e), importers of chemical substances, mixtures, *and articles* must report immediately (generally, within 30 calendar days) information to EPA that reasonably supports the conclusion that a chemical substance presents a substantial risk of injury to health or the environment, unless such information is otherwise known to the EPA administrator.

Other significant reporting requirements include TSCA section 8(a) chemical data reporting. Importers of chemical substances must report information on import volumes and other related information to EPA every four years.[53] Importers must track the volumes of chemical substances and mixtures imported in each calendar year and must be cognizant that lower thresholds apply to chemical substances that are subject to a proposed or final rule, order, or judicial action under TSCA section 4, 5, 6, or 7. Chemical substances imported as part of articles are not subject to the quadrennial Chemical Data Reporting (CDR) rule.

---

49. 40 C.F.R. pt. 712, subpt. B (2023).
50. *Id.* pt. 704, subpt. B.
51. 15 U.S.C. § 2607(c); 40 C.F.R. pt. 717 (2023).
52. 15 U.S.C. § 2607(d); 40 C.F.R. pt. 716 (2023).
53. 40 C.F.R. pt. 711 (2023).

Importers of any PFAS, including imports of PFAS as part of an article, in any quantity between January 1, 2022, and December 31, 2022, are subject to reporting requirements under TSCA section 8(a)(7).[54] This is a broad reporting requirement that contains nearly no exemptions, though streamlined requirements are available for articles importers and small manufacturers that exclusively import articles. Though TSCA section 8(a)(7) PFAS reporting is a one-time reporting requirement that concludes on May 8, 2025, for most reporters, and November 10, 2025, for small articles importers, this requirement reflects the significance of tracking imports, identifying product components, and the fact that reporting requirements for specified chemical substances, mixtures, and articles may be instituted several years after the date of import.

3.5.2 TSCA Section 4 Testing Requirements

Under TSCA section 4, EPA may issue a test rule, negotiate an enforceable consent agreement (ECA), or issue an order that requires manufacturers and importers to conduct specified tests and submit data on chemical substances or mixtures. EPA has interpreted its TSCA section 4 authority as extending broadly to both current importers of a chemical substance and past import activities, such as companies that imported a chemical substance or mixture at any time and in any quantity within the past five years.[55] The potential applicability of a TSCA section 4 test rule, ECA, or order could be foreseen, depending on the prioritization status of an existing chemical for risk evaluation under TSCA section 6 or other regulatory priorities.

3.5.3 TSCA Section 5 Manufacturing and Processing Notices and Use Restrictions

In addition to ensuring compliance with TSCA section 13, companies may not import a chemical substance that is not listed on the TSCA Inventory unless the substance is subject to a specific exemption or notice, such as a low volume exemption (LVE) or low release

54. *Id.* pt. 705.
55. EPA, Policies regarding Manufacturers and Processors Subject to TSCA Section 4(a) Testing (2022), https://www.epa.gov/system/files/documents/2022-08/Policy_Manufacturing_Processing_August_2022.pdf.

and low exposures exemption (LoREX).[56] An importer must submit a premanufacture notice (PMN) or any other applicable TSCA section 5 notice prior to the import of any new chemical substance. Companies must similarly monitor imported chemical substances and mixtures for applicable SNURs and ensure that the shipment of an import does not constitute an activity designated as a "significant new use" under a SNUR without first submitting a significant new use notice (SNUN).[57] Importers should seek confirmation from suppliers that a chemical substance is listed on the TSCA Inventory and determine whether any substance is regulated by a TSCA section 5 SNUR. Importers must also ensure compliance with the requirements of any applicable order under TSCA section 5.

3.5.4 TSCA Section 6 Risk Evaluation and Risk Management

EPA is authorized under TSCA section 6 to implement risk management measures to protect against unreasonable risk of injury to health or the environment. All parties along the value chain—manufacturers, importers, processors, distributors, and commercial users—are potentially subject to section 6 requirements, including chemicals when part of articles. Importers should remain attentive to EPA's risk management rules as EPA continues to complete risk evaluations under amended TSCA. Particularly, importers of articles that were never before subject to TSCA requirements for certain import activities may now be subject to regulation.

3.5.5 TSCA Section 7 Judicial Actions to Address Imminent Hazard

TSCA section 7 authorizes EPA to initiate a judicial action in U.S. district court when the manufacture (including import), processing, distribution in commerce, use, or disposal of a chemical substance, mixture, or article is likely to result in section 7 actions that could include seizure of subject chemicals or mixtures (or any article containing such chemical substances or mixtures), recalls, or public notifications. Though a scarcely used authority, importers should be aware of potential actions.

56. 40 C.F.R. pts. 720, 723 (2023).
57. *Id.* pt. 721.

3.5.6 TSCA Section 12(b) Export Notification Requirements

TSCA section 12(a) states that a chemical substance, mixture, or article that is imported solely for subsequent export *is not* subject to TSCA (other than TSCA section 8). If an importer does not import a chemical substance solely for export, but then subsequently exports the substance, mixture, or article, export notifications are required if the export contains a chemical substance or mixture subject to a proposed or final rule, order, or judicial action under TSCA section 4, 5, 6, or 7.[58] Furthermore, if CBP denies entry of a noncompliant shipment, and the importer chooses to export the shipment to a foreign country, then TSCA section 12(b) notification requirements may apply.

TAKEAWAYS

- Companies that import chemical substances, mixtures, and finished goods or articles must be aware of requirements that apply to their businesses under TSCA section 13 and result from the regulation of imports as "manufacture" under TSCA.
- For complying with TSCA section 13 import certification requirements, companies should gather all requisite information to certify compliance before importing a shipment. This includes preparing, as applicable, supplier certification letters or making other good-faith efforts to determine whether a shipment is TSCA-compliant.
- Obtaining suppler certifications also ensures that importers have enough information to comply with requirements that apply to importers as manufacturers of chemical substances under TSCA.
- Importers must be aware of regulatory developments under TSCA relating to EPA's enforcement priorities, substances undergoing risk evaluation that will be subject to TSCA section 6 risk management rules (including as part of articles), and other emerging regulatory developments under TSCA sections 4, 5, and 8. The rules change quickly, making the marketplace potentially treacherous for the unaware. Companies should be aware of potential requirements that may apply to a substance, mixture, or article before initiating the import.

---

58. *Id.* pt. 707.

4

New and Existing Chemicals: How EPA Evaluates and Manages Risk

Richard E. Engler and Todd J. Stedeford

Key Messages

- EPA's authority under TSCA is very different for the regulation of new and existing chemicals.
- EPA's implementation of regulations on new and existing chemicals both represent challenges and opportunities.
- Innovation plans need to be strategic in accounting for these differences or risk market entry challenges.

The Toxic Substances Control Act (TSCA) divides chemical substances into two categories: existing chemicals and new chemicals. Whether a substance is new or existing is based on whether the substance is listed on the TSCA Chemical Substance Inventory (TSCA Inventory). Any substance listed on the TSCA Inventory is an existing chemical. Any substance not listed on the TSCA Inventory is a new chemical. (*See* Figure 4.1.) This divide is important because

TSCA provides the U.S. Environmental Protection Agency (EPA) with separate, distinct authority and obligations for new and existing chemicals. The two key sections of TSCA that give EPA the authority to review substances and issue protective regulations are section 5,[1] for new chemicals, and section 6,[2] for existing chemicals. Except for certain exemptions discussed in more detail in this chapter, a company may not manufacture or import a new chemical substance unless the company submits a premanufacture notice (PMN), and EPA completes its review, issues a risk determination, and takes the necessary actions required by section 5. After EPA completes its review of a PMN, the submitter may manufacture (or import) the substance and then must file a notice of commencement (NOC). Submitting the NOC places the substance on the TSCA Inventory and changes the substance from "new" to "existing."

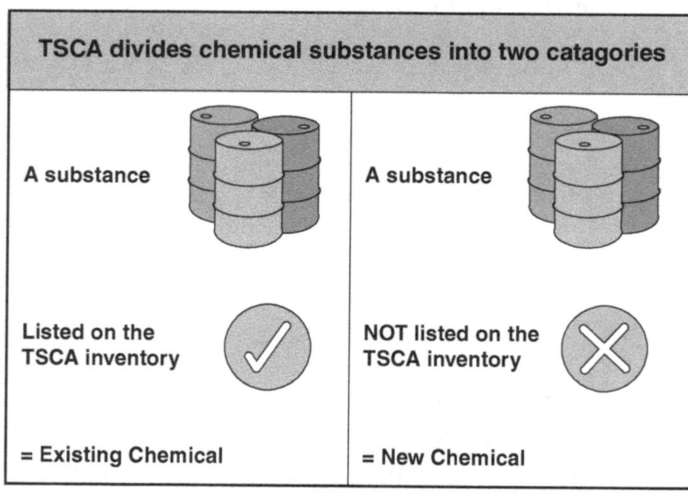

Figure 4.1. TSCA divides chemical substances into two categories

EPA interprets TSCA to also apply to microorganisms that are used for a nonexempt TSCA purpose. For example, microbes that are used to ferment sugars to ethanol for use as fuel is a nonexempt use of the microbe. The same microbe might be used to make ethanol for human consumption, in which case, that use of the microbe and the

1. 15 U.S.C. § 2504.
2. *Id.* § 2505.

ethanol are excluded from TSCA authority. If a substance (or in this case, a microbe) is used for both TSCA and non-TSCA purposes, the manufacturer must comply with the statutory requirements and regulations for each of those controlling statutes. For microorganisms that are not naturally occurring, a microbial commercial activity notice (MCAN) is required.[3] An MCAN is effectively a PMN for a microbe.

4.1 The TSCA Inventory

The TSCA Inventory is central to EPA's regulatory authority and is often thought of or referred to as the list of chemicals in commerce in the United States, but there are a variety of reasons that a substance is not listed on the TSCA Inventory, yet is still permitted in commerce without a PMN. Exemptions will be discussed in more detail in this chapter. The TSCA Inventory is divided into two portions: a public portion and a confidential portion. Substances listed on the public portion of the TSCA Inventory are listed with a Chemical Abstracts Service Registry Number (CAS RN) and a specific Chemical Abstracts (CA) Index Name. Substances listed on the confidential portion of the TSCA Inventory are listed with an Accession Number (AN) and a generic name. ANs are assigned randomly by EPA when the substance is placed on the TSCA Inventory. Existing chemicals are also assigned a commercial status as "active" or "inactive." After enactment of the Frank R. Lautenberg Chemical Safety for the 21st Century Act (Lautenberg), EPA issued regulations that required manufacturers and importers, and allowed processors, to submit notices of activity (NOAs). This process allowed EPA to designate each substance as active or inactive in commerce. About half of the more than 80,000 substances listed on the TSCA Inventory are listed as active. Knowing which substances are active allows EPA to focus its regulatory reviews on those that are active in commerce, leaving the inactive substances to a later time (e.g., if a manufacturer files an NOA to convert an inactive substance to active). There are approximately 42,000 substances listed as active on the TSCA Inventory and another 44,000 listed as inactive.

3. EPA, Microbial Products of Biotechnology: Summary of Regulations under the Toxic Substances Control Act (2012), https://www.epa.gov/sites/production/files/2015-08/documents/biotech_fact_sheet.pdf.

4.2 Chemical Identity

Before beginning a search of the TSCA Inventory to confirm whether a substance is listed, it is important to establish correctly the identity of the substance under the TSCA nomenclature rules and the associated CAS RN or AN. It is unfortunately true that a product may be identified by one CAS RN in the United States under TSCA and a different CAS RN in Europe or various Asian countries. For simple substances, the identity is likely the same, but for variable or complex substances, the identities may diverge because of the different approaches to identity.

There are a variety of ways to establish the correct identity. Generally, a company should seek guidance from an expert in TSCA nomenclature. An expert can help evaluate the commercial intent for the product (e.g., whether a component may be identified as an impurity) and how variability in the product might have to be represented in the identity. These considerations are technical and fact-specific and can vary from country to country. Do not neglect the importance of establishing the correct chemical identity—it is not enough to know the chemistry, it is also essential to understand the TSCA nomenclature rules and that TSCA rules are not the same as the rules used in other countries or regions.

Once the correct identity has been established, a search of the public portion of the TSCA Inventory for the CAS RN may commence. If not listed on the public portion of the TSCA Inventory, entities can submit a bona fide intent to manufacture notice (BFI) to EPA. This is essentially a statement that a submitter has a serious intent to produce or import a chemical and it is not known whether the chemical is listed on the TSCA Inventory. EPA will evaluate the BFI and respond if the substance is listed and, if so, provide the AN and whether the substance is the subject of a regulation (e.g., a significant new use rule (SNUR)). If the substance is not listed on the public or confidential portion of the TSCA Inventory, it may only be manufactured or imported under one of several PMN exemptions.

4.3 PMN Exemptions

PMN exemptions fall into several categories. There are self-executing exemptions, exemptions with limited notification requirements, and exemptions that require notification much like the PMN requirements.

4.3.1 Self-Executing Exemptions

There are several exemptions to the requirement to submit a PMN for a new chemical:

- Chemicals that are not subject to TSCA jurisdiction[4]
- Mixtures;[5] individual components of a mixture are not exempt; each component must be evaluated individually for TSCA compliance
- Substances manufactured or imported for research and development (R&D)[6]
- Substances manufactured exclusively for export and labeled as such[7]
- Byproducts that are burned for fuel (including incineration), disposed of as a waste, including in a landfill or for enriching soil, or used only to extract a component substance (although the extracted component must itself be listed or eligible for another exemption)[8]
- Substances with no separate commercial purpose, such as impurities, substances formed by aging or weathering of another substance, and substances formed during end use (such as a cured adhesive), and nonisolated intermediates[9]
- Substances manufactured or imported as part of noncommercial (e.g., academic) R&D[10]
- Substances imported in finished products that meet the TSCA definition of an "article"; such components must not be released intentionally from the article—a pen is an article, but because the ink is intended to be released, the ink is a substance (or a mixture of substances)[11]

Substances that meet the definition of a "naturally occurring substance"[12] are automatically included on the TSCA Inventory.[13]

4. 40 C.F.R. § 720.30(a) (2023).
5. *Id.* § 720.30(b).
6. *Id.* § 720.30(c).
7. *Id.* § 720.30(e).
8. *Id.* § 720.30(g).
9. *Id.* § 720.30(h).
10. *Id.* § 720.30(i).
11. *Id.* § 720.22(b)(1).
12. *Id.* § 710.4(b).
13. *Id.* § 710.27(b).

Because naturally occurring substances are automatically included on the TSCA Inventory, all naturally occurring substances are existing chemicals regardless of whether each substance is explicitly listed on the TSCA Inventory. Note that to qualify as naturally occurring, it is not sufficient that the substance occur in nature, it may only be processed by one of the nonchemical means specified in the definition.

4.3.2 Limited Notification Exemptions

After reviewing thousands of polymer PMNs in the 1980s and 1990s, EPA established criteria for polymers of low concern and promulgated regulations to exempt such polymers from the PMN requirements (the TSCA Polymer Exemption).[14] If a polymer meets the a priori low-hazard criteria of the TSCA Polymer Exemption, a company may manufacture or import the polymer without first notifying EPA.[15] Polymers manufactured under the TSCA Polymer Exemption are not added to the TSCA Inventory.

Some polymers are excluded from the TSCA Polymer Exemption because EPA cannot conclude that the polymer type will not present an unreasonable risk. For example, polymers that degrade in the environment are not eligible for the TSCA Polymer Exemption.[16] It seems counterintuitive that degradable polymers are not polymers of low concern. It is not that EPA wishes to disincentivize degradable polymers, it is that without knowing what the degradants are, EPA cannot conclude that the polymer and its degradants are not an unreasonable risk.

The January following the first time a company manufactures a particular polymer under the exemption, the company must notify EPA that the company availed itself of the exemption for one or more new polymer(s) in the preceding year. The notification need not include the specific details about the exempt polymer, but the company must keep records documenting that the polymer meets the exemption criteria.

14. Premanufacture Notification Exemptions; Revisions of Exemptions for Polymers; Final Rule, 60 Fed. Reg. 16,316 (Mar. 29, 1995).
15. 40 C.F.R. § 723.250 (2023).
16. *Id.* § 723.250(d)(3).

4.3.3 Exemption Notices

There are several exemption types that require review by EPA prior to manufacture or import of a substance for a nonexempt purpose. The three types are a low volume exemption (LVE), a low release and low exposures exemption (LoREX), and a test marketing exemption (TME). An exemption grants permission to the notice submitter to manufacture or import the substance described under the conditions described in the notice. Other companies (competitors or customers) may not manufacture or import under the authority of the first company's exemption notice.

EPA has 30 days (LVE or LoREX) or 45 days (TME) to review an exemption notice (depending on the notice type). After its review, EPA will either grant or deny the exemption notice. EPA will sometimes request changes to the notice prior to granting the notice. In these cases, EPA's grant is conditioned on the submitter making those changes. Unlike a PMN, if EPA grants an exemption notice, the substance is not added to the TSCA Inventory (the substance is exempt from such listing). Also, unlike a PMN, most aspects of exemption notices are automatically binding on the manufacturer. Manufacturing site, release and exposure conditions, and the specific use are all automatically binding. If a company wishes to change any of those binding conditions, the company must submit a modification notice and wait for EPA to review the modified conditions and grant the modification.

LVEs are the most common type of exemption notice. If EPA grants an LVE, the submitter may manufacture or import (as specified in the LVE) up to ten metric tons of the substance (or a lower quantity if so specified) in a one-year period (365 days from the grant date, not a calendar year).[17] Companies sometimes use an LVE to bridge between R&D and large-scale production. An LVE allows the company to commercialize the substance without the additional time and expense of a PMN. LVEs do not expire but can be revoked.[18]

Another type of exemption notice is a LoREX. LoREXs are not limited to under ten metric tons. Instead, LoREXs are limited to very strict release and exposure quantities. A LoREX allows for large-scale production under very strict controls. Because the LoREX criteria are extremely strict, many submitters will opt for the greater flexibility of an LVE if they can maintain production below ten metric tons.

---

17. *Id.* § 723.50(a)(1)(i).
18. *Id.* § 723.50(h)(2).

The last type of exemption notice is a TME. A TME allows the submitter a limited amount of time (as specified in the TME notice) to include the substance in a product distributed widely for the purposes of test marketing.[19] TMEs are binding on both the quantity specified in the notice and the test marketing timeframe. Because of these limitations, many companies will submit an LVE instead of a TME, unless the ten-metric-ton limit of an LVE is not a sufficient quantity to carry out the test marketing.

4.4 Section 5—New Chemicals Reviews

When a PMN is submitted, EPA must review it and make a determination. TSCA specifies that EPA has 90 days to review a PMN (EPA may extend the review period by an additional 90 days). If EPA fails to make a determination within the review period, EPA must refund the submission fee. As a practical matter, if the end of the review period is approaching, EPA requests that submitters voluntarily suspend the review period, meaning that PMNs do not actually reach the end of the review period because the submitter has "paused" the clock. While such suspensions are nominally voluntary, most submitters assent rather than take a position adverse to EPA and face potential unilateral action by EPA and, if the submitter disagrees with EPA's determination, leaving judicial review as the only remedy.

4.4.1 PMN Determinations

The new chemical review process under TSCA is rigorous. EPA carefully reviews every PMN, MCAN, or significant new use notice (SNUN) submitted according to a detailed step-wise process. EPA must review and make one of the determinations for each submission as specified in section 5(a)(3):[20]

- Substance presents unreasonable risk
- Insufficient information to assess health and environmental effects
- In the absence of sufficient information, the chemical

19. *Id.* § 720.38.
20. 15 U.S.C. § 2604(a)(3).

  - May present an unreasonable risk, *or*
  - Will be produced in substantial quantities, may enter the environment in substantial quantities, or have significant or substantial human exposure
- The chemical is not likely to present unreasonable risk[21]

In each case, EPA must evaluate for "unreasonable risk of injury to health or the environment, without consideration of costs or other nonrisk factors, including an unreasonable risk to a potentially exposed or susceptible subpopulation identified as relevant by the Administrator under the conditions of use."[22] "Conditions of use" (COUs) is an important and ill-defined term that is discussed in more detail later in the chapter.

A finding that a substance "presents" unreasonable risk is an unusual outcome. It requires that EPA have both sufficient hazard and exposure information to conclude that COUs are an unreasonable risk.

Since enactment of Lautenberg, EPA has in almost all circumstances limited its conclusion that a substance is "not likely to present unreasonable risk" to substances for which EPA finds a low hazard for health and the environment (for both acute and chronic endpoints). This means that, in the majority of cases, EPA is making "may present" unreasonable risk and/or "insufficient information" determinations.

4.4.2 Key Terms

There are several key terms that were introduced in 2016. Of particular relevance for section 5 is the term "conditions of use" that includes consideration of "reasonably foreseen" COUs. Congress did not define what is "reasonably foreseen" in the statute or in the legislative history. The Senate Report states that "misuse" is not included in "reasonably foreseen" COUs.[23]

---

21. To grant an exemption notice, EPA must conclude the substance will not present an unreasonable risk. TSCA § 5(h)(1)(A), 15 U.S.C. § 2604(h)(1)(A). This is, nominally, a higher bar than "not likely to present unreasonable risk," but as EPA is implementing TSCA in 2024, EPA interprets the two to be effectively the same and EPA requires a high degree of certainty that there will not be an unreasonable risk.
22. TSCA § 5(a)(3)(C), 15 U.S.C. § 2604(a)(3)(C).
23. Frank R. Lautenberg Chemical Safety for the 21st Century Act, Report Together with Minority Views, S. Rep. No. 114-67, at 7 (2015) [hereinafter Lautenberg Senate Report], https://www.congress.gov/114/crpt/srpt67/CRPT-114srpt67.pdf.

Another key term is "not likely to present unreasonable risk." Congress does not define how likely a circumstance must be to be likely or not. What is clear is that Congress eschewed using the well-established standard of "reasonable certainty of no harm" so "not likely to present unreasonable risk under the [reasonably foreseen] conditions of use" must be less certain than "reasonable certainty of no harm." At the time of this writing, EPA has yet to elucidate its thinking on the limits of what is reasonably foreseen or how unlikely a COU must be to be "not likely."

Another key term is "potentially exposed or susceptible subpopulation." This term includes workers and the general population and includes those that might be at risk for greater exposure or more significant adverse effects and explicitly includes "infants, children, pregnant women, workers, or the elderly." EPA correctly points to this term as a source for its authority to evaluate workplace exposures—that is, the term requires that EPA evaluate risk to workers. What is less clear is that if EPA identifies potential risk to workers, whether EPA is required to issue protective measures under TSCA, that EPA may issue protective measures when Occupational Safety and Health Administration (OSHA) requirements are insufficient, or whether EPA is precluded from issuing protective measures by TSCA section 9(c).[24] As a practical matter, since 2016, EPA assumes that OSHA regulations have no protective effect in the workplace, even though EPA routinely cites to OSHA standards when EPA issues TSCA regulations.

4.4.3 PMN Outcomes

Depending on which determination EPA makes for a PMN, EPA must take one of several actions. If EPA makes a determination that the substance is "not likely to present unreasonable risk," EPA must publish the basis for its determination; this determination is final agency action. The submitter may proceed to commercialize the new substance regardless of how much time remains in the review period.

If EPA makes a "may present unreasonable risk" or an "insufficient information" determination, or some combination thereof, EPA

24. TSCA section 9(c) states: "In exercising any authority under this chapter, the Administrator shall not, for purposes of [section 4(b)(1) of the Occupational Safety and Health Act of 1970], be deemed to be exercising statutory authority to prescribe or enforce standards or regulations affecting occupational safety and health." 15 U.S.C. § 2608(c).

must issue an order under TSCA section 5(e). The order must limit activities "to the extent necessary" to protect against the unreasonable risk identified in the determination. In the majority of cases, EPA negotiates consent orders—orders in which both EPA and the submitter agree to the terms that protect against the risks identified and are commercially acceptable to the submitter and its supply chain.

If EPA makes a "presents unreasonable risk" determination, EPA must issue an order under TSCA section 5(f) and may also propose a rule under TSCA section 6(a). As stated earlier, a "presents" determination is unusual and generally, if EPA comes to this conclusion, the submitter will withdraw the PMN and abandon the technology rather than EPA issuing an order that bans the substance for the intended activity.

Whether EPA issues an order under section 5(e) or 5(f), the order only applies to the submitter, not potential competitors or others in the supply chain (e.g., customers). To extend the protective measures identified in the order to other companies, EPA is required to issue a SNUR within 90 days of issuing the corresponding order—or explain why EPA is not issuing such a SNUR. The SNUR extends the protective measures of the order to others in the market (competitors and/or supply chain partners).

4.4.4 Orders and SNURs

Over the years, EPA has developed a standard set of protective measures from which EPA selects to protect against the risks EPA identifies in its PMN reviews. These protective measures are reflected in 40 C.F.R. Part 721, Subpart B, "Certain Significant New Uses." SNURs may be a combination of significant new uses (SNUs) that are "you must" and "you may not" terms. "You must" terms may include, for example, requirements for use of protective measures in the workplace, hazard communication requirements, and/or a required disposal method. "You may not" terms include limits on use (such as no consumer use) and limits on releases to water. EPA generally selects among the predefined SNUs but can write terms that are specific to a particular substance to reflect the protective measures that are necessary under the circumstances.

A company may not undertake a SNU without submitting a SNUN, waiting for EPA's review and determination, and waiting for EPA to take any necessary action. A SNUN is very much like a PMN, except it is for new COUs, not a new chemical substance. The outcome of a SNUN will, in most cases, also be an order that allows the submitter to undertake the SNU.

Some SNUs are confidential to the submitter of the original notice, so a second company would not know the specific restrictions in the SNUR. The most common instance of this is a production volume limit that is based on the confidential production volume specified in the submission (the SNU is defined as production over the confidential annual production volume). If this is the case, a company that is not privy to that confidential information must submit a BFI in which the company describes its intended COU (e.g., its intended production volume). EPA would respond to the BFI as to whether that COU is a SNU. If the intended COU is not a SNU, the company may proceed with its commercial plans without the time and expense of a SNUN.

Whenever EPA issues a regulation in an order and/or a SNUR, any company that manufactures, imports, processes, distributes, uses, or disposes of that substance must maintain records of compliance with the order/SNUR and keep records of the company's suppliers and customers of the substance or any product containing the substance. The records must document how the company is complying with the protective measures specified (e.g., no production above a production volume limit). In some cases, measurements or monitoring is required. If EPA inspects a facility and such records are not available, EPA is likely to assert that the facility is not compliant with the order or SNUR. In addition, orders and SNURs trigger or modify other TSCA obligations both for the company and the supply chain partners. For example, export of a product that contains a substance with an order or SNUR triggers export notifications under section 12(b). (See Chapter 5 for more details.) Orders and SNURs also change reporting obligations under the quadrennial Chemical Data Reporting (CDR) rule, both by voiding some exemptions and lowering the reporting threshold from 25,000 pounds to 2,500 pounds.[25]

This enforcement risk (that the lack of a record is deemed to be an instance of noncompliance), along with the implications that an order or SNUR is an indication of the substance being particularly hazardous, tends to lead to commercial deselection of chemicals that carry such regulations. While it is logical to conclude that operating in compliance with an order or SNUR means that EPA has reviewed

25. 40 C.F.R. pt. 711 (2023).

such operations and concluded the allowed COUs do not pose unreasonable risk, this is not the typical commercial reaction of supply chain partners. Whether this view changes as orders and SNURs become more the norm than the exception remains to be seen.

The tendency of customers to view adversely orders and SNURs leads to a phenomenon called the "new chemicals bias." This refers to a "bias" against a new chemical that is subject to a protective measure when compared to an existing substance of equal or greater hazard that is not (or not yet) subject to such measures. While it is true that EPA is required to review all existing substances and will, eventually, establish protective measures for each substance it reviews, as a practical matter, at a pace of three to five years per substance and five substances per year—EPA's intended pace of review in 2024—EPA will never review the vast majority of the more than 40,000 existing chemicals on the TSCA Inventory. As a result, new chemicals that are subject to section 5 restrictions may languish commercially.

The "new chemicals bias" is a critical consideration for a company as it plans innovation cycles and market entries. If a business is to develop new chemical substances, it must account for the new chemicals bias if the company intends to supply TSCA markets. Avoiding or diminishing the effect of the new chemicals bias occurs only if the chemical supplies uses not covered by TSCA (e.g., food, drugs, cosmetics) or supplies markets outside of the United States.

4.5 Section 6—Existing Chemicals Review

When TSCA was originally enacted in October 1976, it granted EPA the authority to regulate existing chemical substances. This authority was, however, curtailed significantly in October 1991 when the U.S. Court of Appeals for the Fifth Circuit vacated a final rule EPA issued under TSCA section 6 to prohibit the future manufacturing, processing, and distribution of asbestos in nearly all products.[26] The court's primary concern with EPA's final rule was that it moved to ban asbestos without evaluating (and presumably rejecting) the least burdensome alternatives, as required under TSCA section 6(a) at that time.[27] Thereafter,

26. Corrosion Proof Fittings v. EPA, 947 F.2d 1201 (5th Cir. 1991), https://law.justia.com/cases/federal/appellate-courts/F2/947/1201/153685/.

27. *Id.*

EPA avoided using its TSCA section 6 authority to regulate additional existing chemical substances except in cooperation with industry. This weakness served as part of the basis for prompting congressional interest in amending TSCA. The U.S. Congress identified three specific shortcomings under TSCA section 6 that required action, namely the absence of a requirement for EPA to systematically assess all existing chemical substances, no direction to EPA on the criteria for identifying existing chemical substances that warrant evaluation, and the requirement that EPA use the "least burdensome" regulatory option.[28] The 2016 TSCA amendments addressed these shortcomings by including requirements on EPA to prioritize all existing chemical substances and to perform risk evaluations on existing chemical substances that EPA designates as high priority. In addition, the 2016 TSCA amendments removed the "least burdensome" limitation. The following sections will discuss each of these amendments.

4.6 Prioritization

The 2016 TSCA amendments require EPA to prioritize existing chemical substances for risk evaluation and make determinations for those substances as either high-priority or low-priority substances (i.e., HPS or LPS).[29] The prioritization process is formally initiated once EPA publishes a notice in the *Federal Register* identifying the existing chemical substance as a candidate for prioritization, which includes a 90-calendar-day public comment period during which interested persons may submit information to EPA.[30]

At the close of the public comment period, EPA performs a screening review of the candidate chemical substances against seven criteria/considerations, as discussed in Chapter 2. These considerations are informed by EPA's initial prioritization process and any information received during the public comment period.[31] EPA evaluates this information against specific qualitative and quantitative benchmarks for identifying whether an existing chemical substance is a high hazard

28. Lautenberg Senate Report, *supra* note 23, at 4.
29. 40 C.F.R. pt. 702, subpt. A (2023); Procedures for Prioritization of Chemicals for Risk Evaluation under the Toxic Substances Control Act, 82 Fed. Reg. 33,753, 33,762 (July 20, 2017).
30. 40 C.F.R. § 702.7(d) (2023); 82 Fed. Reg. at 33,763.
31. 40 C.F.R. § 702.9 (2023); 82 Fed. Reg. at 33,763.

concern (e.g., a known human carcinogen) and/or a high exposure concern (e.g., produced or imported in quantities of greater than one million pounds per year).[32] (*See* Figure 4.2.) Thereafter, EPA will publish its proposed HPS or LPS designations for the candidate substances in the *Federal Register* and provide a 90-calendar-day public comment period.[33] If the available information is insufficient for EPA to make an HPS or LPS designation, EPA must designate such a substance as an HPS. Once EPA designates a substance as a potential HPS, it is unlikely that EPA will later conclude that it is, in fact, low priority, so companies should expect any proposed HPS to receive that final designation.

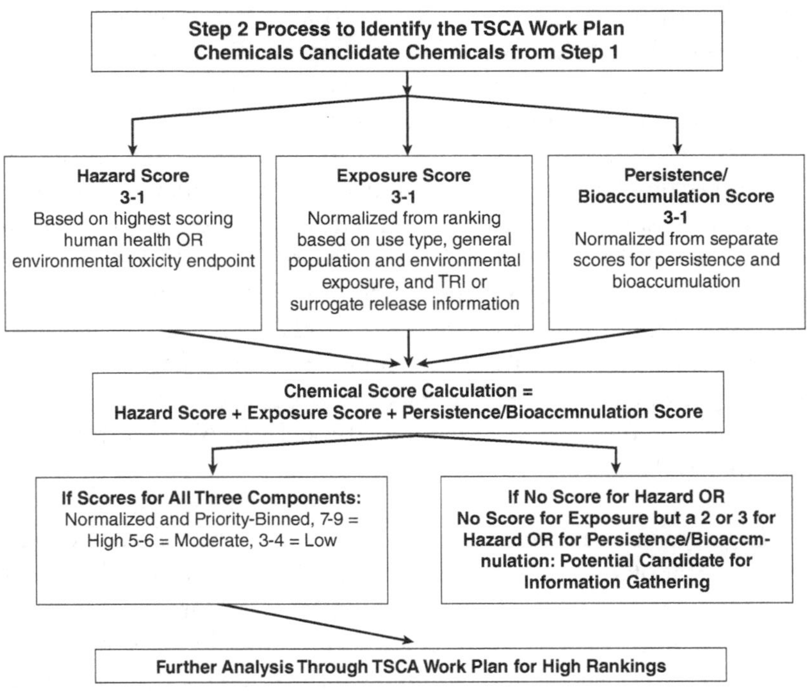

Figure 4.2. EPA's screening process to identify candidate chemicals for prioritization for risk evaluation

Source: EPA, TSCA Work Plan Chemicals: Methods Document 6 (2012), https://www.epa.gov/sites/default/files/2014-03/documents/work_plan_methods_document_web_final.pdf.

32. EPA, TSCA Work Plan Chemicals: Methods Document 8–9, 11–12 (2012), https://www.epa.gov/sites/default/files/2014-03/documents/work_plan_methods_document_web_final.pdf.
33. 40 C.F.R. § 702.9(g) (2023); 82 Fed. Reg. at 33,764.

In 2024, EPA identified 15 substances as potential candidates for the five substances next in line for prioritization and sought public input. EPA then issued data call-in rules for the 15 substances and one substance's degradant. EPA is apparently taking this "pre-prioritization" approach to allow more flexibility in choosing substances for prioritization, to allow more public input on which substance(s) should be up next, and to give EPA time to gather data on the substances. EPA's experience with the 30 substances that it had designated as HPSs in earlier rounds led EPA to move data gathering earlier in the process. EPA is now using data call-in rules and may issue test orders under TSCA section 4 to fill key data gaps. EPA had issued test rules on substances that had already entered risk evaluation,[34] but EPA found that data generation, even under a test rule, is a more protracted process and generating data was delaying EPA's risk evaluations of those substances.

EPA's initiation of its prioritization process creates potential financial obligations on manufacturers (including importers) of these chemical substances. Once EPA initiates its prioritization process on candidate substances, defined as the date that EPA publishes its notice in the *Federal Register*, manufacturers (including importers) are responsible for funding a risk evaluation if EPA makes a final designation that the candidate substance is an HPS,[35] which EPA will almost assuredly do. This financial obligation applies unless one of two conditions is met by certification through EPA's Central Data Exchange (CDX):[36]

1. The manufacturer (including importer) had already ceased manufacturing prior to the defined cutoff dates and will not manufacture (including import) for five years.
2. The manufacturer (including importer) has not manufactured the chemical substance in the five-year period preceding publication of the preliminary lists.

34. *See, e.g.*, *List of Chemicals Subject to Section 4 Test Orders*, EPA, https://www.epa.gov/assessing-and-managing-chemicals-under-tsca/list-chemicals-subject-section-4-test-orders (last updated Oct. 9, 2024).

35. *See, e.g.*, Final Lists Identifying Manufacturers Subject to Fee Obligations for EPA-Initiated Risk Evaluations under Section 6 of the Toxic Substances Control Act (TSCA); Notice of Availability, 85 Fed. Reg. 55,283, 55,284 (Sept. 4, 2020).

36. *Id.*

If a company cannot certify to one of these conditions, manufacturers (including importers) are required to make (collectively) two payments to EPA totaling $857,000 for small businesses and $4,287,000 for other businesses.[37] These substantial costs are shared by fee payers according to a formula that EPA promulgated in the TSCA fee rule.[38] Companies may, however, form a consortium and allocate costs in a way agreed upon by members.

If EPA continues to publish a pre-prioritization list of candidates for prioritization, a company could use that signal as a decision point whether the company will continue to manufacture or import that substance and face paying a share of the risk evaluation fee as well as participating in the section 6 process (discussed more in the following section).

4.7 Risk Evaluation

The 2016 TSCA amendments include "risk evaluation" as a new term of art within the TSCA risk assessment context. Congress did not, however, define this term in the 2016 TSCA amendments and EPA did not provide a codified regulatory definition for this term in its original 2017 framework rule nor its updated 2024 framework rule.[39] It is, therefore, important to understand what these terms mean within the context of EPA's activities under TSCA section 6. We provide context for these terms in the following subsections. Thereafter, we discuss the key components of TSCA risk evaluations, including the timelines for these documents, areas to focus on when reviewing these documents, which are typically thousands of pages in length, and how EPA identifies unreasonable risks.

37. Fees for the Administration of the Toxic Substances Control Act (TSCA), 89 Fed. Reg. 12,961, 12,966 (Feb. 21, 2024).
38. 40 C.F.R. § 700.45(f) (2023).
39. Procedures for Chemical Risk Evaluation under the Amended Toxic Substances Control Act, 82 Fed. Reg. 7,562, 7,575–76 (Jan. 19, 2017); Procedures for Chemical Risk Evaluation under the Toxic Substances Control Act (TSCA), 89 Fed. Reg. 37,028, 37,052 (May 3, 2024).

4.7.1 Risk Assessment versus Risk Evaluation

In 1983, the U.S. National Research Council (NRC) described the following four components of a risk assessment: (1) hazard identification; (2) dose-response assessment; (3) exposure assessment; and (4) risk characterization.[40] (*See* Figure 4.3.) NRC defined each of these components as follows:

- Hazard identification: The determination of whether a particular chemical is or is not causally linked to particular health effects.
- Dose-response assessment: The determination of the relation between the magnitude of exposure and the probability of occurrence of the health effects in question.
- Exposure assessment: The determination of the extent of human exposure before or after application of regulatory controls.
- Risk characterization: The description of the nature and often the magnitude of human risk, including attendant uncertainty.[41]

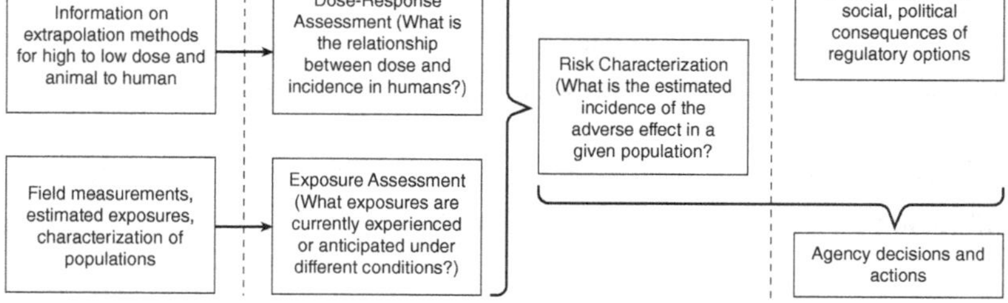

Figure 4.3. Elements of risk assessment and risk management

Source: NRC, Risk Assessment in the Federal Government: Managing the Process (1983), https://doi.org/10.17226/366.

The 2016 TSCA amendments require EPA to perform a risk assessment on HPSs that includes a determination of unreasonable

40. NRC, Risk Assessment in the Federal Government: Managing the Process (1983), https://doi.org/10.17226/366.
41. *Id.* at 3.

risk without consideration of cost or other nonrisk factors.[42] A TSCA risk evaluation, therefore, consists of the risk assessment *and* the unreasonable risk determination.

4.7.2 Components of a Risk Evaluation

TSCA risk evaluations consist of five main components, including (1) a scope; (2) a hazard assessment (including a dose-response assessment); (3) an exposure assessment; (4) a risk characterization; and (5) a risk determination.[43] These five components are published as two primary deliverables for public comment: the draft scope (component 1) and the draft risk evaluation (components 2–5). If an HPS is in a company's supply chain, whether because it manufactures, imports, processes, or uses the HPS, it is critical that a company monitor and participate in the risk evaluation process to ensure that the company's interests are represented. If a company is a downstream customer of a manufacturer or importer, it risks having EPA ban a COU that may be commercially relevant to the downstream entity if EPA does not have sufficient facts to conclude that the COU is not an unreasonable risk. Unlike the past, when a downstream customer could rely on a supplier to ensure regulatory requirements did not burden unduly customers, with EPA's current approach, a supplier is probably not able to represent relevant COUs during the risk evaluation, resulting in EPA having insufficient information and concluding that a COU is an unreasonable risk, necessitating a ban. If a key HPS is in a company's supply chain, it is advisable to join or create a consortium of similarly situated companies to share the burden of paying the fees (if applicable), commenting on draft and final work products, and sharing the cost of testing (if required). Consortia do have administrative overhead costs, but the efficiency of developing joint comments, sharing the cost of scientific experts, and developing and executing advocacy strategy can easily make up for the overhead.

The first step in EPA's risk evaluation process is publication of the draft scope. The draft scope is essentially a roadmap of what EPA intends on doing and includes "the hazards, exposures, conditions of use, and potentially exposed or susceptible subpopulations

42. TSCA § 6(b)(4)(F)(iii), 15 U.S.C. § 2607(b)(4)(F)(iii).
43. 89 Fed. Reg. at 37,053.

the Administrator expects to consider."[44] EPA codified these requirements to also include the following:

> A description of the *reasonably available information and scientific approaches* EPA plans to use in the risk evaluation.
>
> A *conceptual model* that describes the actual or predicted relationships between the chemical substance, its associated conditions of use through predicted exposure scenarios, and the identified human and environmental receptors and human and ecological health hazards.
>
> An *analysis plan* that includes hypotheses and descriptions about the relationships identified in the conceptual model and the approaches and strategies EPA intends to use to assess exposure and hazard effects, and to characterize risk; and a description, including quality, of the data, information, methods, and models, that EPA intends to use in the analysis and how uncertainty and variability will be characterized.[45]

EPA's goal is to publish the draft scope in the *Federal Register* concurrent with its proposed designation of a chemical substance as an HPS but no later than three months after EPA initiates a risk evaluation on the chemical substance (i.e., the date EPA makes a final HPS designation).[46] EPA's publication of the draft scope represents the first opportunity for the public to provide feedback to EPA, during a public comment period of no less than 45 calendar days, on its intended plan for developing the draft risk evaluation.[47] This is the first opportunity to check EPA's work. Is EPA taking a reasonable approach to hazard? Does EPA's conceptual model represent relevant commercial interests? If not, be sure to comment for the record. Thereafter, EPA will publish the final scope no later than six months after initiation of the draft risk evaluation.[48]

EPA's draft risk evaluations on HPSs address the four components identified by NRC in 1983 and include a risk determination, as required under TSCA. Once EPA publishes a notice of availability in the *Federal Register* for a draft risk evaluation, EPA will open a docket to facilitate receipt of public comments for a period of not fewer than 60 calendar days.[49] This stage-gate is more critical to review than the

44. TSCA § 6(b)(4)(D), 15 U.S.C. § 2607(b)(4)(D).
45. 89 Fed. Reg. at 37,053 (emphasis added).
46. *Id.* at 37,055.
47. *Id.*
48. *Id.*
49. *Id.*

scope. It is important to ensure that EPA is representing accurately all relevant COUs. It is also recommended that entities confirm EPA is identifying relevant COUs as an unreasonable risk. It can be prejudicial if EPA concludes formally that a COU is an unreasonable risk.

After EPA publishes the draft risk evaluation, EPA performs an external peer review on the draft risk evaluation. The peer review is typically performed by the TSCA Science Advisory Committee on Chemicals (SACC). The timing of the external peer review may, however, be less than a week after the close of the public comment period.[50] EPA has also held at least one external peer review prior to the close of the public comment period.[51] We mention these timelines because the external peer reviewers are unlikely to have time to review the public comments submitted on the draft risk evaluation. On the other hand, comments submitted on the scope of the risk evaluation should be available to the review committee, so such comments can lay the groundwork for questions that the SACC should consider. The fact that the SACC is likely not going to review comments on the draft risk evaluation should not deter persons from submitting public comments. The comments build an administrative record, which may be needed as part of future legal challenges on EPA's final risk management rule. The ideal administrative record demonstrates consistent, repeated comments making both scientific and legal arguments.

EPA is required to publish a notice of availability in the *Federal Register* for a final risk evaluation, no later than three years after it initiated the risk evaluation (i.e., the publication date in the *Federal Register* that EPA designated the chemical substance as an HPS).[52] EPA may, however, extend this timeline by no more than six months, provided that the total time elapsed between initiating the risk evaluation and publishing the final risk evaluation does not exceed

50. 1,4-Dioxane; Draft Supplement to the TSCA Risk Evaluation; Science Advisory Committee on Chemicals (SACC) Meeting; Notice of Meeting and Request for Comment, 88 Fed. Reg. 43,562 (July 10, 2023) (close of public comment period: September 8, 2023; external peer review meeting: September 12–15, 2023).
51. Draft Toxic Substances Control Act (TSCA) Risk Evaluations and TSCA Science Advisory Committee on Chemicals (SACC) Meetings; Cyclic Aliphatic Bromide Cluster (HBCD) and 1,4-Dioxane; Notice of Availability and Public Meetings, 84 Fed. Reg. 31,315 (July 1, 2019) (close of public comment period: August 30, 2019; external peer review meeting: July 29–August 2, 2019).
52. 40 C.F.R. § 702.43(d)(1) (2024); 89 Fed. Reg. at 37,055.

3.5 years.[53] In its initial ten risk evaluations, EPA was close to meeting these deadlines. EPA has not met those deadlines with the next 20 HPSs.

4.7.3 Public Comment Focus Areas

The exposure assessment and hazard identification (including dose-response assessment) are typically the most contested sections of EPA's risk evaluations, as these directly inform EPA's risk determination (i.e., whether EPA's predicted exposures exceed the identified hazard benchmarks and therefore present an unreasonable risk). Potentially regulated entities should, therefore, focus on these sections when EPA publishes notice of availability on a draft risk evaluation for public comment, which lasts no fewer than 60 calendar days,[54] but may not last more than 60 days. This may seem like an ample amount of time to review two sections of a draft risk evaluation and provide comments and/or additional data. We note, however, that these sections can encompass hundreds of pages of primary text and include appendices and supplemental files, even for substances that have limited commercial uses.[55] It is important to monitor EPA's progress from prioritization, through scoping, to risk evaluation, so that robust comments on the risk evaluation can be prepared and submitted timely.

EPA's human health exposure assessments include exposures to workers, the general population, and, if relevant, consumers. EPA's evaluation of worker exposures is typically the driver for unreasonable risk determinations, in no small part because EPA assumes little, if any, engineering controls (in the absence of data showing otherwise) and that workers do not use any personal protective equipment (PPE). This discussion is focused on worker exposures. EPA's exposure assessments on workers are generally informed by monitoring data provided by regulated entities and/or published data sets from inspections performed by OSHA and the U.S. National Institute for Occupational

53. 40 C.F.R. § 702.43(d)(2) (2024); 89 Fed. Reg. at 37,055.
54. 40 C.F.R. § 702.43(c) (2024); 89 Fed. Reg. at 37,055.
55. *See, e.g.*, *Risk Evaluation for Tris(2-chloroethyl) Phosphate (TCEP)*, EPA, https://www.epa.gov/assessing-and-managing-chemicals-under-tsca/risk-evaluation-tris2-chloroethyl-phosphate-tcep (last updated Sept. 26, 2024).

Safety and Health (NIOSH).[56] In the absence of worker exposure/environmental release data, EPA uses modeling software to generate exposure/release estimates to inform its risk characterizations for each COU.[57] EPA's models are, however, highly conservative and almost always driving EPA's determination of unreasonable risks. A representative example is discussed in this section.

EPA develops worker exposure model estimates via the inhalation and dermal pathways (ingestion is very unusual in a workplace setting, most ingestion exposures result from drinking water). EPA's dermal exposure models for workers utilize estimates that are oftentimes unrealistic, but companies rarely have dermal exposure data to refute EPA's conservative models. Similarly, without industrial hygiene monitoring data for inhalation, EPA will assume uncontrolled exposures to vapors or, if aerosol, dust, or mist is expected, exposure to particulates up to the OSHA limit for nuisance dust (15 milligrams per cubic meter (mg/m^3)). Because of these overly conservative assumptions, EPA will almost always find unreasonable risk for unprotected exposures and because EPA now issues a single determination for each substance,[58] EPA will conclude that each substance is an unreasonable risk, thereby triggering EPA to issue a risk management rule for each substance it evaluates. This approach has been challenged by litigants, but unless and until the litigants prevail in the various lawsuits, EPA will continue to identify each risk evaluation substance as an unreasonable risk—the only question will be whether the risk management conditions are based on the best available science for both hazard endpoints and exposure metrics.

EPA's hazard identification (including dose-response assessment) is typically informed by data obtained from toxicological studies on experimental animals (e.g., rats or mice). This is an appropriate approach when human data are lacking, which is almost always the case. EPA has been using the lowest effect level observed across a number of studies, regardless of the quality of the study or whether the

---

56. *Chemical Exposure Health Data*, OSHA, https://www.osha.gov/opengov/health-samples (last visited Sept. 27, 2024); *Health Hazard Evaluations (HHEs)*, NIOSH, https://www2a.cdc.gov/hhe/search.asp (last updated Apr. 11, 2016).
57. *ChemSTEER—Chemical Screening Tool for Exposures and Environmental Releases*, EPA, https://www.epa.gov/tsca-screening-tools/chemsteer-chemical-screening-tool-exposures-and-environmental-releases (last updated Feb. 8, 2024).
58. Procedures for Prioritization of Chemicals for Risk Evaluation under the Toxic Substances Control Act, 82 Fed. Reg. 33,753 (July 20, 2017).

effect or effect level is reproducible. EPA further assumes a linear low-dose extrapolation for assessing cancer risks from chemical substances that have been shown to cause cancer in experimental animals and/or in humans, even when a threshold for carcinogenicity is observed. We provide representative examples for each of these issues.

EPA's human health risk determinations are directly informed by points of departure (PODs) (e.g., no-observed-adverse-effect levels (NOAEL)). A POD represents the concentration of a chemical substance that may or may not cause an adverse effect in, for example, experimental animals in a particular study. EPA typically selects the lowest POD available for quantifying risks, even when the POD and the reported adverse effect(s) are not reproducible in more robust studies. Take, for example, EPA's risk evaluation on trichloroethylene (TCE). In that risk evaluation, EPA concluded that the best available science and weight of scientific evidence supported using a POD from a study on TCE that identified immunological effects in mice,[59] despite another study that reported developmental effects at much lower levels,[60] even though subsequent studies could not reproduce the effect.[61] Members of the SACC questioned the quality of that study.[62] Despite this, EPA relied on the questionable quality study as the basis for its proposed risk management rule on TCE.[63] EPA takes a similar, overly conservative approach for carcinogens. Absent a well-elucidated mode of action (MOA), EPA will depart from its long-standing guidance, which permits some uncertainties with the

---

59. EPA, Risk Evaluation for Trichloroethylene—CASRN: 79-01-6 280 (2020) (740R18008), https://www.epa.gov/sites/default/files/2020-11/documents/1._risk_evaluation_for_trichloroethylene_tce_casrn_79-01-6.pdf.
60. *Id.* Paula D. Johnson et al., *Threshold of Trichloroethylene Contamination in Maternal Drinking Waters Affecting Fetal Heart Development in the Rat*, 111 Env't Health Persps. 289 (2003), https://www.ncbi.nlm.nih.gov/pmc/articles/PMC1241384/pdf/ehp0111-000289.pdf.
61. Jeffrey W. Fisher et al., *Trichloroethylene, Trichloroacetic Acid, and Dichloroacetic Acid: Do They Affect Fetal Rat Heart Development?*, 20 Int'l J. Toxicology 257 (2001), https://journals.sagepub.com/doi/10.1080/109158101753252992; John M. DeSesso et al., *Trichloroethylene in Drinking Water throughout Gestation Did Not Produce Congenital Heart Defects in Sprague Dawley Rats*, 111 Birth Defects Rsch. 1217 (2019), https://www.ncbi.nlm.nih.gov/pmc/articles/PMC7432160/pdf/BDR2-111-1217.pdf.
62. EPA, TSCA Science Advisory Committee on Chemicals Meeting Minutes and Final Report No. 2020-4, Peer Review for EPA Draft Risk Evaluation for Trichloroethylene (TCE), March 24–27, 2020, Held via Phone and Webcast (Virtual Meeting) 65–66 (2020), https://downloads.regulations.gov/EPA-HQ-OPPT-2019-0500-0111/content.pdf.
63. Trichloroethylene (TCE); Regulation under the Toxic Substances Control Act (TSCA), 88 Fed. Reg. 74,712, 74,791 (Oct. 31, 2023).

MOA,[64] and assume that a substance is carcinogenic at all doses. While these may seem like esoteric, scientific disagreements, they can make an enormous difference in the risk management outcome and can be the difference between EPA banning a substance entirely (as EPA proposed for TCE) and requiring reasonable workplace protection standards. Careful, expert evaluation of the science that underlies EPA's risk determination and risk management is critical to ensure that EPA is using the best available science and promulgating well-supported risk management rules.

4.7.4 EPA's Approaches for Identifying Unreasonable Risks

Neither the original TSCA nor the 2016 TSCA amendments defined "unreasonable risk," and EPA chose not to define this term in its original 2017 framework rule nor its updated 2024 framework rule. EPA typically informs this determination using specific human health hazard benchmarks for acute or chronic noncancer effects that include the application of uncertainty factors or for chronic cancer effects by calculation of excess cancer risks. EPA also uses a quantitative approach for determining unreasonable risks to environmental receptors (e.g., fish) known as a risk quotient (RQ) approach. The exact details of these approaches are not necessary to understand their potential impact, but it is important to understand conceptually each to appreciate the magnitude of the impact an EPA determination of unreasonable risk may cause. We, therefore, explain each of these approaches in this section.

For acute and chronic noncancer effects and for HPSs with a threshold carcinogenic MOA, EPA uses a margin of exposure (MOE) approach for identifying unreasonable risks. One way to understand this approach is to select the POD—the most sensitive toxicity level usually derived from a mammalian toxicity study—and divide it by an uncertainty factor that reflects the uncertainty of the applicability of the POD to humans. The result is an exposure level below which EPA would conclude there is no unreasonable risk. EPA does not strictly follow this approach in its risk evaluations, but EPA's actual approach yields the same mathematical result. In any case, higher uncertainty leads to lower acceptable exposure levels.

64. EPA, Guidelines for Carcinogen Risk Assessment 1-10 n.2 (2005) (EPA/630/P-03-001B), https://www3.epa.gov/airtoxics/cancer_guidelines_final_3-25-05.pdf.

For cancer risks that EPA assesses using a linear low-dose extrapolation, EPA applies an approach that quantifies incremental cancer risks at any nonzero level of human exposure. EPA's benchmark for cancer in the general population is one excess cancer case in a population of 1,000,000; for workers, EPA uses one excess cancer case in a population of 10,000.

EPA quantifies acute and chronic risks to environmental receptors (e.g., fish) with the RQ approach. In the RQ approach, EPA simply divides a predicted surface water concentration by a "concentration of concern" (CoC) that is based on the most sensitive aquatic species (fish, invertebrates, or algae). If the calculated concentration exceeds the CoC, EPA concludes there is an unreasonable risk.

Because the exposure and hazard evaluations form the basis for EPA's identification of unreasonable risk and its final risk determination, it is, therefore, important to evaluate critically these sections and to document all deficiencies as part of public comments. Be sure to repeat such criticisms if EPA has not addressed them in early stages of its evaluation. This will preserve these arguments and demonstrate that they were not waived during the administrative process leading up to EPA's risk management rulemaking activities in case a company (or a group) wishes to file a legal challenge to EPA's final rule.

EPA initiates two types of risk evaluations. Those initiated by EPA through its prioritization process, or those requested by manufacturers for EPA to perform (i.e., manufacturer-requested risk evaluations (MRREs)). Although originally contemplated to allow manufacturers to request risk evaluation and concomitant federal preemption of state regulations, with the changes to EPA's risk evaluation framework rule,[65] there are very limited advantages for a manufacturer to request a risk evaluation. Unless EPA updates its framework rule, many question the wisdom of seeking an MRRE due to the costs, the near certainty that EPA will make a determination of unreasonable risk for the substance, and the potential liabilities and inferences that may stem from this determination.

65. *See, e.g.*, Procedures for Chemical Risk Evaluation under the Toxic Substances Control Act (TSCA), 89 Fed Reg. 37,028, 37,045 (May 3, 2024).

4.8 Risk Management

Once EPA publishes the final risk evaluation in the *Federal Register*, it is required to propose a risk management rule on the HPS no later than one year after the final risk evaluation was published if EPA concludes that the HPS presents an unreasonable risk of injury to health or the environment. As part of the rulemaking, EPA must apply one or more of the requirements listed under TSCA section 6(a) (e.g., bans, labeling requirements, and/or workplace controls) "to the extent necessary so that the chemical substance or mixture no longer presents such risk." EPA must also publish the final risk management rule no later than two years after the date the final risk evaluation was published.

When developing draft risk management rules, EPA is required to propose a regulatory action and at least one primary alternative regulatory action. Unlike EPA's risk evaluations, EPA is required to consider the benefits and cost effectiveness of its regulatory risk management actions, per TSCA section 6(c)(2)(A). EPA's proposed and final risk management rules have focused on applying prohibitions, requiring compliance with workplace chemical protection programs (WCPPs) for nonprohibited COUs and for COUs with time-limited exemptions under TSCA section 6(g), and identifying de minimis thresholds for the HPSs in products. Each of these regulatory options, if (when) finalized, carry significant implications for businesses. We discuss these options in the following subsections with reference to EPA's proposed and final risk management rules.

4.8.1 Prohibitions

On May 3, 2023, EPA published its proposed risk management rule on methylene chloride with its stated intent to prohibit most industrial and commercial COUs (e.g., plastic and rubber products manufacturing, including polycarbonate manufacturing).[66] During the public comment period, potentially regulated entities submitted industrial hygiene monitoring data, which demonstrated to EPA's satisfaction for specific COUs (e.g., plastic and rubber products manufacturing, including polycarbonate manufacturing) that EPA's initial concerns

66. Methylene Chloride; Regulation under the Toxic Substances Control Act (TSCA), 88 Fed. Reg. 28,284, 28,307 (May 3, 2023).

about compliance with the WCPP "due to insufficient information at the time of proposal" were not warranted.[67] EPA's final risk management rule permits this COU because of the demonstrated ability of manufacturers to comply with EPA's WCPP.[68]

The final methylene chloride rule suggests that EPA will prohibit specific COUs unless potentially regulated entities can provide data that demonstrate an ability to comply with EPA's WCPP prior to EPA issuing its final risk management rule. If EPA does move forward with prohibiting a specific COU, it is required to set an appropriate transition period, to the extent practicable, based on the availability of technically and economically feasible alternatives that will be reasonably available when the prohibition takes effect. We caution, however, that EPA's identification of alternatives should not serve as a selection mechanism for regulated entities. For example, EPA's alternatives assessment for methylene chloride included existing chemical substances (e.g., benzene and ethylbenzene) that EPA will likely evaluate and prohibit under TSCA section 6 in the future.[69]

4.8.2 WCPPs

EPA's WCPPs typically include comparable provisions to other legally binding workplace monitoring requirements (e.g., OSHA). WCPPs consist of eight-hour time-weighted average (TWA) existing chemical exposure limits (ECELs), action levels based on the ECELs (i.e., half of the ECEL), and 15-minute short-term exposure limits (STELs). These requirements are, however, typically far lower than existing occupational exposure limits. For example, EPA's eight-hour TWA ECEL for methylene chloride is two parts per million (ppm), whereas OSHA's eight-hour TWA permissible exposure limit (PEL) is 25 ppm.[70] EPA's decreased values may serve as a point of contention

67. Methylene Chloride; Regulation under the Toxic Substances Control Act (TSCA), 89 Fed. Reg. 39,254, 39,262 (May 8, 2024).
68. *Id.* at 39,263.
69. Richard E. Engler & Todd. J. Stedeford, *What Are the Key Elements and Likely Impact of the EPA's Proposed Rule for Methylene Chloride?*, CHEM. WATCH (June 21, 2023), https://www.eli.org/sites/default/files/files-general/CW%20Insight%20-%20methylene%20chloride%20-%20Richard%20E%20Engler%20and%20Todd%20J%20Stedeford%20article%20%2800398852xAA4DC%29.PDF.
70. 40 C.F.R. § 751.109(c)(1) (2024); 89 Fed. Reg. at 39,297; OSHA, METHYLENE CHLORIDE 3 (2003) (OSHA 3144-06R), https://www.osha.gov/sites/default/files/publications/osha3144.pdf.

with potentially regulated entities, but EPA justifies correctly that its WCPPs, including the ECELs, are developed to mitigate unreasonable risks to sensitive populations under TSCA, which OSHA's PELs may not contemplate.[71]

The substantive issues with EPA's WCPPs include its use of questionable science when quantifying exposures to workers and deriving ECELs that may not comport with the scientific standards under TSCA section 26. Several representative examples are available, including EPA's proposed risk management activities on chrysotile asbestos, *N*-methyl pyrrolidone (NMP), and TCE, as discussed previously.

For chrysotile asbestos, EPA estimated worker exposures from occupational monitoring data, more than half of which were below the limit of detection (LOD), using its 1994 *Guidelines for Statistical Analysis of Occupational Exposure Data*. These guidelines recommend "replacing non-detects with the LOD or LOQ [limit of quantification] divided by two or divided by the square root of two, depending on the skewness of the data distributions."[72] EPA's most recent guidelines state, however, that "[w]hen computing the mean of a set of asbestos measurements, samples that are 'nondetect' [i.e., below the LOD] should be evaluated using a value of zero, not ½ the analytical sensitivity."[73]

For NMP, EPA's proposed risk management rule includes a WCPP with dermal protection requirements, based on a study that reported an adverse effect (i.e., reduced fertility) that was not reproducible in two subsequent studies.[74] EPA rated the reduced fertility study as "High" quality in the final risk evaluation on NMP, despite assigning

71. 88 Fed. Reg. at 28,288.

72. EPA, Risk Evaluation for Asbestos Part I: Chrysotile Asbestos 82 (2020) (EPA-740-R1-8012), https://www.epa.gov/sites/default/files/2020-12/documents/1_risk_evaluation_for_asbestos_part_1_chrysotile_asbestos.pdf; EPA, Guidelines for Statistical Analysis of Occupational Exposure Data 48 (1994), https://www.epa.gov/sites/default/files/2015-09/documents/stat_guide_occ.pdf.

73. Office of Solid Waste and Emergency Response, EPA, OSWER Directive No. 9200.0-68, Framework for Investigating Asbestos-Contaminated Superfund Sites 19 (2008) (footnote omitted), https://semspub.epa.gov/work/HQ/175329.pdf.

74. N-Methylpyrrolidone (NMP); Regulation under the Toxic Substances Control Act (TSCA), 89 Fed. Reg. 51,134 (June 14, 2024). For discussion, see Letter from NMP Producers Group, Inc., to Information Quality Guidelines Staff, EPA, re: Request for Correction of Information on the Toxic Substances Control Act (TSCA) Risk Evaluation for N-Methylpyrrolidone (Apr. 19, 2023), https://www.epa.gov/system/files/documents/2023-05/RFC%2023001%20N-Methylpyrrolidone.pdf.

a lower quality rating when EPA sponsored an evaluation of NMP through the Organisation for Economic Co-operation and Development (OECD).[75] More recently yet prior to the TSCA risk evaluation on NMP, EPA had concluded that the reduced fertility study was not the most relevant for quantifying risks because it was an inconsistent finding "when looking at the complete database."[76]

The abovementioned examples may seem troubling, and we agree that they are. We mention these because of the importance of providing public comments on EPA's draft risk evaluations and proposed risk management rules. As we indicated previously, public comments on EPA's draft risk evaluations are unlikely to result in substantive changes to EPA's final risk evaluations. The public comments must, however, be submitted at each stage of the administrative process to preserve potential legal challenges if (when) EPA proposes and finalizes risk management rules, including WCPPs, based on questionable science.

4.8.3 Time-Limited Exemptions

Under TSCA section 6(g), EPA may grant a time-limited exemption for a specific COU if EPA concludes that one of the following conditions apply: (1) the COU is critical or essential and no technically or economically feasible alternative is available; (2) the COU, if for example prohibited, would significantly disrupt the national economy, natural security, or critical infrastructure; or (3) the COU provides a substantial benefit to health, environment, or public safety.[77]

These conditions are fact-specific and require supporting information to convince EPA with determining that one of the conditions apply. EPA has included time-limited exemptions as part of its final risk management rules. These exemptions, however, require compliance with EPA's WCPPs and have been limited to specific COUs. For example, EPA granted time-limited exemptions for methylene

75. OECD, SIDS Initial Assessment Report for SIAM 24: 1-methyl-2-pyrrolidinone 41 (2007), https://hpvchemicals.oecd.org/ui/SponsoredChemicals.aspx (click on "Pyrrolidinone, 1-methyl- (CAS 872-50-4)," then click on file titled "SIDS_872504.zip").
76. EPA, TSCA Work Plan Chemical Risk Assessment: N-Methylpyrrolidone: Paint Stripper Use, CASRN: 872-50-4, at 51 (2015) (EPA Document No. 740-R1-5002), https://www.epa.gov/sites/default/files/2015-11/documents/nmp_ra_3_23_15_final.pdf.
77. 15 U.S.C. § 2605(g).

chloride for specific COUs in civilian aviation and those used by the National Aeronautics and Space Administration.[78]

4.8.4 De Minimis Thresholds

EPA is authorized under TSCA section 6(a)(2)(A)(ii) to establish, prohibit, or restrict the concentration of an HPS more than a specified level.[79] TSCA section 6 does not, however, include a requirement for EPA to set a de minimis threshold for an HPS that EPA concludes to present an unreasonable risk of injury to health or the environment. EPA has, however, taken steps to establish de minimis thresholds as part of its proposed and final risk management rules. This is an important component of EPA's risk management activities because it alleviates potentially regulated entities of proving a negative—that is, the absence of an HPS in its COUs. We caution potentially regulated entities that EPA's de minimis thresholds will likely follow those established by OSHA under its Hazard Communication Standard at 29 C.F.R. § 1910.1200, which applies, for example, a threshold of 0.1 weight percent for carcinogens. EPA applied this same value as the de minimis threshold for methylene chloride, whereby those products with concentrations of methylene chloride below 0.1 weight percent would not be subject to EPA's final risk management rule.[80]

4.8.5 Implications and Next Steps

EPA's risk management activities under TSCA section 6 will result in transactional costs that must be considered at both the proposed and final stages. For example, if a potentially regulated entity exports or intends to export an HPS that is the subject of a proposed or final TSCA risk management rule, that entity is required to notify EPA of the export or intent to export, per TSCA section 12(b)(2). Entities are also required to certify that imports of an HPS that are subject to a promulgated TSCA risk management rule comply with the requirements of that rule. For further discussion on these topics, refer to Chapter 5 (exports) and Chapter 3 (imports).

---

78. *See, e.g.*, Methylene Chloride; Regulation under the Toxic Substances Control Act (TSCA), 89 Fed. Reg. 39,254, 39,255 (May 8, 2024).
79. 15 U.S.C. § 2605(a)(2)(A)(ii).
80. 89 Fed. Reg. at 39,268.

Beyond the previously mentioned requirements, business entities should consider their options for challenging EPA's final risk management rules that include prohibitions in the absence of data demonstrating an ability to comply with EPA's WCPP at the time of proposal. EPA has concluded that compliance with a WCPP, including an ECEL, will mitigate unreasonable risks.[81] Therefore, EPA's inclusion of prohibitions in its final rules in the absence of data appears to go beyond the "extent necessary" provisions of TSCA, although this has not been the subject of litigation. After all, EPA's WCPP is a de facto ban for entities that are unable to comply; therefore, it is unclear why EPA chose to ban specific COUs rather than requiring documented compliance with a WCPP.

The scientific underpinnings of EPA's final risk management rules in the form of WCPPs may also provide an opportunity for challenge, as indicated, for chrysotile asbestos, NMP, and TCE. We caution, however, that like the "extent necessary" provision of TSCA, the scientific standards under TSCA section 26 have not been subjected to legal interpretation through litigation.

Takeaways

- An understanding of TSCA sections 5 and 6 and how EPA is implementing these two key sections is vital to understanding regulatory obligations and the related business risks and opportunities.
- Careful strategic planning is needed to understand the regulatory obligations to which a new chemical can be expected to be subject.
- Similarly, it is critical to anticipate future regulations that may be applicable to existing chemicals, and plan accordingly to compete in today's markets.
- Failure to anticipate chemical regulatory challenges could blunt commercial opportunities or invite limitations on market access that could have been avoided with better planning.
- Depending on the specific requirements of the individual regulations under section 5 or 6, there may be specific requirements

81. *Id.* at 39,275.

Not all of the abovementioned actions are *final* rulemakings. While export notification is triggered only by final TSCA section 4 test rules or final enforceable consent agreements (ECAs), and not proposed test rules or ECAs, all proposed TSCA section 5 or 6 rules and pending TSCA section 5 or 7 actions trigger the export notification requirement.

It is important to note that when EPA requires data through a TSCA section 4 test rule, the requirement to provide data to EPA will expire or "sunset" after a specific period. Once the testing requirement has expired, the fact that a chemical substance was the subject of a test rule in the past does not trigger an export notification. Obtaining data through a TSCA section 4 test rule may give EPA cause to pursue a rulemaking under TSCA sections 5, 6, or 7, however, so EPA rulemakings should be reviewed to confirm that notification has not been triggered by a different TSCA action.

Export notification is required only for chemical substances and mixtures known to be in an exported material or article. No testing is required to determine whether the material contains a chemical substance or mixture subject to the export notification requirements.

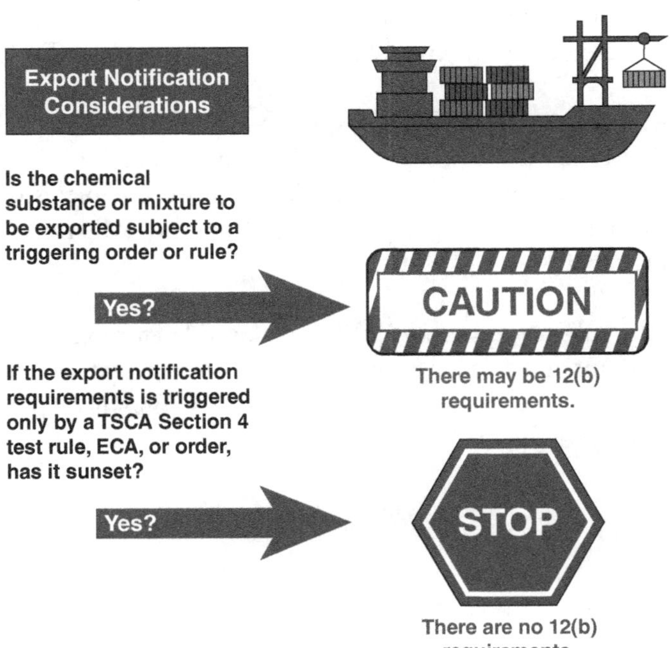

Figure 5.1. Export notification considerations

5.2.2 Chemical Substances Exempt from Notification

5.2.2.1 Export-Only Chemicals

Under TSCA section 12(a), a chemical substance, mixture, or article is exempt from TSCA requirements, other than recordkeeping, if

- it is manufactured, processed, or distributed solely for export; or
- it is labeled as such.[2]

The exemption from TSCA requirements does not apply, however, if EPA finds that the chemical substance, mixture, or article "presents an unreasonable risk of injury to health within the United States or to the environment of the United States."[3] As EPA proposes and issues final risk management rules under the Frank R. Lautenberg Chemical Safety for the 21st Century Act, EPA is including such findings. For example, in its 2024 final risk management rule for methylene chloride, EPA notes that, pursuant to TSCA section 12(a)(2), the rule "applies to methylene chloride even if being manufactured, processed, or distributed in commerce solely for export from the United States because EPA has determined that methylene chloride presents an unreasonable risk to health within the United States."[4]

The exemption from TSCA requirements other than recordkeeping explicitly applies to new chemicals and premanufacture notice (PMN) requirements. Under the regulations, new chemicals that are manufactured solely for export are exempt from the PMN notification requirements if

- the substance is labeled that it is intended for export; and
- the manufacturer knows that the person to whom the substance is being distributed intends to export it or process it solely for export.[5]

2. TSCA § 12(a), 15 U.S.C. § 2611(a).
3. TSCA § 12(a)(2), 15 U.S.C. § 2611(a)(2).
4. Methylene Chloride; Regulation under the Toxic Substances Control Act (TSCA), 89 Fed. Reg. 39,254, 39,272 (May 8, 2024).
5. 40 C.F.R. § 720.30(e) (2023).

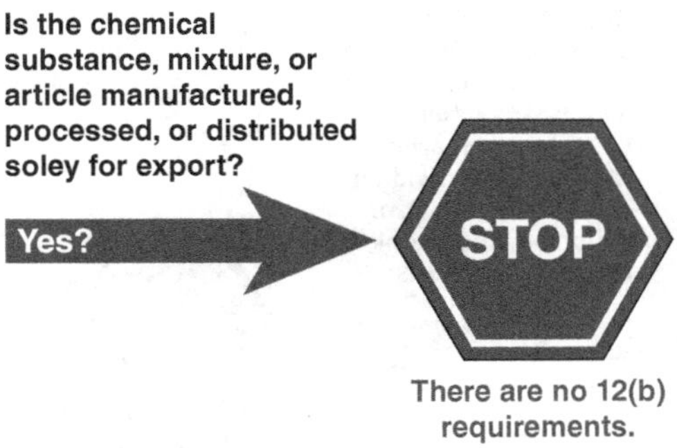

Figure 5.2. Export notification considerations

5.2.2.2 Articles

Articles are generally exempt from TSCA section 12(b) export notification. As described in more detail in Chapter 2, an "article" is defined as

> a manufactured item (1) which is formed to a specific shape or design during manufacture, (2) which has end use function(s) dependent in whole or in part upon its shape or design during end use, and (3) which has either no change of chemical composition during its end use or only those changes of composition which have no commercial purpose separate from that of the article, and that result from a chemical reaction that occurs upon end use of other chemical substances, mixtures, or articles; except that fluids and particles are not considered articles regardless of shape or design.[6]

Certain articles are ineligible for exemption from the export notification requirements, however. Articles that are not exempt include polychlorinated biphenyl (PCB) articles being exported for purposes other than disposal.[7] Articles addressed in individual TSCA sections 5, 6, or 7 actions are also not exempt. For example, EPA proposed in November 2023 to require export notification for decabromodiphenyl ether (decaBDE)-containing wire and cable for nuclear power generation facilities.[8] As EPA issues more risk management rules, more articles may require export notification.

6. *Id.* § 704.3.
7. *Id.* § 707.60(d).
8. Decabromodiphenyl Ether and Phenol, Isopropylated Phosphate (3:1); Revision to the Regulation of Persistent, Bioaccumulative, and Toxic Chemicals under the Toxic Substances Control Act (TSCA), 88 Fed. Reg. 82,287, 82,299–300 (Nov. 24, 2023).

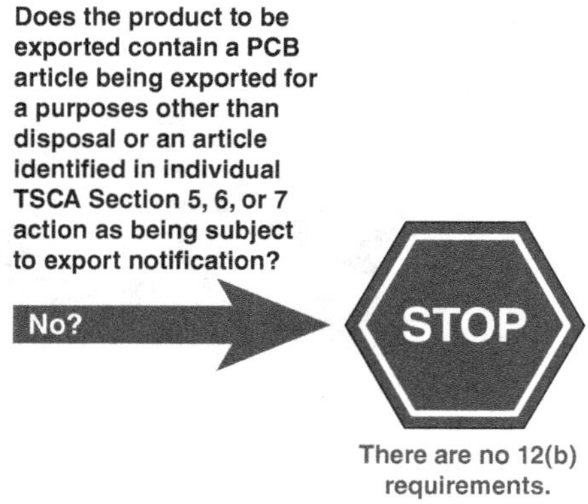

Figure 5.3. Export notification considerations

5.2.2.3 *De Minimis Level*

If the amount of the regulated chemical substance or mixture being exported is small enough, no export notification is required. Generally, this amount is a concentration of less than 1 percent (by weight or volume).[9] If the chemical substance or mixture being exported is a known or potential human carcinogen, however, then the de minimis level is less than 0.1 percent by weight or volume.[10] Under the regulations, a chemical substance is considered a known or potential human carcinogen if it meets one of the following criteria:

- The National Toxicology Program (NTP) lists the chemical substance or mixture as "known to be a human carcinogen" or "reasonably anticipated to be a human carcinogen" in its *Report on Carcinogens*.[11]
- The International Agency for Research on Cancer (IARC) classifies the chemical substance or mixture as "carcinogenic to humans" (Group 1), "probably carcinogenic to humans" (Group 2A), or "possibly carcinogenic to humans" (Group 2B) in its *Monographs and Supplements on the Evaluation of Carcinogenic Risks to Humans*.[12]

---

9. 40 C.F.R. § 707.60(c)(1) (2023).
10. *Id.* § 707.60(c)(2).
11. *15th Report on Carcinogens*, NTP, https://ntp.niehs.nih.gov/whatwestudy/assessments/cancer/roc (last updated Feb. 13, 2024). Exporters should make sure that they are using the latest edition of the *Report on Carcinogens*.
12. IARC Monographs and Supplements are available on the IARC website at *Publications*, IARC, https://monographs.iarc.who.int/cards_page/publications-monographs/ (last visited Sept. 27, 2024).

- The chemical substance is alpha-naphthylamine (CAS RN 134-32-7) or 4-nitrobiphenyl (CAS RN 92-93-3).

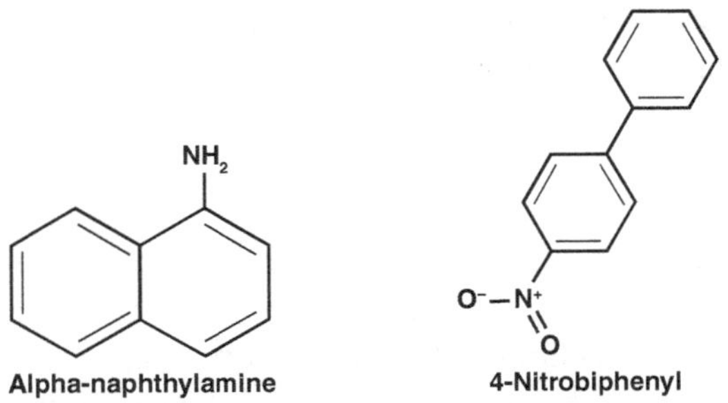

Figure 5.4. Chemical structures

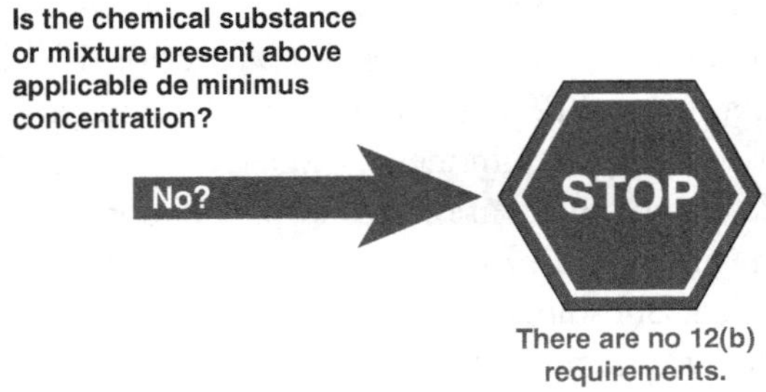

Figure 5.5. Export notification considerations

5.2.3 Required Information

TSCA section 12(b) export notifications must include the following information:

- The name of the chemical substance as it appears in the TSCA action triggering the notification requirement. If a confidential product is exported, a generic name and accession number must be used.
- The name and address of the exporter.
- The country or countries of import.
- Date(s) of export or intended export.
- The TSCA sections (4, 5, 6, and/or 7) under which EPA has taken action. A single export notification may refer to more

than one section of TSCA if the exported chemical is the subject of multiple TSCA actions.[13]

In 2023, EPA amended the export notification regulations to require that all export notifications be submitted electronically using EPA's Central Data Exchange (CDX).[14]

5.2.4 CBI

Exporters may assert a confidential business information (CBI) claim for any information submitted to EPA in a TSCA section 12(b) export notice. The claim must be made at the time the information is submitted to EPA. CBI claims must be substantiated at the time they are made. Despite any CBI claims, EPA's notice to foreign governments will identify the regulated chemical and summarize the regulatory action or note the availability of data under section 4 or 5(b).[15]

EPA clarified in 2023 that it is generally not necessary to provide confidential chemical identities in a TSCA section 12(b) export notification. According to EPA, its chemical import and export regulations "never included such a requirement, though some submitters unnecessarily provided such information anyway."[16] Exporters notifying EPA about a chemical substance that is on the confidential portion of the TSCA Chemical Substance Inventory can identify the chemical substance by a generic name and accession number, or by any other non-confidential identifier under which it is listed on EPA's TSCA section 12(b) reporting list maintained by EPA and available in CDX.[17]

5.2.5 Timing for Export Notifications

The export notification requirements apply to export to other countries and do not apply to exports to territories or possessions of the United States. The requirements apply only to the first export to a particular country, including territories and possessions, so it is important to be aware of the territories and possessions of other countries.

13. 40 C.F.R. § 707.67 (2023).
14. Confidential Business Information Claims under the Toxic Substances Control Act (TSCA), 88 Fed. Reg. 37,155 (June 7, 2023) (codified at 40 C.F.R. § 707.65(c)).
15. 40 C.F.R. § 707.70(b) (2023).
16. 88 Fed. Reg. at 37,162.
17. 40 C.F.R. §§ 707.67(a), 707.65(c) (2023).

For example, an export notification submitted for an export to Bermuda would satisfy the reporting requirements to England or any other territory or possession of the United Kingdom.

The timing of the export notification varies depending on the reason for the notification. For chemical substances and mixtures subject to regulation under TSCA section 5(f), 6, or 7, TSCA section 12(b) export notices must be submitted to EPA for the first export or intended export to a particular country within each calendar year that the TSCA section 12(b) requirements apply. For chemical substances or mixtures subject to a TSCA section 4 test rule, a section 5(a)(2) rule, a section 5(e) order, or a section 5(b) rule, only a *one-time* export notice must be submitted for the first export of a chemical substance or mixture to a particular country.

Export notifications must be made through CDX within seven days of forming the intent to export or on the date of export, whichever is earlier. According to the regulations, a notice based on an intent to export "must be based on a definite contractual obligation, or an equivalent intra-company agreement, to export the regulated chemical."[18]

If a proposed rule triggers the export notification, the requirement to submit an export notification for the chemical substance or mixture begins 30 days after EPA publishes the proposed rule in the *Federal Register*.[19]

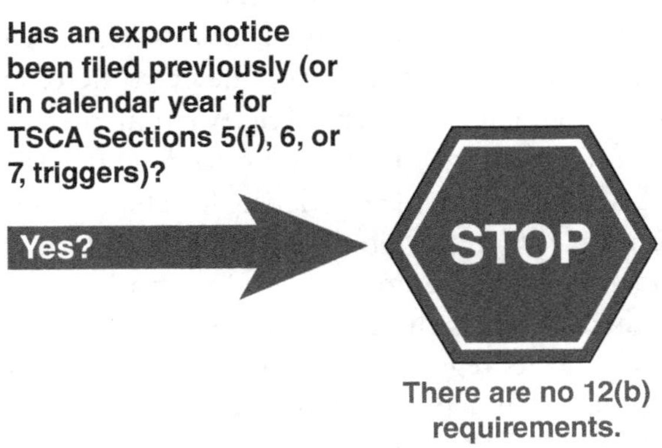

Figure 5.6. Export notification considerations

18. *Id.* § 707.65(a)(2).
19. *Id.* § 707.65(b).

5.3 EPA's Notice to Importing Countries

EPA will notify the country of destination within five days of EPA's receipt of a TSCA section 12(b) export notice. The notification will include:

- The identity of the chemical substance
- A summary of the regulatory action EPA has taken or the availability of data
- A copy of the pertinent *Federal Register* notice on the EPA regulatory action taken
- The name of an EPA contact for further information

EPA will provide information claimed as CBI to the country of destination. In such cases, EPA will notify the country of destination that the notice contains CBI and request the country of destination to take appropriate measures to safeguard the information claimed as CBI.[20]

5.4 Recordkeeping

Under TSCA, EPA may inspect any facility at which chemical substances or mixtures are manufactured, processed, or stored prior to or following their distribution in commerce to determine whether the exporter is in compliance with TSCA requirements. Documents that the exporter may wish to maintain to demonstrate compliance with TSCA section 12 include all labels for chemicals and mixtures exported under TSCA section 12(a), TSCA section 12(b) export notices, and any correspondence with EPA regarding a chemical substance's or mixture's compliance with TSCA section 12(b). TSCA section 12(b) and its regulations do not specify how long exporters should maintain documents demonstrating compliance with TSCA. Generally, however, TSCA regulations provide that documents must be maintained for five years.

20. *Id.* § 707.75(c); Chemical Imports and Exports; Notification of Export, 45 Fed. Reg. 82,844, 82,847 (Dec. 16, 1980).

5.5 Export Requirements for PCBs

As noted in Section 5.2.2.2, although notice of export is generally not required for articles, notice is required for PCB articles.[21] No notice of export is required for the export of PCBs if they are present in a concentration of less than or equal to 50 parts per million (by weight or volume).[22] EPA has promulgated specific regulations regarding the transboundary shipment of PCBs for disposal.[23]

5.6 Export Requirements for Mercury and Mercury Compounds

The Mercury Export Ban Act of 2008 prohibits the export of elemental mercury unless a person successfully petitions EPA for an "essential use" exemption.[24] Effective January 1, 2020, the 2016 Frank R. Lautenberg Chemical Safety for the 21st Century Act expanded the export prohibition of mercury from elemental mercury to certain mercury compounds: mercury (I) chloride or calomel (CAS RN 10112-91-1); mercury (II) oxide (CAS RN 21908-53-2); mercury (II) sulfate (CAS RN 7783-35-9); mercury (II) nitrate (CAS RN 10045-94-0); and cinnabar or mercury sulphide (CAS RN 1344-48-5).[25] EPA has the authority to add any mercury compound to this list after determining that exporting any additional mercury compound for the purpose of regenerating elemental mercury is technically feasible. In addition, any person may petition EPA to add a mercury compound to the published list. There is an exemption from the prohibition of exports of these mercury compounds if such exports are to member countries of the Organisation for Economic Co-operation and Development (OECD) for "environmentally sound disposal, on the condition that no mercury or mercury compounds so exported are to be recovered, recycled, or reclaimed for use, or directly reused, after such export."[26]

21. 40 C.F.R. § 707.60(b), (d) (2023).
22. *Id.* § 707.60(c)(3).
23. *Id.* pt. 761, subpt. F.
24. TSCA § 12(c)(1), (4), 15 U.S.C. § 2611(c)(1), (4); Mercury Export Ban Act of 2008, Pub. L. No. 110-414, 122 Stat. 4341.
25. Mercury Compounds; Prohibition of Export, 81 Fed. Reg. 58,926, 58,927 (Aug. 26, 2016).
26. TSCA § 12(c)(7)(D), 15 U.S.C. § 2611(c)(7)(D).

TAKEAWAYS

- The exporter is the one with the power and responsibility for controlling the shipment of the chemical substance outside of the customs territory of the United States.
- Just because a TSCA section 4 test rule has sunset, export notification may still be required. Exporters will need to check whether EPA has initiated rulemaking under TSCA sections 5, 6, or 7 for the chemical substance or mixture.
- New chemicals manufactured only for export are exempt from PMN requirements.
- To avoid costly penalties, exporters should have a system in place to ensure timely compliance with applicable export requirements.

6

TSCA and Commercial Transactions: What to Look For

Lisa R. Burchi

Key Messages

- TSCA compliance is an integral component of due diligence in commercial transactions.
- What diligence is due depends on the extent to which the target company or asset at issue is involved in the manufacture, import, processing, distribution, and/or use of chemical substances or mixtures regulated under TSCA.
- Critically important is the understanding that TSCA's jurisdictional reach is enormous and increasingly includes commercial products that contain chemicals of interest to EPA, especially appliances, electronics, textiles, and related finished products that are defined as "articles" under TSCA.
- While TSCA compliance is one motivating factor to step up due diligence, a far more consequential factor is avoiding problems with business distribution. Market access can be denied, product recalls may ensue, and reputational

damage may occur; all are foreseeable consequences of TSCA noncompliance.

- EPA provides meaningful incentives, including 100 percent penalty mitigation, for "new owners" to conduct TSCA compliance due diligence before or upon acquisition.
- Companies must prepare to transfer licenses, assign agreements, and otherwise ensure the smooth transition of TSCA obligations and responsibilities.

6.1 Overview

"Due diligence" is defined as

> the process of investigation carried on usually by a disinterested third party (as an accounting or law firm) on behalf of a party contemplating a business transaction (as a corporate acquisition or merger, loan of finances, or especially purchase of securities) for the purpose of providing information with which to evaluate the advantages and risks involved.[1]

All companies engaged in a transaction (e.g., sale, merger, spin-off, divestiture) know the value of conducting a comprehensive appraisal of business assets and liabilities undertaken by a prospective buyer to evaluate its commercial potential. It goes without saying that sellers prepare, and buyers review, information related to various aspects of a business's operations and finances as part of due diligence.

Regulatory compliance and considerations can be part of that due diligence as well, providing the buyer with some insight into current and potentially upcoming regulatory issues based on the seller's product line and sites. Many entities are not as aware, however, that there can be legal, regulatory, and practical considerations under the Toxic Substances Control Act (TSCA) when researching a company that is engaged in the manufacture (including import), processing, sales/distribution, or use of chemical substances, including chemical substances as part of mixtures and articles, as these terms are defined in Chapters 2 and 3.

For many years, the commercial and regulatory implications of TSCA compliance have been under-assessed in standard due

1. *Due Diligence*, Merriam-Webster Dictionary, https://www.merriam-webster.com/dictionary/due%20diligence#:~:text=%3A%20the%20care%20that%20a%20prudent,risks%20affecting%20a%20business%20transaction (last visited Sept. 27, 2024).

diligence. Given the dramatic implications of the U.S. Environmental Protection Agency's (EPA's) implementation of TSCA and its greatly expanded scope, due diligence is one area businesspeople can ill afford to botch. Due diligence fit for TSCA purposes can identify regulatory and commercial risks and elicit essential information regarding potential risks for impacted chemical substances that are an integral part of the transaction. For example, learning that a company manufactures or processes a substance that is under EPA scrutiny or subject to a TSCA section 5(e) consent order or significant new use rule (SNUR) can have dramatic implications regarding the bottom line, or even whether the deal should proceed. From a commercial perspective, EPA's existing or even prospective regulations can result in restrictions that prevent the sale of certain products, seriously diminish uses of those products and the revenue derived from them, or invite the need for additional, expensive data development or capital improvements to address manufacturing requirements EPA regulation imposes. These all can significantly affect a deal's bottom line.

Not only is there a need for a company to conduct due diligence prior to completing a business transaction, but there also can be strong incentives under TSCA to do so. The reasons are twofold. First, regardless of any contractual indemnifications and assignment of liabilities such that costs, including penalties and the cost of remedial measures, are borne by the seller for noncompliance during the time the seller was responsible, EPA will not typically negotiate or initiate enforcement action against that seller if the seller no longer owns the company. Instead, the new entity could be responsible for any payments or other requirements. The new entity is whose name might appear on a press release announcing any settlement for noncompliance or a complaint filed in court. While the new owner can seek indemnification from the seller based on their contractual arrangements, there are other potential business consequences—costly lawsuits, reputational damage, diminished brand trust, the cost of business disruptions while compliance is achieved—that cannot be so easily managed contractually.

Second, EPA has developed what it calls the "Audit Policy" that can provide opportunities to avoid any penalties for violations that are discovered and self-confessed to EPA, provided certain conditions are satisfied.[2] EPA developed a specialized audit policy specifically

2. Incentives for Self-Policing: Discovery, Disclosure, Correction, and Prevention of Violations, 65 Fed. Reg. 19,618 (Apr. 11, 2000).

for new owners ("New Owner Interim Approach") and tailored the conditions to be satisfied for penalty avoidance to ensure that buyers are motivated to utilize this policy for violations discovered during or after the due diligence process.[3] This self-disclosure option for new owners may be more important now than ever before, as EPA's enforcement under TSCA has been robust in recent years, with the maximum per penalty amount now more than $48,000.[4] Since this penalty amount can be per shipment or sale of a product, or per manufacturing or importing event, one can imagine how a violation related to one product can give rise to hundreds of separate offenses and six-figure penalty amounts.

When due diligence and all other aspects related to an acquisition, divesture, or other transaction are complete, there are certain licenses and rights that must be transferred officially from the seller to the new company. These transfers are needed to inform EPA that a new entity will be stepping into the shoes of the previous company and taking all rights and responsibilities regarding those licenses, rights, and other obligations. EPA's written procedures and template agreements to transfer certain TSCA rules or orders to a successor in interest provide assistance with this process and transition.

6.2 Determining the Scope of TSCA Due Diligence

As part of environmental due diligence when considering the acquisition of another company, an acquiring company can conduct a review of the TSCA status of a seller's products and processes. How comprehensive any TSCA due diligence should be depends on several factors. First and foremost to consider is the nature of the business and whether the business being acquired is engaged in activities that would trigger more rigorous TSCA requirements. Companies

3. Interim Approach to Applying the Audit Policy to New Owners, 73 Fed. Reg. 44,991 (Aug. 1, 2008). Although it has never been issued in final and is referred to as an "interim approach," it is relied upon by EPA as if issued in final and is called the "New Owner Audit Policy" in its 2021 "Frequently Asked Questions" document. Office of Enforcement and Compliance Assurance, EPA, EPA's Audit Policy Program: Frequently Asked Questions i (2021) [hereinafter Audit Policy FAQ], https://www.epa.gov/sites/default/files/2021-02/documents/epaauditpolicyprogramfaqs2021.pdf.
4. Civil Monetary Penalty Inflation Adjustment, 88 Fed. Reg. 89,309, 89,312 (Dec. 27, 2023).

routinely engaged in the manufacturing of chemical substances are the types most clearly subject to TSCA requirements. Perhaps less understood is that TSCA equates manufacturing with importation, so that any company that imports chemical substances, including when components of mixtures (e.g., paints, alloys), can be subject to significant TSCA regulations. Companies that engage only in processing, activities including formulating and blending, distribution, and/or exportation may have less regulatory requirements, but TSCA is still applicable.

In addition to the types of activities in which the acquiring company is engaged, the types of chemical substances, mixtures, and/or articles that are imported, domestically purchased, or used can trigger vastly different requirements. There are, for example, certain substances subject to TSCA section 5 SNURs that trigger various compliance requirements, including the use of personal protective equipment, restrictions on use in consumer products, and prohibitions of discharge to water. There is a growing list of substances being reviewed by EPA under TSCA section 6 with the potential worst-case scenario if EPA implements regulations prohibiting manufacture, import, processing, distribution, and/or use of the substance. There is also the class of substances of notoriety more recently, per- and polyfluoroalkyl substances (PFAS), that if intentionally present in any product present significant TSCA challenges and are worthy of a due diligence deeper dive.

Thus, while the scope of TSCA due diligence may differ depending on the business to be acquired, some form of TSCA due diligence should be conducted to assist the buyer in ascertaining whether and how TSCA's regulations can impact a business, and then whether any existing practices or products could lead to business disruptions, enforcement penalties, and other costs.

The parties initially also must determine the timing for any TSCA due diligence, such as those TSCA issues that will be reviewed prior to the closing (i.e., the effective date for the acquisition, typically set forth in an agreement) and those that may be reviewed as part of a post-closing audit. This decision depends on similar factors, and companies that are involved routinely in the manufacturing or importing of chemical substances, mixtures, and articles are the type of business that would require a more rigorous review prior to any deal closing. Other companies engage in other activities (e.g., processing, distributing, using, disposing) with chemical substances, mixtures, and articles where TSCA compliance should still be investigated, but perhaps a thorough examination may not be possible or necessary before any deal closes. In those latter cases, certain aspects of TSCA compliance can be more important to review up front than others.

Timing decisions also hinge on how potential problems once identified will be addressed and who will pay the cost. Issues identified prior to the date of acquisition provide opportunities for such issues to be addressed prior to that date, which likely would be addressed by the seller at its cost. Issues identified after the date of acquisition still can be addressed by the seller pursuant to terms set forth in the closing agreement, but otherwise likely would need to be addressed, and paid for, by the buyer. Regardless of the time of discovery, buyers can mitigate the impact of noncompliance that could result in enforcement and penalties by self-reporting under the New Owner Interim Approach. Even if the New Owner Interim Approach is not available (i.e., one of the conditions cannot be met), there still may be options for penalty mitigation under the Audit Policy or an applicable enforcement response policy (ERP).

To ensure these issues are appropriately vetted, a buyer should confirm that its due diligence team includes expertise in TSCA's jurisdiction and regulations. In determining the scope of any due diligence review under TSCA, various EPA resources can be very helpful:

- EPA's "Toxic Substances Control Act (TSCA) New and Existing Chemicals Inspection Manual" provides guidance to inspectors conducting inspections and thus indicates those areas where EPA focuses its attention for compliance.[5]
- EPA's guidance document "Protocol for Conducting Environmental Compliance Audits of Facilities with PCBs, Asbestos, and Lead-Based Paint Regulated under TSCA" provides information from EPA to support entities conducting their own environmental auditing related to (1) the use, disposal, cleanup, and storage of polychlorinated biphenyls (PCBs); (2) the removal of asbestos from buildings and its ultimate

5. Office of Enforcement and Compliance Assurance, EPA, Toxic Substances Control Act (TSCA) New and Existing Chemicals Inspection Manual (2022), https://www.epa.gov/system/files/documents/2022-04/tscanewandexistingchemicalinspectionsmanual.pdf.

disposal; and/or (3) notifications, training, and work practice standards for lead-based paint.[6]

- EPA's "Compliance Monitoring Strategy for the Toxic Substances Control Act (TSCA)" provides guidance to EPA regions as to how to "[a]ddress the most significant TSCA-regulated problems" and "[p]romote compliance generally throughout the various TSCA-regulated universes," thus providing additional guidance regarding those TSCA issues that EPA inspectors are instructed to prioritize.[7]
- EPA's TSCA ERPs set forth EPA's enforcement options and penalty calculation formulas so that companies can understand EPA's varying authority and resulting company consequences, depending on the alleged violation at issue.[8]

6.3 Conducting Due Diligence—General Issues

In preparing for the sale of its business, a seller understands that some type of due diligence will be conducted, and, these days, the seller typically creates an electronic data room to allow the electronic storage and viewing of documents related to the sale. There are various motivations for doing so, including but not limited to planning for the foreseeable due diligence inquiries of any serious potential buyer. To maintain confidentiality, information can be provided pursuant to a nondisclosure agreement.

6. Office of Enforcement and Compliance Assurance, EPA, Protocol for Conducting Environmental Compliance Audits of Facilities with PCBs, Asbestos, and Lead-Based Paint Regulated under TSCA (2000), https://www.epa.gov/sites/production/files/documents/apcol-tsca.pdf.
7. Office of Enforcement and Compliance Assurance, EPA, Compliance Monitoring Strategy for the Toxic Substances Control Act (TSCA) (2016), https://www.epa.gov/sites/default/files/2014-01/documents/tsca-cms.pdf.
8. EPA, Enforcement Response Policy for Test Rules under Section 4 of the Toxic Substances Control Act (1986), https://www.epa.gov/sites/default/files/documents/tscasec4ruleserp-052886.pdf; EPA, TSCA Section 5 Enforcement Response Policy (1988, as amended 1989 and 1993) [hereinafter Section 5 ERP], https://www.epa.gov/sites/default/files/2016-06/documents/amendedtscasection5-erp.pdf; EPA, The Enforcement Response Policy for Reporting and Recordkeeping Rules and Requirements for TSCA Sections 8, 12, and 13 (revised 1999), https://www.epa.gov/sites/default/files/documents/erp8_12r.pdf; EPA, Polychlorinated Biphenyls (PCB) Penalty Policy (1990), https://www.epa.gov/sites/default/files/documents/pcbpen.pdf; EPA, Section 1018—Disclosure Rule Enforcement Response and Penalty Policy (2007), https://www.epa.gov/sites/default/files/documents/1018erpp-1207.pdf.

There is certain general information that can assist in determining a company's level of understanding of, and compliance with, regulatory requirements. This section includes the types of questions that can be posed and documents that can be requested by a potential buyer as part of TSCA due diligence and in turn the type of information and documents that a seller could review and prepare in anticipation of such requests. The questions that follow are intended to start generally and then, depending on those responses, move on to more granular issues. Depending on the types of documents available and the target company's understanding of its requirements, an acquiring company can adjust the level of due diligence needed to make informed business decisions.

One of the first questions that should be asked is whether the company to be acquired believes it is subject to any requirements under TSCA section 4, 5, 8, 12, or 13 and, if so, whether it has available TSCA compliance policies and procedures. Although not a regulatory requirement under TSCA, written TSCA standard operating procedures (SOPs) can provide significant information regarding whether and how regulatory requirements are satisfied. Comprehensive and well-documented policies and/or compliance management systems can be indicative of a company's thorough TSCA compliance approach. Lack of such documentation is a red flag when investigating a company that appears to be subject to significant TSCA requirements.

One subset of questions or document requests relates to the availability of compliance procedures and/or training that confirms the seller has a system in place before making any changes to its procurement of substances, manufacturing processes, or related activities. If a company has no management of systems to ensure changes are reviewed and approved prior to implementation, there can be significant regulatory impacts that are not considered or addressed. For example, an employee may find a less expensive source for a particular raw material, a not uncommon event given global supply chain dynamics. The employee may have made a change without understanding that if the substance is no longer supplied by a domestic source, the company could be considered an importer of record, triggering additional TSCA regulatory requirements. Companies with suitable training and/or change management processes in place are much better able to limit the possibility of noncompliance.

A further inquiry related to compliance procedures is to determine if the seller has ever conducted its own audit or a review of its procedures. Copies of internal company audit reports, or even a description of such audits and their findings, can be instructive in assessing the strength of a company's compliance programs and what steps were taken to address adverse findings, if any.

General TSCA due diligence also can inquire how a company stays informed of evolving TSCA requirements. Regulatory requirements change rapidly, so establishing whether and how a company monitors EPA, state, and global chemical regulations for new requirements, guidance, and trends is another way to assess a company's general compliance efforts.

A revealing due diligence inquiry is whether the seller has ever been involved in a prior enforcement proceeding based on TSCA noncompliance. Past enforcement by EPA is no secret and can be investigated independently,[9] but considering potential challenges (e.g., a company name change), the onus of disclosing should be with the seller. Reviewing enforcement history documents not only provides important information regarding the strengths and weaknesses of a TSCA compliance program but also can be particularly relevant to the buyer. There may be, for example, remediation efforts or penalty payments that will affect the transaction and the potential buyer's responsibilities.

There are likely contracts and agreements in place related to the manufacture, importation, processing, use, testing, distribution, and/or disposal of chemical substances, mixtures, or articles pertinent to TSCA. An important component of TSCA due diligence is determining the scope of all such agreements, whether any rights and/or obligations are transferred upon acquisition or can be assigned, and what if any steps may be necessary upon completion of the acquisition.

At the conclusion of this general TSCA due diligence review, a potential buyer should have some indication of how TSCA regulations and compliance can impact the acquisition. Depending on whether all or most of the following statements are true, the potential buyer and its due diligence team can determine whether further review is required:

9. EPA's administrative enforcement docket, https://yosemite.epa.gov/OA/RHC/EPAAdmin.nsf, can be searched for companies that have settled matters where EPA has alleged violations and issued a consent agreement and final order. EPA's Enforcement and Compliance History Online (ECHO), https://echo.epa.gov/, provides an online searchable database of various EPA enforcement actions.

- There is no manufacture, importation, processing, distribution, and/or use of chemical substances, mixtures, and articles that are subject to regulation under TSCA.
- There are no exports of any chemical substances (on their own or as components of a mixture).
- There is no processing of chemical substances or mixtures.
- There are no activities that would create chemical reactions.
- There are no research and development (R&D) activities with or testing of chemical substances or mixtures.
- There are no chemical components defined as PFAS.

6.4 Conducting Due Diligence—Specific Issues

If an acquiring company understands or learns that the business for sale is engaged in activities for which significant TSCA compliance is required (e.g., manufacturing or importation of chemical substances or mixtures; manufacturing, importing, or even processing certain chemical substances "of concern" that trigger additional TSCA requirements), then the TSCA due diligence can be more thorough.

6.4.1 CBI

One overarching issue to consider throughout the due diligence process is whether the company at issue has information it claims as confidential business information (CBI). EPA's procedures for claiming CBI changed significantly in 2023, and there are new and amended procedures to assert and maintain those claims.[10] If a company has claimed information as CBI, it should be able to provide an explanation as to the basis for that claim and whether that CBI has been submitted to EPA and, if required, substantiated. A prospective buyer should be aware of a company's CBI claims and whether those claims have been treated and supported as such pursuant to EPA's regulations. Lack of adherence to EPA's process can result in loss of protection of that CBI status. For CBI claims properly asserted and maintained, there are considerations post-acquisition to ensure continued CBI protection (e.g., updating contact information).

---

10. Confidential Business Information Claims under the Toxic Substances Control Act (TSCA), 88 Fed. Reg. 37,155, 37,169 (June 7, 2023).

6.4.2 TSCA Inventory Listing and Exemptions

For more comprehensive due diligence reviews, potential buyers can confirm that all substances (including those in mixtures or released from articles) manufactured, imported, or processed are listed on the TSCA Chemical Substance Inventory (TSCA Inventory) or exempt from listing, as well as confirm that all those substances listed on the TSCA Inventory are "active."[11] This is the type of information that EPA would routinely request as part of any inspection, and the requirement to be listed on the TSCA Inventory or exempt from listing prior to any commercial manufacture or import is one of the paramount issues upon which EPA would focus in any inspection. In fact, EPA's TSCA Section 5 ERP not only considers the commercial manufacture or import of a chemical substance not listed on the TSCA Inventory or exempt from listing as one of the more serious violations under TSCA section 5, but also EPA considers each day of production or importation of a new chemical substance in violation of the section 5 notification requirements to constitute a new (or "per-day") violation.[12] Any indication that a substance is manufactured (including imported), processed, used, or sold/distributed but is not listed on the TSCA Inventory or subject to an exclusion or exemption is a red flag that the seller may be in violation of TSCA, and the buyer may be at risk for penalties and business disruptions if it continues.

Sellers should have available for review information regarding those chemical substances manufactured, imported, processed, or used, including chemical name, Chemical Abstracts Service Registry Number (CAS RN), whether the chemical substance is listed on the public or confidential TSCA Inventory or exempt from TSCA Inventory listing, the active status of that substance, and the basis or source for the information provided (e.g., safety data sheets (SDSs), supplier certifications). For businesses engaged in manufacture involving chemical reactions, a technically skilled person should be part of the due diligence team to review production chemistry and confirm that the reaction products are as represented.

At a minimum, this TSCA due diligence inquiry can provide buyers with pertinent information regarding the seller's compliance,

---

11. TSCA § 8(b), 15 U.S.C. § 2607(b); 40 C.F.R. pt. 710 (2023). *See also How to Access the TSCA Inventory*, EPA, https://www.epa.gov/tsca-inventory/how-access-tsca-inventory (last updated Sept. 11, 2024).
12. Section 5 ERP, *supra* note 8, at 15.

as well as its attitude toward TSCA compliance. Considering the importance of the information at issue and perhaps the knowledge that this is information that could be readily requested by EPA as part of an inspection, accurate and complete information regarding the TSCA status of all chemical substances and mixtures (including articles that contain chemical substances and mixtures) can be indicative of TSCA compliance generally, while insufficient or incomplete answers and documentation can be a red flag. This is not to say that lack of complete and meticulous records is a red flag per se, as there are complexities and nuances regarding TSCA compliance that must be considered. One particular issue is whether there are chemical identities that are maintained as confidential by a supplier and how the seller manages those issues and confirms TSCA compliance despite not knowing the specific chemical identity. On the more extreme side, if the seller has no, or hit-or-miss, TSCA Inventory records and has not thoroughly analyzed the chemistry and components of its products, it may be the case that the buyer could discover problems after the acquisition, with the potential for production interruptions, customer disputes, and penalties that can follow.

Related to TSCA Inventory listing requirements are the following questions and document requests. An answer of "yes" to any of these questions indicates serious engagement in TSCA issues.

- Has the seller filed premanufacture notices (PMNs)? If the company is engaged in new chemistry, it is important to understand the scope and responsibilities for such substances. Where possible, it is helpful to obtain copies of the PMNs. If there are "new" chemical substances that are not listed on the TSCA Inventory or subject to an exemption, the substance could not be manufactured (including imported) until a PMN is filed, the applicable review period has expired, and the responsible entity complies with any restrictions imposed by EPA.
- Has EPA issued a test marketing exemption (TME), low volume exemption (LVE), and/or low releases and low exposures exemption (LoREX) for any of the seller's chemical substances? If so, a buyer may wish to review those exemptions and the conditions in place under those exemptions. Issues related to these exemptions also raise questions regarding the transfer of those exemptions to new or related entities, as discussed later in the chapter.

- Is the seller relying on an R&D exemption? If so, a buyer can determine whether the requirements of the R&D exemption are satisfied (e.g., availability of a log for the quantity of the R&D substance manufactured (or imported)). Depending on the extent of reliance on the R&D exemption, due diligence could include a review of laboratory operations and relevant documents (e.g., labels, production logs) to determine if substances that are the subject of the R&D exemption satisfy R&D exemption requirements. If the seller is not in compliance with the requirements of the R&D exemption and another exclusion or exemption does not apply, then there may be a TSCA violation, and the buyer may be at risk for penalties and business disruptions if such activities continue.
- Is the seller relying on a polymer exemption? If so, a buyer can determine whether the requirements for the polymer exemption are met (e.g., availability of required reports to EPA and recordkeeping). Depending on the extent of reliance on the polymer exemption, due diligence also could include a review of practices and relevant documents (e.g., representative structural diagrams) to determine that substances qualify and satisfy the polymer exemption requirements. If the seller is not in compliance with a polymer exemption and another exclusion or exemption does not apply, there may be a TSCA violation, and the buyer may be at risk for penalties and business disruptions if such activities continue.

6.4.3 TSCA Section 5 or 6 Rules or Orders

Substances for which EPA has proposed or issued rules or orders under TSCA section 5 or 6 are especially important, as this suggests EPA is devoting or has devoted focused regulatory scrutiny for which regulatory requirements apply or will apply. Companies can seek to avoid any manufacture, import, processing, distribution, or use of these substances, but that is not always feasible or necessary. Additional requirements or restrictions under TSCA sections 5 and 6 are increasingly becoming part of the TSCA landscape, and the goal of a prospective buyer may be understanding and managing these requirements rather than considering this a deal-breaker.

To assess TSCA compliance and make informed decisions regarding the level of TSCA compliance the seller is interested or willing to address, the following questions and document reviews are most important:

- Are there section 5(e) or 5(f) orders applicable to any substances manufactured (including import), processed, used, disposed of, or purchased? If yes, the buyer can seek to review the section 5 order with particular attention to the conditions and restrictions imposed on a substance subject to such an order and whether the seller is complying with those conditions and restrictions.
- Are there SNURs applicable to any substances manufactured (including import), processed, distributed, used, disposed of, or purchased? If so, EPA's regulations at 40 C.F.R. Part 721 sets forth all issued SNURs,[13] but there can be chemical identities or other information claimed as confidential that requires the seller to provide additional information sufficient to satisfy the buyer's due diligence. The buyer then can review those SNURs with particular attention to the conditions and restrictions imposed on the substance and whether the seller is complying with those conditions and restrictions. One requirement to highlight is that companies that intend to manufacture or process for commercial purposes a chemical substance subject to a SNUR and intend to distribute the substance in commerce can have certain notification requirements to downstream recipients or the need to otherwise demonstrate the recipient knows of the SNUR and/or cannot undertake any significant new use described in the SNUR.[14]
- Are there substances the seller manufactures (including imports), processes, uses, distributes, and/or disposes of that EPA has designated or is considering designating as high priority for risk evaluation, or that are otherwise undergoing risk evaluation, under TSCA section 6? If so, the buyer's due diligence must review and assess the potential obligations, risks, and fees associated with that substance.
- Are there substances the seller manufactures (including imports), processes, uses, distributes, or disposes of that are subject to bans or restrictions under TSCA section 5 or 6?

13. 40 C.F.R. pt. 721 (2023).
14. *Id.* § 721.5(a)(2).

If so, the buyer can seek documents or information to determine that the seller's practices for such substances are compliant with those restrictions.

6.4.4 TSCA Section 8 Rules and Orders

EPA's regulations implementing TSCA section 8 requirements set forth reporting and recordkeeping requirements. From an EPA enforcement perspective, potential violations of these requirements can sometimes be considered "low-hanging fruit," since it can be a straightforward case for EPA to demonstrate that a report was required to be submitted but was not or that a report was submitted but its contents are incorrect. EPA often prioritizes these infractions for enforcement because they are easy to catch and easy to prove. For this reason, determining what reporting and recordkeeping requirements apply and how those requirements are satisfied can be of extreme interest to a prospective buyer.

To assess TSCA compliance and make informed decisions regarding the level of TSCA compliance the seller is interested or willing to address, the following questions and document reviews are most important:

- Has the seller submitted information under the Chemical Data Reporting (CDR) rule? If yes, the most recently submitted CDR report and the underlying information that the CDR report is based on should be reviewed. The basis for and documentation of any exemptions from CDR reporting (e.g., no manufacture/import, production quantities less than 25,000 pounds) also can be reviewed. The report provides insight into substances manufactured in or imported into the United States, including as part of mixtures.
- Has the seller submitted reports pursuant to section 8(e)? If yes, these reports can be reviewed. If no such reports have been submitted, it could be important to determine and review any decisions as to why reporting was not required and/or confirm there are systems in place to review potential information under section 8(e) and provide training regarding these requirements. Even if required reporting was made, the fact that a TSCA section 8(e) report was filed reflects commercial sensitivities that should be addressed. Does the

chemical look like a problem in the making? Is it regulated in other jurisdictions? Will downstream processors and users resist it based on toxicity concerns? All these issues need to be considered.

- Does the seller have records of allegations of significant adverse reactions under section 8(c)? If yes, these should be reviewed. If not, it would be important to confirm there are systems in place to review potential information under section 8(c) and provide training regarding these requirements.
- Are any of the substances identified subject to section 8(d) rules? If yes, there may be follow-up questions for additional information regarding who was required to report, what was required to be reported, and any submissions or exemptions from submissions under section 8(d) chemicals.

6.4.5 TSCA Section 12 (Export) and Section 13 (Import) Requirements

Companies engaged in the importation and exportation of chemical substances and mixtures can trigger TSCA regulatory requirements. Export notifications under section 12(b) are only required for those substances that are subject to certain proposed and/or final rules and orders under TSCA sections 4, 5, 6, and 7. There are exemptions (e.g., exports must contain a section 12(b) substance above specified de minimis concentrations) and specific requirements for when and how often export notifications must be submitted. The actual preparation of a section 12(b) export notification is not complicated. The arguably most important issue from a due diligence perspective is whether there is a system in place to flag, report, and track these requirements.

TSCA section 13 import certification requirements also are not complicated—a single sentence with language specified by EPA in its regulations on import documentation can suffice. Challenges can arise depending on certain factors, particularly the quantity of chemical substances and mixtures imported and whether chemical identities are claimed as confidential by the foreign supplier. As with section 12, any due diligence should focus first on the procedures in place that track when importations will take place, including the TSCA compliance reviews that occur prior to importation and how import certifications are prepared and managed. The use of import brokers can be helpful but is not dispositive of compliance, because in many cases a broker's ability to comply with section 13 is possible only when the importing company provides the broker with needed information to make the certifications.

6.4.6 TSCA Section 4 Rules or Orders

TSCA section 4 authorizes EPA to issue test rules when certain criteria are satisfied, requiring the development of adequate test data on the health and environmental effects of chemical substances and mixtures. A buyer can inquire and determine whether there are any substances that the seller manufactures (including imports) or processes that are subject to section 4 test rules, orders, or consent agreements. If so, the buyer can request to review documents indicating compliance with any rules, orders, or consent agreements (e.g., letter of intent to test, exemption applications). If there is any incomplete testing, the buyer can seek information to understand the responsibilities and costs that will be incurred in conducting any such required, but not yet completed, testing. Test rules, orders, and consent agreements also trigger export notification requirements.

6.4.7 TSCA Articles

Chemical substances that are parts of finished goods, or "articles," under TSCA and not intended to be released are sometimes exempt from certain TSCA requirements, including but not limited to PMN submissions and CDR reporting. Increasingly, however, EPA has greatly limited the so-called article exemption and is regulating chemical substances as part of articles. This trend is expected to continue.

One recent example involves phenol, isopropylated phosphate (3:1) (PIP 3:1), a substance identified by EPA in a 2014 "Work Plan for Chemical Assessments"[15] as a persistent, bioaccumulative, and toxic substance for which EPA was required to take "expedited" regulatory action. That action involved a proposed rule issued in July 2019 where EPA sought comments on its proposal to, in part, prohibit the processing and distribution in commerce of PIP (3:1), and the

15. Office of Pollution Prevention and Toxics, EPA, TSCA Work Plan for Chemical Assessments: 2014 Update (2014), https://www.epa.gov/sites/default/files/2015-01/documents/tsca_work_plan_chemicals_2014_update-final.pdf.

products or articles containing the chemical substance, for all uses with limited exemptions. Despite the drastic nature of EPA's proposal, surprisingly few entities sounded the alarm in comments and urged EPA to consider the catastrophic implications of a hard stop on the importation of articles containing PIP (3:1). Several sectors, including the electronics and semiconductor industries, realized that most finished goods that plugged into the wall contain PIP (3:1). EPA and industry eventually negotiated delayed compliance dates, but the PIP (3:1) experience remains a cautionary tale regarding TSCA's potential reach and impact for industries manufacturing (including importing), processing, and distributing articles containing chemicals regulated under TSCA.

To address potential compliance and market access issues for articles, due diligence should include inquiring whether any TSCA rules for chemical substances apply such that products included in a transaction might be implicated. If any such substances are identified, it is critically important to determine how the seller has addressed any regulatory requirements or otherwise modified its TSCA compliance practices to ensure these otherwise exempt articles have not fallen through the cracks. While contractual representation and warranty provisions may help to make an aggrieved party whole, the business disruption, denial of market access, and diminished brand implications of inadequate TSCA due diligence can be catastrophic, with long-lasting implications.

6.5 Issues for Seller Following Discovery of Violations before or during Due Diligence, or after Acquisition

While preparing for the due diligence of potential buyers would seem standard, some due diligence on the seller's part may not be. The extent of a seller's due diligence prior to the transaction can depend on several factors, including the nature of the seller's business and the structure of the transaction. The motivations to do so can vary as well. A seller's own due diligence could assist in determining if there are compliance problems and, if so, how to disclose or otherwise address those issues. Identified compliance issues could impact any sale (or the purchase price) or indemnifications set forth in a closing agreement, which may be important to know up front. When it issued the New Owner Interim Approach, EPA noted that it "received comments suggesting that such incentives for new owners might have a beneficial effect on negotiations, encouraging prospective sellers to address violations before closing, or giving prospective buyers leverage to negotiate for the seller to correct violations found during due diligence."[16] The seller thus has incentives to ensure that any due diligence it conducts that could identify a violation of TSCA is managed to maximize its ability to satisfy the conditions under EPA's penalty mitigation policies.

Even if the scope of TSCA due diligence is limited prior to the date of acquisition, it is possible that a violation will be discovered during such a review and the seller will need to be prepared to address that possibility. On this point, it should be noted that EPA has not provided the seller with the same additional incentives to conduct due diligence as it has provided to the buyer under the New Owner Interim Approach, to be discussed in the next section. The seller likely cannot shield evidence of violations in a closing agreement and indeed EPA, in the New Owner Interim Approach, stated that if sellers attempted "to include 'no-tell' clauses in their transaction or indemnity agreements, such clauses may well be voidable as contrary to the public interest."[17]

Indemnification provisions specific to TSCA can address which entity will pay for penalties assessed by EPA for TSCA violations arising before the acquisition and which entity is responsible for costs resulting from business interruptions caused by TSCA violations existing before the acquisition. TSCA personnel and environmental lawyers should review the applicable clauses to ensure they capture appropriate warranties, representations, and indemnifications for potential applicable TSCA claims. In rare cases, there is a risk to the seller that after the acquisition, a buyer will obtain penalty mitigation under the New Owner Interim Approach, and EPA will seek penalties from the seller for its role in causing the violation. EPA states: "In situations where the violations demonstrate potentially widespread or recurring noncompliance, or a potential endangerment to human health or the environment, EPA may decide to bring an enforcement action against the prior owner."[18] As such, a seller should consider

16. Interim Approach to Applying the Audit Policy to New Owners, 73 Fed. Reg. 44,991, 45,004 (Aug. 1, 2008).
17. *Id.*
18. Audit Policy FAQ, *supra* note 3, at 14.

how it will respond to any violation discovered before, or potentially after, the acquisition.

If there are any liabilities imposed on the seller, those liabilities may pass to the buyer after acquisition, depending on the structure of the transaction. More importantly, however, from a buyer's perspective, if the violations continue during operations of the business, the buyer will be violating TSCA from the first day of its acquisition.

6.6 Issues for Buyer Following Discovery of Violations during Due Diligence or after Date of Acquisition—New Owner Interim Approach

Since 1995, EPA has had in place the Audit Policy intended to encourage regulated entities to "voluntarily discover, disclose, correct and prevent violations of Federal environmental law."[19] EPA's objective is straightforward, namely, the enhanced protection of human health and the environment by incentivizing companies to come forward with their environmental law violations. EPA's general Audit Policy does not offer penalty waivers or mitigation unless certain conditions are met, including that the alleged violation was discovered as part of a periodic audit or compliance management system.[20] Due diligence conducted as part of a sale is not considered systematic or periodic, thus potentially eliminating self-disclosure in this scenario.

Recognizing that "new owners may be particularly well-situated and highly motivated to focus on, and invest in, making a clean start for their new facilities by addressing environmental noncompliance,"[21] EPA in 2008 issued the New Owner Interim Approach to provide incentives for new owners to self-report.[22] The Audit Policy and the New Owner Interim Approach are not limited to TSCA, but rather apply to all environmental statutes administered by EPA.

The fact that this approach remains "interim" should not be mistaken as EPA's lack of commitment to implement the policy and provide some flexibility for new owners. EPA reaffirmed its commitment

19. Incentives for Self-Policing: Discovery, Disclosure, Correction, and Prevention of Violations, 65 Fed. Reg. 19,618 (Apr. 11, 2000).
20. *Id.* at 19,625.
21. Enhancing Environmental Outcomes from Audit Policy Disclosures through Tailored Incentives for New Owners; Notice, 72 Fed. Reg. 27,116 (May 14, 2007).
22. 65 Fed. Reg. at 19,618.

to the policy for new owners in May 2018.[23] In the "Audit Policy Program: Frequently Asked Questions" (Audit Policy FAQ) document issued in 2021 regarding EPA's audit policies, EPA dropped the "interim approach" language and referred to it as the "New Owner Audit Policy."[24] In its preamble to the New Owner Interim Approach, EPA states the following regarding its reasoning for developing this policy:

> Through applying a clear, transparent, and easily administered Interim Approach to resolving disclosures from new owners, the Agency seeks to use the Audit Policy to leverage its ability to make effective use of scarce government resources. If procedural and transaction costs can be minimized for regulators and self-disclosing new owners, EPA anticipates that the opportunity to work with new owners as they make clean starts at their new facilities can help secure higher quality environmental improvements more quickly and effectively than might otherwise occur.[25]

The incentives set forth in the New Owner Interim Approach are numerous. The most obvious benefit is that if a new owner qualifies under the New Owner Interim Approach, EPA will not assess any penalties against that new owner for violations occurring for the period before the date of acquisition. EPA describes these penalties as relating to both "economic benefit" and "gravity" penalties. With regard to economic benefit, this refers to EPA's policy to ensure that EPA will recognize and, if need be, reflect the "economic benefit" (e.g., operating costs) that were gained because of an entity's noncompliance and resulted in an unfair economic advantage over its compliant competitors. The "gravity" component of a civil penalty refers to that portion that is over and above the economic benefit.

If EPA does calculate economic benefit penalties associated with avoided operation and maintenance costs, EPA can assess those penalties against the new owner, but will only do so from the date of acquisition.[26] If EPA calculates economic benefit penalties associated with

---

23. *See* Press Release, EPA, EPA Announces Renewed Emphasis on Self-Disclosed Violation Policies (May 15, 2018), https://www.epa.gov/sites/default/files/2018-05/documents/refreshannouncementfordisclosures.pdf.
24. Audit Policy FAQ, *supra* note 3, at i.
25. Interim Approach to Applying the Audit Policy to New Owners, 73 Fed. Reg. 44,991, 44,992 (Aug. 1, 2008).
26. *Id.* at 44,998.

delayed capital expenditures or with unfair competitive advantage, EPA also can assess those penalties against the new owner, but only if the new owner does not correct the violations in accordance with the Audit Policy (i.e., within 60 days of discovery or another reasonable timeframe to which EPA has agreed). In reality, the calculation of economic benefits can be a challenging analysis, and EPA is more typically inclined not to investigate this component under the Audit Policy or New Owner Interim Approach, unless the facts present a strong case for such investigation.[27]

There are disadvantages to self-reporting. Most notable is the possibility that EPA will determine that the Audit Policy conditions have not been met and thus EPA will not significantly reduce penalties or not reduce penalties at all.

In the Audit Policy, EPA sets forth nine conditions that must all be met for an entity to be eligible for 100 percent mitigation of any gravity-based civil penalties that otherwise could be assessed by EPA in settlement of the disclosed violations. In its New Owner Interim Approach, EPA tailors the conditions of the Audit Policy to address certain facts and circumstances particular to the new owner scenario. First, EPA had to define who is a "new owner." Under the New Owner Interim Approach, an entity is considered a "new owner" when it certifies to the following criteria:

> a. Prior to the transaction, the new owner was not responsible for environmental compliance at the facility which is the subject of the disclosure, did not cause the violations being disclosed and could not have prevented their occurrence;
>
> b. The violation which is the subject of the disclosure originated with the prior owner; and
>
> c. Prior to the transaction, neither the buyer nor the seller had the largest ownership share of the other entity, and they did not have a common corporate parent.[28]

This definition is intended to ensure that "new" owners in certain transactions cannot qualify for beneficial treatment under the New

27. Audit Policy FAQ, *supra* note 3, at 9 ("While EPA still reserves the right to recover any economic benefit—particularly where not doing so would put a law-abiding competitor at a clear competitive disadvantage—EPA generally defers to the relevant program penalty policies governing the statutory or regulatory requirement at issue.").
28. 73 Fed. Reg. at 44,995.

Owner Interim Approach. In one example, EPA states that the New Owner Interim Approach could apply to a "new owner which, prior to the transaction, was a silent or inactive partner in a joint venture, and then purchased the rest of the business and became the active owner, so long as its prior share was less than the largest, and the new owner can certify to the first criterion" regarding lack of operational control at the facility.[29] In another example, a new owner that is the product of a merger may benefit from the New Owner Interim Approach, "so long as neither party had previously held the greatest ownership share of the entity with which it merged."[30] For stock transactions, EPA states that penalty mitigation is not envisioned for situations where the buyer and seller previously had a common corporate parent:

> EPA assumes, for purposes of interpreting this criterion, that the corporate parent was in control of the prior owner, the "new" owner, and facility operations. Accordingly, where two companies have a common corporate parent and one subsidiary buys another, the acquiring entity is not sufficiently "new" to warrant this tailored application of the Audit Policy.[31]

For entities that qualify as "new owners," the New Owner Interim Approach applies when that new owner certifies to the criteria of the "new owner" definition and meets all the conditions of the Audit Policy, as modified for new owners. Not all of the Audit Policy conditions have been modified to address new owners. In fact, there are four Audit Policy conditions that are the same under the New Owner Interim Approach, acknowledging that EPA already addressed specific circumstances for new owners in its Audit Policy. These unmodified Audit Policy conditions are those related to discovery, correction/remediation, prevention of recurrence, and no repeat violations.

- **Discovery and Disclosure Independent of Government or Third-Party Plaintiff (Condition 4).** The Audit Policy and New Owner Interim Approach provide that violations must be discovered and disclosed before EPA or another government agency likely would have identified the problem either

---

29. *Id.* at 44,996.
30. *Id.*
31. *Id. See also* AUDIT POLICY FAQ, *supra* note 3, at 12–14.

through its own investigative work or from information received through a third party.

- **Correction and Remediation (Condition 5).** The Audit Policy and New Owner Interim Approach provide that a self-disclosing entity must correct the disclosed violation within 60 calendar days from the date of discovery, certify in writing that the violation has been corrected, and take appropriate measures as required by law to remedy any environmental or human harm due to the violation. EPA recognizes that not all violations can be corrected in the 60-day timeframe, and thus may allow for an extension of time for corrections that require significant expenditures, involve technically complex issues, or involve decisions for which an entity seeks or is required to obtain EPA, state, or local input or approval.
- **Prevent Recurrence (Condition 6).** The Audit Policy and New Owner Interim Approach provide that the disclosing entity must agree in writing to take steps to prevent a recurrence of the violation after it has been disclosed and corrected.
- **No Repeat Violations (Condition 7).** For a self-disclosure to receive Audit Policy or New Owner Interim Approach consideration, the same or a closely related violation must have not occurred at the same facility within the past three years. When the facility is part of a multifacility organization, the Audit Policy and New Owner Interim Approach are not available if the same or a closely related violation occurred as part of a pattern of violations at one or more of these facilities within the past five years. In the case of a facility that has been newly acquired, the Audit Policy acknowledges that the existence of a violation prior to the acquisition does not trigger the repeat violations exclusion as to the new owner. This means that the acquired entity's history of violations will not prevent the acquiring entity from obtaining mitigation.

EPA formally modified five of the Audit Policy's preconditions in its New Owner Interim Approach, even if some of these changes had been implemented previously. These modifications reflect EPA's recognition of the factual differences in the acquisition context and in an attempt to expand the violations eligible for penalty mitigation or other incentives as applied to new owners.

The first modified condition is one regarding systematic discovery (Condition 1). EPA recognizes that a new owner's preclosing due diligence is by its nature a one-time event and thus will waive the "periodic" or systematic element of this condition for violations discovered through preacquisition due diligence and allow such disclosures to be considered for full penalty mitigation.[32]

The second modified condition relates to voluntary discovery (Condition 2). The Audit Policy states that the disclosed violation "must have been identified voluntarily, and not through a monitoring, sampling, or auditing procedure that is required by statute, regulation, permit, judicial or administrative order, or consent agreement."[33] Examples EPA provides of discovery that would not be voluntary and would not be eligible for penalty mitigation include "emissions violations detected through a required continuous emissions monitor, violations of NPDES [National Pollutant Discharge Elimination System] discharge limits found through prescribed monitoring, and violations discovered through a compliance audit required to be performed by the terms of a consent order or settlement agreement."[34] The Audit Policy and Audit Policy FAQ outline one exemption in the new owner context for Clean Air Act violations discovered at newly acquired facilities as part of the new owner's reexamination of facility compliance under Title V.[35] In the New Owner Interim Approach, EPA expanded its interpretation of the voluntary discovery condition in the new owner context to allow consideration of all violations that would otherwise be ineligible for Audit Policy consideration because they are already required to be identified through a legally mandated monitoring, sampling, or auditing protocol, and thus not "voluntarily discovered." New owners that enter into an audit agreement or disclose violations before the first instance when the monitoring, sampling, or auditing is required would not be disqualified based on this condition.[36]

The third modified condition relates to prompt disclosure (Condition 3). The Audit Policy provides that violations must be promptly disclosed in writing, within 21 days of discovery.[37] Under the New

32. 73 Fed. Reg. at 44,999–45,000.
33. Incentives for Self-Policing: Discovery, Disclosure, Correction, and Prevention of Violations, 65 Fed. Reg. 19,618, 19,621 (Apr. 11, 2000).
34. *Id.*
35. *Id.*; Audit Policy FAQ, *supra* note 3, at 2–3.
36. 73 Fed. Reg. at 45,000; *EPA's Interim Approach to Applying the Audit Policy to New Owners*, EPA, https://www.epa.gov/compliance/epas-interim-approach-applying-audit-policy-new-owners (last updated Mar. 22, 2024).
37. 65 Fed. Reg. at 19,621–22.

Owner Interim Approach, for violations discovered before the date of acquisition, a new owner has up to 45 days after the date of acquisition to disclose the violations. For violations discovered after the date of acquisition, a new owner must disclose violations within 21 days after discovery or within 45 days after the date of acquisition, whichever time period is longer. In the busy period just after acquisition, this extended definition of "prompt" provides new owners more time to decide and prepare to come forward with its due diligence findings. A new owner also can seek to enter into an audit agreement with EPA any time during the first nine months after the date of acquisition, and if executed, "the clock stops" with regard to the prompt disclosure condition for any violations discovered thereafter and disclosed in accordance with the agreement.[38] In no case, however, can an acquiring entity seek New Owner Interim Approach benefits after nine months from the date of acquisition.

EPA also modified the condition regarding other violations excluded (Condition 8). The Audit Policy excludes violations that resulted in serious actual harm or may have presented an imminent and substantial endangerment.[39] Where violations that gave rise to serious actual harm or an imminent and substantial endangerment began before the new owner's acquisition, EPA allows such violations to be eligible under the New Owner Interim Approach, absent a fatality, community evacuation, or other seriously injurious or catastrophic event.[40] This again is to encourage new owners to come forward and correct significant violations, which is one of EPA's main goals in promoting this New Owner Interim Approach.

The final modified condition relates to cooperation (Condition 9). EPA modified the cooperation condition of the Audit Policy only to make clear that the disclosing entity must cooperate with EPA in determining whether all Audit Policy conditions—as they have been modified by the New Owner Interim Approach—have been met.[41] This information can include providing information to support that an entity meets EPA's definition of "new owner."

38. 73 Fed. Reg. at 45,001.
39. 65 Fed. Reg. at 19,623.
40. 73 Fed. Reg. at 45,003.
41. *Id.* at 45,003–04.

6.7 Post-Acquisition TSCA Obligations

As part of any acquisition and the resulting agreements that are executed to complete the transaction, there are issues specific to TSCA to address. For example, depending on the type of transactions, there may be requirements to submit to EPA documentation to effectuate the transfer of certain rights and liabilities to the successor entity:

> Because a company's status as a successor in interest is determined by state law, EPA is not in a position to advise a company regarding whether it is a successor in interest to a company that has submitted a particular section 5 notice. A company may wish to consult competent counsel on this question.[42]

Some of these issues may be more complex if the seller is not exiting the market entirely, as there are potential TSCA implications, for example, if both companies manufacture the same substances that are subject to rules, orders, or PMN exemptions.

Generally, as part of an acquisition, the buyer will have the possession and control of TSCA documents and records. Sellers and buyers should consider the legal or practical reasons for the seller to have copies of, or access to, certain TSCA-related records and files, either to address potential liabilities or indemnifications or because the seller will continue to manufacture (including importing), process, use, distribute, or dispose of the substances after the acquisition.

Specific post-acquisition issues for TSCA provisions include the following.

6.7.1 Section 5 PMNs

The buyer will need all PMNs, the notice of commencement (NOC), and records documenting compliance with all exemptions from PMN requirements that the seller relied upon. EPA's website sets forth the following regarding the transfer of the rights and responsibilities of a PMN to a successor company after the NOC has been filed or in cases where the NOC has not yet been filed:

42. *Filing a Pre-manufacture Notice with EPA—"Transfer Notice" Requirement*, EPA, https://www.epa.gov/reviewing-new-chemicals-under-toxic-substances-control-act-tsca/filing-pre-manufacture-notice-epa#transfer (last updated Sept. 23, 2024).

- As a general matter, if the company newly associated with the chemical substance is a successor in interest under applicable state law, that company in effect becomes the submitter of the section 5 notice.
    - Except where otherwise required pursuant to a TSCA section 5(e) or 5(f) Consent Order, a successor in interest to a company that filed a PMN with EPA need not submit another PMN for that same chemical substance in order to commence manufacture, regardless of whether the chemical substance is on the TSCA Inventory. The successor in interest would need to file a Notice of Commencement with EPA pursuant to 40 CFR 720.102 if commencing manufacture of a chemical substance that is not yet on the TSCA Inventory.
    - A company that has taken over a product line but who is not a successor in interest under applicable state law may have to file its own PMN before commencing manufacture if the substance is not yet on the TSCA Inventory.
    - Because a company's status as a successor in interest is determined by state law, EPA is not in a position to advise a company regarding whether it is a successor in interest to a company that has submitted a particular section 5 notice. A company may wish to consult competent counsel on this question.[43]

6.7.2 Section 5(e) Orders

TSCA section 5(e) orders are binding to the signatory of that order. If the order and its conditions will be transferred to the buyer, EPA's website states the following:

- In general, section 5(e) Consent Orders signed after mid-1996 contain "successor liability" requirements including submission of a "Notice of Transfer" form, whereas Orders issued before then do not.
- For older Orders lacking a "Notice of Transfer" form, EPA recommends using the section 5(e) Consent Order Transfer Notice form.
- Note that EPA's policy is that section 5(e) Consent Orders may be transferred from the original Company to a Successor

43. *Id.*

in Interest only after EPA receives a notice of commencement of manufacture or import ("NOC") for the PMN substance from the Company pursuant to 40 CFR 720.102.[44]

When needed, EPA has developed a template "transfer notice" form for section 5(e) consent orders, which is excerpted from EPA's "boilerplate" TSCA section 5(e) consent order.[45]

6.7.3 LVE and LoREX Exemptions

LVE and LoREX exemption are binding to the signatory of those exemption documents. If the LVE or LoREX exemption and its conditions will be transferred to the buyer, EPA has developed three template transfer agreements: (1) transfer notice form for LVEs processed before May 30, 1995; (2) transfer notice form for LVEs processed on or after May 30, 1995; and (3) transfer notice form for LoREX exemptions processed on or after May 30, 1995.[46]

It should be noted that only one party to the transaction can rely on the LVE. If the seller remains in the business and both entities wish to rely upon an LVE exemption, it is possible that EPA will approve LVEs to multiple parties based on its analysis of the substance and the cumulative volumes.

6.7.4 TME

Regarding TMEs, EPA states: "Due to their short-term nature, EPA views Test Market Exemptions under 40 CFR 720.38 as non-transferable; thus there is no form to transfer a TME."[47]

6.7.5 Section 8

Depending on the timing and form of the acquisition, the buyer may be required to report under the CDR rule for manufacture and importation prior to the acquisition. EPA guidance sets forth several

44. *Successor Transfer Forms under TSCA Section 5*, EPA, https://www.epa.gov/reviewing-new-chemicals-under-toxic-substances-control-act-tsca/successor-transfer-forms-under-tsca (last updated June 3, 2024).
45. EPA, "Transfer Notice" Form for Section 5(e) Consent Orders, https://www.epa.gov/sites/default/files/2016-09/documents/sucesr5e.pdf.
46. *Successor Transfer Forms under TSCA Section 5*, *supra* note 44.
47. *Id.*

examples to assist companies to determine reporting obligations after changes to company ownership or legal identity.[48]

Regarding the transfer of section 8(c) records, EPA states:

> (1) If a firm ceases to do business, the successor must receive and keep all the records that must be kept under this part.
>
> (2) If a firm ceases to do business and there is no successor to receive and keep the records for the prescribed period, these records must be transmitted to EPA.[49]

Companies also should note that records of significant adverse reactions to the health of employees shall be retained for a period of 30 years from the date such reactions were first reported to or known by the person maintaining such records.[50]

6.7.6 Section 4

The buyer will need pertinent records relating to any test rules, orders, consent agreements, cost sharing, or exemptions from such section 4 requirements. If there are any cost-sharing agreements, the buyer as the successor may need to notify or otherwise comply with requirements set forth in those agreements. If the seller and buyer will be prospectively manufacturing a substance subject to a section 4 test rule, membership in any cost-sharing agreements and the allocation of testing costs also must be determined.

6.7.7 Section 12(b)

A buyer stepping into the shoes of the seller may be able to rely upon past export notifications and should be provided those records. As a new corporate entity, the buyer cannot rely on the export notifications filed by the seller. Instead, the buyer can continue the practices of the seller or develop its own to ensure that export notifications are submitted properly and timely. In-house or outside regulatory and/or legal counsel can be consulted to determine how section 12(b) requirements are to be satisfied prospectively.

---

48. EPA, Fact Sheet: Reporting after Changes to Company Ownership or Legal Identity (2020), https://www.epa.gov/chemical-data-reporting/fact-sheet-reporting-after-changes-company-ownership-or-legal-identity-2020.
49. 40 C.F.R. § 717.15(e) (2023).
50. *Id.* § 717.15(d).

6.7.8 Submissions to EPA with CBI Claims

Various documents submitted to EPA can claim information as confidential. EPA's 2023 rule sets forth the requirements to make a CBI claim, including when such a claim must be substantiated. In the final rule regarding changes in company ownership, EPA states:

> In circumstances where ownership of the company or unit of a company has changed, such that contact information for one or more prior TSCA submissions that include confidentiality claims is affected, a notice of transfer of ownership must be directed to EPA via CDX [Central Data Exchange]. Instructions for providing this notice and for requesting access to copies of a prior TSCA submission are available at *https://cdx.epa.gov/*.[51]

EPA has issued guidance in the form of questions and answers regarding the "maintenance of CBI contact/ownership questions."[52] For example, EPA states:

> **How does a new owner of a CBI claim need to update this information? Can it be asserted and substantiated during any reporting activity, such as CDR? i.e., by substantiating the transfer, which includes the parties, the type of transfer, and all other required information?**
>
> CBI claims are asserted on a submission-by-submission basis. If one company acquires another company or unit of another company, the new owner of the company or business unit may assert CBI claims on its own behalf going forward. If a new person becomes the company contact for a given submission, they should create a new CDX account for themselves, and then they may assert or maintain and support new or existing CBI claims on behalf of the company. CBI claims are usually treated as specific to the individual submission. One exception to this general rule is that confidential chemical identities, once actually disclosed or otherwise shown to be no longer treated as CBI, will no longer be eligible for confidential [TSCA] Inventory treatment and cannot generally be claimed as CBI anymore. However, other information pertaining to the chemical, like production volume or site identity, may be claimed as CBI in the future. Confidential chemical identities

51. Confidential Business Information Claims under the Toxic Substances Control Act (TSCA), 88 Fed. Reg. 37,155, 37,169 (June 7, 2023).
52. *Final Rule: Requirements for Confidential Business Information Claims under TSCA—Maintenance of CBI Contact/Ownership Questions*, EPA, https://www.epa.gov/tsca-cbi/final-rule-requirements-confidential-business-information-claims-under-tsca#Maintenance%20of%20CBI%20contact/ownership%20questions (last updated July 22, 2024).

may also be claimed as confidential by more than one company, but if any manufacturer or processor of that substance withdraws the claim, has the claim denied, or otherwise discloses the fact that the substance is manufactured or processed for non-exempt commercial purposes in the US, the substance identity is no longer eligible for confidential treatment. The transfer of ownership of a company or part of a company need not be substantiated, except that CBI claims in a notice of transfer form must be substantiated.[53]

Takeaways

- Considering EPA's intense focus on TSCA compliance and the extensive commercial disruption failed due diligence can invite, companies can ill afford to overlook TSCA requirements when conducting due diligence as part of commercial transactions.
- TSCA is not a niche regulatory program uniquely applicable to large-quantity chemical manufacturers with little relevance to product manufacturers. TSCA's outsized relevance to a broad and growing range of entities and product lines has caught many in business off guard and resulted in significant commercial disruption and compliance penalties. While traditional contractual provisions can mitigate some of the commercial consequences of failed due diligence, all of these consequences can be avoided by stepping up due diligence to ensure the full impact of the Frank R. Lautenberg Chemical Safety for the 21st Century Act ("new TSCA") is reflected in the diligence due in transactions triggering TSCA jurisdiction.
- A company engaged in TSCA activities and selling its business should take steps to prepare the information and documentation a potential buyer would seek as part of TSCA due diligence.
- A company considering the purchase of a business should familiarize itself with EPA's New Owner Interim Approach to take advantage of its incentives for penalty avoidance when TSCA violations are discovered during or after the due diligence process.

53. *Id.* (Question 4).

7

PFAS and TSCA

Lynn L. Bergeson and Carla N. Hutton

Key Messages

- PFAS are defined disparately around the world and in the United States and are increasingly the subject of restriction and phaseouts.
- TSCA is well-situated to regulate the introduction of new PFAS chemicals, but less well suited to regulate existing PFAS, as current litigation reflects.
- Businesses must be relentless in identifying PFAS in their supply chains, and either prepare to defend their continued use or begin to prepare for their elimination.

7.1 PFAS and TSCA

In recent years, regulatory interest in chemicals defined as per- and polyfluoroalkyl substances (PFAS) has exploded. Internationally, governments have greatly accelerated their review and regulation of PFAS. Closer to home, federal and state agencies are implementing legislative and regulatory measures that are causing significant business disruption and uncertainty across many product sectors. Our focus in this chapter is on the regulation of PFAS under the Toxic Substances Control Act (TSCA), the limitations that the U.S. Environmental Protection Agency (EPA) applies to them, and business strategies that might be considered in supporting existing and commercializing new PFAS despite the demonizing this broad class of substances is enduring globally. We appreciate that some PFAS are appropriately regulated and deserving of careful review and restriction. Not all PFAS are harmful, however, and EPA recognizes that the properties and functionalities of PFAS meeting TSCA's stringent standards can be commercialized.

7.2 What Is a PFAS?

Before delving into all the ways that EPA is using TSCA to regulate PFAS, a note about how EPA defines PFAS. EPA's significant new use rule (SNUR) for certain perfluoroalkyl sulfonates,[1] first issued in 2002, lists specific chemical substances by Chemical Abstracts Service Registry Number (CAS RN). Over time, EPA's understanding of PFAS has evolved. In the past, EPA viewed PFAS as a limited number of chemicals with known identities that can easily be regulated through SNURs. Instead, PFAS is a class number in the thousands, with EPA's CompTox Chemicals Dashboard listing more than 14,000 PFAS.[2] The vast number of PFAS and the limited data for most of them have prompted EPA to reconsider its approach to regulating them. Recent TSCA actions, such as the September 2023 "Framework for TSCA New Chemicals Review of PFAS Premanufacture Notices (PMNs) and Significant New Use Notices (SNUNs)" (the Framework) and the October 2023 TSCA section 8(a)(7) reporting and recordkeeping rule, address PFAS as a class rather than focusing on single chemicals. EPA's section 8(a)(7) reporting and recordkeeping rule defines PFAS as a chemical substance with one of the following three structures:

- $R\text{-}(CF_2)\text{-}CF(R')R''$, where both the CF_2 and CF moieties are saturated carbons (Figure 7.1)

1. 40 C.F.R. § 721.9582 (2023).
2. *Navigation Panel to PFAS Structure Lists: PFASSTRUCTV5—August 2022*, EPA Comp-Tox Chem. Dashboard v2.4.1, https://comptox.epa.gov/dashboard/chemical-lists/PFASSTRUCT (last visited Sept. 27, 2024).

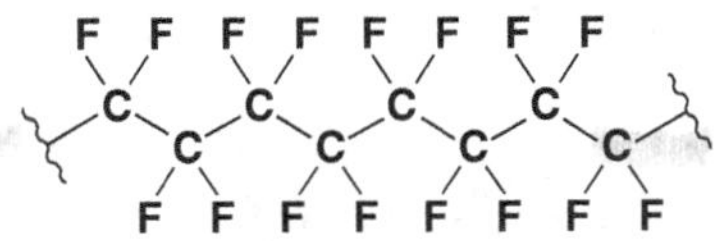

Figure 7.1. R-(CF_2)-CF(R')R", where both the CF_2 and CF moieties are saturated carbons

- R-CF_2OCF_2-R', where R and R' can either be F, O, or saturated carbons (Figure 7.2)

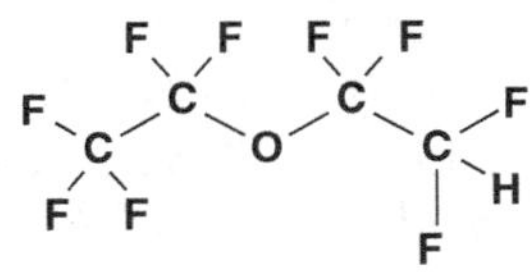

Figure 7.2. R-CF_2OCF_2-R', where R and R' can either be F, O, or saturated carbons

- $CF_3C(CF_3)$R'R", where R' and R" can either be F or saturated carbons (Figure 7.3)

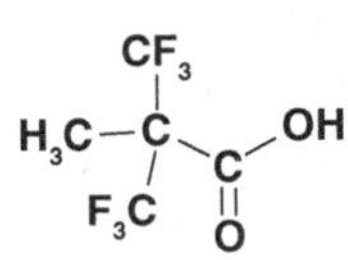

Figure 7.3. $CF_3C(CF_3)$R'R", where R' and R" can either be F or saturated carbons

This definition is not necessarily used by EPA as a whole, however. It also does not align with definitions used by state government agencies,[3] the European Commission, and the Organisation for Economic Co-operation and Development (OECD).

3. Some states, for example, adopt the Organisation for Economic Co-operation and Development (OECD) definition of PFAS, but limit the definition to "intentionally added" substances. Other states limit their prohibitions to certain product classes like cosmetics, ski wax, textiles, and a wide variety of other products. Care must be taken to understand the definition of PFAS and the dates any prohibition becomes effective in a state, as they vary widely.

7.3 PFAS as New Chemicals

Although EPA has not banned PFAS, the agency has used its authority under TSCA section 5 to make it significantly more difficult to introduce new PFAS into commerce or to resume manufacture (including import) or processing of inactive PFAS without EPA review. EPA has issued three SNURs that apply to certain PFAS and has proposed to make PFAS categorically ineligible for certain PMN exemptions. EPA also brought an enforcement action against a company for violating one of the SNURs despite the company's fluorination process predating the issuance of the SNUR. This section provides an overview of the SNURs that apply to PFAS, highlights where the new chemical review process differs for PFAS, and examines how EPA has handled the unknowing production of PFAS.

7.3.1 SNURs for Certain Perfluoroalkyl Sulfonates and LCPFAC Chemical Substances

Regulatory concern with PFAS is not new. In 2000, the company 3M voluntarily committed to terminating production of perfluorooctanyl sulfonate (PFOS).[4] PFOS (Figure 7.4) is considered a "long-chain" PFAS, having an eight carbon fluorocarbon chain and a sulfonic acid functional group and is widely regarded as a uniquely persistent and ubiquitous chemical. It was added to Appendix B of the Stockholm Convention on Persistent Organic Pollutants in 2009.

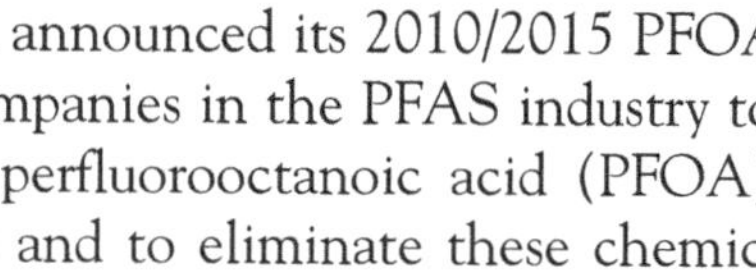

Figure 7.4. PFOS

In 2006, EPA announced its 2010/2015 PFOA Stewardship Program, inviting companies in the PFAS industry to commit to reducing emissions of perfluorooctanoic acid (PFOA) (Figure 7.5) and related chemicals and to eliminate these chemicals from emissions

4. Press Release, EPA, EPA and 3M Announce Phase Out of PFOS (May 16, 2000), https://www.epa.gov/archive/epapages/newsroom_archive/newsreleases/33aa946e6cb11f35852568e1005246b4.html.

and products by 2015.[5] As companies voluntarily phased out PFOS and PFOA, significantly reducing the use of PFAS, EPA has taken steps under TSCA to "close the door" to ensure that the manufacture (including import) of PFAS does not resume without the agency's review of the significant new use (SNU).

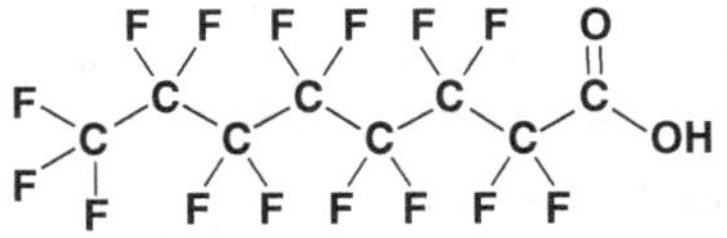

Figure 7.5. PFOA

EPA first issued a SNUR for certain perfluoroalkyl sulfonates in 2002 and has amended it several times, most recently in 2013, to add additional PFAS.[6] The SNUR designates the manufacture (including import) of the listed PFAS as a SNU. This means that manufacturers and importers must submit a SNUN to EPA at least 90 days before manufacturing or importing a listed PFAS. The SNUR includes several very specific, limited, and technical uses that were determined to be ongoing and are exempt from the notification requirement.

EPA issued a SNUR in 2013 to designate the manufacture (including import) and processing of long-chain perfluoroalkyl carboxylate (LCPFAC) chemical substances for use as part of carpets or for treating carpet as a SNU.[7] The rule is notable for making the article exemption[8] inapplicable to persons who import or process the LCPFAC chemical substances as part of carpets. According to EPA, the article exemption assumes that there is generally no exposure to the chemical substances in articles. Exposure to LCPFAC chemical substances could occur during the carpet manufacture process and during the life of the finished carpet, however, and exposure would

5. *Fact Sheet: 2010/2015 PFOA Stewardship Program*, EPA, https://www.epa.gov/assessing-and-managing-chemicals-under-tsca/fact-sheet-20102015-pfoa-stewardship-program (last updated Mar. 18, 2024).
6. Perfluoroalkyl Sulfonates; Significant New Use Rule, 67 Fed. Reg. 11,008 (Mar. 11, 2002); Perfluoroalkyl Sulfonates; Significant New Use Rule, 67 Fed. Reg. 72,854 (Dec. 9, 2002); Perfluoroalkyl Sulfonates; Significant New Use Rule, 72 Fed. Reg. 57,222 (Oct. 9, 2007); Perfluoroalkyl Sulfonates and Long-Chain Perfluoroalkyl Carboxylate Chemical Substances; Final Significant New Use Rule, 78 Fed. Reg. 62,443 (Oct. 22, 2013).
7. 78 Fed. Reg. at 62,443.
8. 40 C.F.R. § 721.45(f) (2023).

increase if LCPFAC chemical substances were incorporated into carpets and then imported.

In 2020, EPA amended the SNUR for LCPFAC chemical substances to designate as a SNU the manufacture (including import) or processing of LCPFAC chemical substances listed in the SNUR for any use that was no longer ongoing after December 31, 2015.[9] EPA also amended the SNUR to add as a SNU the manufacture (including import) or processing of all other LCPFAC chemical substances, including PFOA and its salts, for which there were no ongoing uses as of January 21, 2015.

The 2020 SNUR for LCPFAC chemical substances made the article exemption inapplicable for persons importing LCPFAC chemical substances listed in the SNUR, including PFOA and its salts, as part of a surface coating on articles. According to EPA, the release of LCPFAC chemical substances from surface coatings had been shown to occur and such releases could reasonably be expected to expose article users and the public to the LCPFAC chemical substances. Similarly, according to EPA, the import of articles with such surface coatings would also create a "reasonable potential" for exposure, allowing EPA to find affirmatively under TSCA section 5(a)(5) that notification for import is justified. The 2020 rule also amended the SNUR for perfluoroalkyl sulfonate chemical substances to make the article exemption inapplicable for persons who import perfluoroalkyl sulfonate chemical substances as part of carpets. EPA found affirmatively under TSCA section 5(a)(5) that notification for import was justified because of the potential for exposure to perfluoroalkyl sulfonate chemical substances as part of carpets.

Although making the article exemption inapplicable for persons who import or process LCPFAC or perfluoroalkyl sulfonate chemical substances as part of carpets or LCPFAC chemical substances as part of a surface coating on articles was novel at the time, it is now known that the class of PFAS numbers in the thousands and that they are used in much more than carpets and surface coatings. While these SNURs will allow EPA to evaluate the conditions of use (COUs) associated with any SNU, today it seems obvious that these SNURs capture only a few of the overwhelming number of PFAS for only a handful of uses.

9. Long-Chain Perfluoroalkyl Carboxylate and Perfluoroalkyl Sulfonate Chemical Substances; Significant New Use Rule, 85 Fed. Reg. 45,109 (July 27, 2020).

7.3.2 SNUR for PFAS Designated as Inactive on the TSCA Inventory

In January 2024, EPA issued a SNUR for PFAS designated as inactive on the TSCA Chemical Substance Inventory (TSCA Inventory).[10] For the purposes of the SNUR, EPA defines PFAS as

- R-(CF_2)-CF(R')R", where both the CF_2 and CF moieties are saturated carbons (Figure 7.1)
- R-CF_2OCF_2-R', where R and R' can either be F, O, or saturated carbons (Figure 7.2)
- $CF_3C(CF_3)$R'R", where R' and R" can either be F or saturated carbons (Figure 7.3)

According to EPA, the chemical substances subject to the SNUR are the 329 PFAS that are both currently designated as inactive on the TSCA Inventory and that are not subject to an existing SNUR. Of the 329 PFAS, 30 have specific chemical identities that have been claimed as confidential business information (CBI) and have generic names that do not contain "fluor" or "fluorine." EPA provided a list of the 299 inactive PFAS that do not mask "fluor" or "fluorine" in the generic name in the public docket.[11] According to EPA, because the SNUR uses a structural definition of PFAS, EPA "need not take additional steps to list the 30 inactive PFAS that are not subject to an existing SNUR and whose generic names do not contain 'fluor' or 'fluorine.'"[12]

EPA notes in the SNUR for inactive PFAS that the TSCA Inventory Notification (Active-Inactive) Requirements rule did not require reporting of commercial activity for several activities,

> including, but not limited to, importing or processing of inactive PFAS-containing articles, and manufacturing (including importing) or processing of inactive PFAS as impurities, byproducts not used for commercial purposes, small quantities solely for R&D [research and

10. Per- and Poly-Fluoroalkyl Chemical Substances Designated as Inactive on the TSCA Inventory; Significant New Use Rule, 89 Fed. Reg. 1,822 (Jan. 11, 2024); 40 C.F.R. § 721.11777 (2024).
11. EPA, List of Select Chemicals Subject to the Final Significant New Use Rule Per- and Poly-fluoroalkyl Chemical Substances Designated as Inactive on the TSCA Inventory, https://www.regulations.gov/document/EPA-HQ-OPPT-2022-0867-0029 (posted by EPA on Jan. 11, 2024).
12. 89 Fed. Reg. at 1,824.

> development], for test marketing purposes, as a non-isolated intermediate, or solely for export from the United States.[13]

As a result, EPA could not conclude that there were not ongoing uses of inactive PFAS for those activities, and the SNUR does not designate these activities as SNUs. The new uses under the SNUR are manufacture (including import) or processing of inactive PFAS for any use except:

(1) Importing or processing of inactive PFAS-containing articles
(2) Manufacture (including import) or processing of inactive PFAS:
    - As impurities
    - As byproducts not used for commercial purposes
    - In small quantities solely for R&D
    - For test marketing purposes
    - For use as a nonisolated intermediate
    - Solely for export from the United States

Requiring a SNUN for the manufacture, import, and processing of a PFAS believed inactive will allow EPA to evaluate the PFAS and determine whether the use may present an unreasonable risk to human health or the environment. Because EPA's basis for determining these PFAS are inactive was the lack of a notice of arrival (NOA), EPA concluded that it could not make the article exemption inapplicable here given that such a use would have been exempt from NOA reporting.

7.3.3 LVEs and LoREXs

7.3.3.1 PFAS LVE Policy

In April 2021, EPA announced a new PFAS low volume exemption (LVE) policy.[14] Although EPA had allowed some new PFAS to enter the market through LVEs, EPA stated that "[g]iven the complexity of

13. *Id.* at 1,825.
14. Press Release, EPA, EPA Announces Changes to Prevent Unsafe New PFAS from Entering the Market (Apr. 27, 2021), https://www.epa.gov/chemicals-under-tsca/epa-announces-changes-prevent-unsafe-new-pfas-entering-market.

PFAS chemistry, potential health effects, and their longevity and persistence in the environment,"[15] EPA expected that PFAS are unlikely to be eligible for this kind of exemption. By requiring that a PMN be submitted for a new PFAS, EPA ensures that it has more time to review the PFAS (90 days under the PMN process versus 30 days for LVEs).

7.3.3.2 PFAS LVE Stewardship Program

EPA followed up on its new PFAS LVE policy by announcing[16] a PFAS LVE Stewardship Program.[17] According to EPA's announcement, there were approximately 600 PFAS with currently granted LVEs. Through the program, EPA seeks to work with companies to encourage the voluntary withdrawal of previously granted LVEs for PFAS. To participate, companies with previously granted PFAS LVEs may choose to withdraw voluntarily their LVEs and certify that they will no longer manufacture or import those PFAS. Alternatively, companies may choose to withdraw voluntarily their LVEs following submission and review of a PMN, which will provide for a robust safety review and the imposition of appropriate and enforceable protections for human health and the environment.

7.3.3.3 Petitions to Revoke PFAS LVEs and LoREXs

On October 13, 2022, Earthjustice, on behalf of a coalition of environmental organizations and community advocates, petitioned EPA to revoke the approval of approximately 600 PFAS that were granted through LVEs or low releases and low exposures exemptions (LoREXs).[18] In its press release on the matter, Earthjustice states that these exemptions "allow EPA to approve chemicals through lax safety reviews only if it 'will not present an unreasonable risk' to humans or

15. *Id.*
16. Press Release, EPA, EPA Launches Stewardship Program to Reduce PFAS in the Marketplace (July 14, 2021), https://www.epa.gov/chemicals-under-tsca/epa-launches-stewardship-program-reduce-pfas-marketplace.
17. *PFAS Low Volume Exemption Stewardship Program*, EPA, https://www.epa.gov/reviewing-new-chemicals-under-toxic-substances-control-act-tsca/pfas-low-volume-exemption (last updated Sept. 4, 2024).
18. Earthjustice, Petition to the United States Environmental Protection Agency to Revoke the Approval of Approximately 600 Per- and Polyfluoroalkyl Substances (PFAS) That Were Granted through Low-Volume or Low-Release and Low-Exposure Exemptions to the Premanufacture Notice Requirements of the Toxic Substances Control Act (Oct. 13, 2022), https://earthjustice.org/documents/legal-document/petition-to-remove-half-of-forever-chemicals-in-commerce.

the environment."[19] According to Earthjustice, PFAS do not meet that standard, and EPA must revoke previously granted LVEs and LoREXs for PFAS. The petition follows an April 27, 2021, petition filed by Earthjustice on behalf of many of the same petitioners, and it incorporates the 2021 petition by reference.

7.3.3.4 PFAS Eligibility for LVEs and LoREXs

On May 26, 2023, as part of a proposed rule that would amend the new chemicals procedural regulations under TSCA, EPA proposed making PFAS categorically ineligible for LVEs and LoREXs.[20] Making PFAS ineligible for an LVE or LoREX would require companies to submit a PMN, allowing EPA to review more thoroughly all new PFAS. EPA proposed to define PFAS as a chemical substance containing at least one of the following structures:

- R-(CF_2)-CF(R')R", where both the CF_2 and CF moieties are saturated carbons (Figure 7.1)
- R-CF_2OCF_2-R', where R and R' can either be F, O, or saturated carbons (Figure 7.2)
- $CF_3C(CF_3)$R'R", where R' and R" can either be F or saturated carbons (Figure 7.3)

Although not yet a final rule, EPA's proposal to make PFAS categorically ineligible for LVEs and LoREXs is a logical next step from its PFAS LVE policy. Persons who wish to manufacture a PFAS not on the TSCA Inventory would instead be required to submit a PMN at least 90 days prior to commencing manufacture for a nonexempt commercial purpose, and EPA would have more time to evaluate the safety of the PFAS.

19. Press Release, Earthjustice, Half of "Forever Chemicals" in Commerce Approved through EPA Loopholes (Oct. 13, 2022), https://earthjustice.org/press/2022/half-of-forever-chemicals-in-commerce-approved-through-epa-loopholes.
20. Updates to New Chemicals Regulations under the Toxic Substances Control Act (TSCA), 88 Fed. Reg. 34,100 (May 26, 2023).

7.3.4 Framework for Addressing New PFAS and New Uses of PFAS

In September 2023, EPA released the Framework.[21] When reviewing new PFAS or SNUs of existing PFAS, EPA will use the Framework to guide its review to ensure the PFAS will not be harmful to health or the environment. The Framework uses a structural definition, identifying PFAS as a chemical substance with one of the following three structures:

- R-(CF_2)-CF(R')R", where both the CF_2 and CF moieties are saturated carbons (Figure 7.1)
- R-CF_2OCF_2-R', where R and R' can either be F, O, or saturated carbons (Figure 7.2)
- $CF_3C(CF_3)$R'R", where R' and R" can either be F or saturated carbons (Figure 7.3)

EPA notes that, based on data showing that a PFAS could break down into other PFAS that are more stable and deleterious, it will consider potential metabolites and degradants, as well as the substance itself, when reviewing PFAS under TSCA section 5.

If the new substance meets one of the three structures, EPA will then consider the available hazard information to determine whether the PFAS is a persistent, bioaccumulative, and toxic (PBT) chemical. Spoiler: EPA states in the Framework that "[t]here is a large body of evidence that most PFAS are PBT chemicals."[22] EPA acknowledges that only a small number of PFAS have been well studied, but of that small number, most are PBTs.

EPA next considers exposure. Since PBTs are persistent and bioaccumulate, if the PFAS is PBT, EPA will assess environmental releases and worker exposures and consider exposures to the general population, consumers, and the environment throughout the life cycle of the PFAS. Another spoiler: EPA states that it "generally expects that most PFAS will be PBT."[23] If there are sufficient data for EPA to determine that the PFAS is not PBT, then the typical new chemical assessment process will apply.

---

21. EPA, Framework for TSCA New Chemicals Review of PFAS Premanufacture Notices (PMNs) and Significant New Use Notices (SNUNs) (2023), https://www.epa.gov/system/files/documents/2023-06/PFAS%20Framework_Public%20Release_6-28-23_Final_508c.pdf.
22. *Id.* at 5 n.8.
23. *Id.* at 6.

If EPA determines that the data submitted with the PMN or SNUN or otherwise reasonably available are insufficient, EPA will issue a test order under TSCA section 5(e). EPA may identify testing needs concerning information on physical chemical properties, environmental fate and effects, and human health effects.

As noted in Chapter 4, when reviewing a PMN or SNUN, EPA must make one of five possible determinations, with the actions resulting in an order issued under TSCA section 5(e) or action taken under TSCA section 5(f), unless EPA finds that the substance or SNU is not likely to present an unreasonable risk. Another spoiler: EPA states that it "believes that PBT PFAS are unlikely to receive a determination of 'not likely' to present an unreasonable risk."[24]

7.3.5 Issues to Consider before Submitting a PMN or SNUN

Entities seeking to use PFAS regulated by a SNUR in a way designated as a SNU must submit a SNUN that includes sufficient information to address EPA's concerns for that PFAS. In addition to the substantial delays faced by most PMNs, the lead time for a PFAS will be much longer because the submitter will have to develop a robust data set to inform EPA's assessment.

The National PFAS Testing Strategy discussed in Section 7.4.1 includes a tiered-testing strategy that EPA intends to require for PFAS notified as new chemical substances or new uses under TSCA section 5. The PFAS Testing Strategy is, however, limited to evaluating potential human health hazards for PFAS. In a SNUN (or PMN), it is important to consider the timing and staging of testing to address potential human health hazard concerns that would be addressed by the tiered-testing strategy. The first tier in EPA's PFAS Testing Strategy will probably take six to 12 years and cost up to $250,000 (as of 2024). Tiers II and III testing could take up to seven years and cost more than $5 million. It will also be important to address environmental hazard and fate concerns. Ecotoxicity and fate testing will add additional costs but could be performed in parallel with the mammalian testing.

It is of course true that testing is not required to submit a SNUN (or PMN). Absent extensive testing, EPA's determination will likely be that it has insufficient information, however, and EPA will impose

---

24. *Id.* at 9.

an order with an up-front ban pending testing to address the range of mammalian, ecotoxicity, and fate endpoints.

7.4 Test Orders

7.4.1 National PFAS Testing Strategy

As part of EPA's 2021 PFAS Strategic Roadmap,[25] EPA released the National PFAS Testing Strategy.[26] Using the PFAS Testing Strategy, EPA sorted PFAS into smaller categories based on similarity, reviewed the existing data available for each category, and selected PFAS for which it will issue TSCA test orders requiring manufacturers to provide toxicity data.

As of June 2024, EPA has issued four test orders,[27] and two of the four have been judicially challenged. After receiving the first PFAS test order, for 6:2 fluorotelomer sulfonamide betaine (6:2 FTSB), National Foam, Inc. filed suit in the U.S. Court of Appeals for the District of Columbia Circuit, arguing that it never purchased, possessed, handled, or otherwise used 6:2 FTSB as a chemical substance within the meaning of TSCA section 3(2), but rather used it only as a component of a mixture purchased from an independent vendor. EPA ultimately granted National Foam's testing exemption request, and in

25. EPA, PFAS Strategic Roadmap: EPA's Commitments to Action 2021–2024 (2021), https://www.epa.gov/system/files/documents/2021-10/pfas-roadmap_final-508.pdf.
26. EPA, National PFAS Testing Strategy: Identification of Candidate Per- and Polyfluoroalkyl Substances (PFAS) for Testing (2021), https://www.epa.gov/system/files/documents/2021-10/pfas-natl-test-strategy.pdf.
27. Press Release, EPA, EPA Issues First Test Order under National Testing Strategy for PFAS in Commercial Fire Fighting Foam and Other Uses (June 6, 2022), https://www.epa.gov/newsreleases/epa-issues-first-test-order-under-national-testing-strategy-pfas-commercial-fire; Press Release, EPA, EPA Issues Next Test Order under National Testing Strategy for PFAS Used in Plastics, Chemical Manufacturing (Jan. 4, 2023), https://www.epa.gov/newsreleases/epa-issues-next-test-order-under-national-testing-strategy-pfas-used-plastics-chemical; Press Release, EPA, EPA Issues Next Test Order under National Testing Strategy for PFAS Used in Chemical Manufacturing (Aug. 15, 2023), https://www.epa.gov/newsreleases/epa-issues-next-test-order-under-national-testing-strategy-pfas-used-chemical; Press Release, EPA, EPA Issues PFAS Test Order as Part of National Testing Strategy (Mar. 25, 2024), https://www.epa.gov/newsreleases/epa-issues-pfas-test-order-part-national-testing-strategy-0.

May 2023, the parties asked the court to hold the case in abeyance pending completion of testing by other order recipients.[28]

On March 9, 2023, DuPont de Nemours filed suit in the U.S. Court of Appeals for the Third Circuit, challenging EPA's second PFAS test order, for trifluoro(trifluoromethyl)oxirane (HFPO). In May 2023, EPA determined that DuPont de Nemours does not manufacture HFPO, and the court granted the parties' motion to dismiss the case.[29]

The PFAS Testing Strategy is an admirable approach given the overwhelming number of PFAS and the lack of data available. Identifying single chemicals for testing to provide information about similar ones, thereby allowing EPA to take regulatory action, seems simple enough. The difficulty has proven to be in determining what data are already available, selecting the tests for the test order, and identifying the companies that manufacture the particular PFAS.

7.4.2 TSCA Section 21 Petition Seeking Section 4 Test Rule for 54 PFAS

Before EPA issued its National PFAS Testing Strategy in 2021, on October 14, 2020, a coalition of North Carolina nongovernmental organizations (NGOs) petitioned EPA under TSCA section 21 for a TSCA section 4 test rule for 54 PFAS manufactured by the Chemours Company at its chemical production facility in Fayetteville, North Carolina.[30] After EPA rejected the 2020 petition, the North Carolina public health and environmental justice organizations filed suit on January 7, 2021, in the U.S. District Court for the Northern District of California at San Francisco seeking judicial review of EPA's denial.[31] Petitioners asked the court to compel EPA to initiate a proceeding under TSCA section 4(a) to issue a rule or order requiring Chemours to fund the studies identified in the petition.

28. National Foam v. EPA, No. 22-1208 (D.C. Cir. filed Aug. 15, 2022). As of May 3, 2024, the test order testing is ongoing and there has been no potential or actual extinguishment of testing obligations.
29. DuPont de Nemours Inc. v. EPA, No. 23-1444 (3d Cir. May 22, 2023).
30. The October 13, 2020, petition, EPA's letter acknowledging the petition, and EPA's response to the petition are available on EPA's web page *Support Documents for PFAS Testing Section 21 Petition*, https://www.epa.gov/assessing-and-managing-chemicals-under-tsca/support-documents-pfas-testing-section-21-petition (last updated Jan. 22, 2024).
31. Ctr. for Env't Health (CEH) v. Nishida, No. 21-cv-1535 (N.D. Cal. filed Jan. 7, 2021).

EPA reconsidered its denial of the TSCA section 21 petition, and on December 28, 2021, announced that it granted the petition because the priority substances identified in its National PFAS Testing Strategy include many of the chemicals identified in the petition, as well as additional PFAS to inform additional categories where data are lacking.[32] The case was then transferred from the U.S. District Court for the Northern District of California to the U.S. District Court for the Eastern District of North Carolina.[33] On June 23, 2022, EPA filed a motion to dismiss, arguing that it had granted the petition and was commencing "an appropriate proceeding" in accordance with TSCA section 4 so judicial review was no longer needed in this case. Petitioners opposed EPA's motion, noting that in "granting" their petition, EPA declined to require testing on 47 of the 54 PFAS listed in the petition, and therefore judicial review was still necessary for those 47 PFAS that had not been granted testing.

On March 30, 2023, the U.S. District Court for the Eastern District of North Carolina granted EPA's motion to dismiss, finding that EPA granted the NGOs' 2020 petition and that the court lacks jurisdiction to review a petition that has been granted. Petitioners filed an appeal in the U.S. Court of Appeals for the Fourth Circuit on August 7, 2023, claiming that the lower court wrongly concluded that EPA "granted" their petition; that the court misinterpreted TSCA by concluding that EPA could grant the petition on the basis of a preexisting testing strategy with different objectives; and that the court misread TSCA by concluding that neither the petitioners nor the court could compel EPA to issue test rules or orders requiring specific studies on particular chemicals. On October 10, 2023, EPA filed its response brief, maintaining the lower court correctly determined that EPA granted the petition and correctly dismissed their complaint. The court heard oral arguments on January 23, 2024, and on June 10, 2024, the court affirmed the district court's decision, with one of the three judges concurring in part and dissenting in part.[34] According to the court, EPA "appropriately followed the TSCA's requirements

32. Press Release, EPA, EPA Grants Petition to Order Testing on Human Health Hazards of PFAS (Dec. 28, 2021), https://www.epa.gov/newsreleases/epa-grants-petition-order-testing-human-health-hazards-pfas.
33. CEH v. Nishida, No. 7:22-cv-00073-M (E.D.N.C. May 9, 2022).
34. CEH v. Regan, No. 23-1476 (4th Cir. June 10, 2024), https://www.ca4.uscourts.gov/opinions/231476.P.pdf.

when choosing to treat PFAS as a class."[35] Once EPA determines that testing is necessary, "TSCA then tasks the EPA with 'determining the protocols and methodologies' necessary to conduct those tests so that it can specify how testing must be conducted in its final rule or order."[36] The court stated that not only did EPA not effectively deny petitioners' petition by not adopting their proposed testing program, "by promptly commencing a proceeding for determining how to best test PFAS, the EPA gave Petitioners all that they were entitled to receive."[37] One judge concurred with the majority opinion's determination that EPA properly granted the petition with respect to the 39 PFAS that fell with the 6,504-member group defined by EPA's National PFAS Testing Strategy but stated that EPA's decision not to include within that group 15 of the 45 PFAS set forth in the petition rendered its decision a partial denial subject to de novo review.

7.5 Enforcement Issues

7.5.1 Ski Wax

In May 2020, EPA issued a press release announcing a final agreement with Swix Sport USA resolving TSCA violations associated with the importation of noncompliant ski wax products containing PFAS.[38] According to the press release, Swix agreed to pay a fine and develop a $1 million educational program to raise awareness in ski communities about PFAS chemicals in ski waxes. EPA states that Swix violated the TSCA PMN requirements and import certification requirements when it imported ski wax products containing six different PFAS chemicals on at least 83 occasions that were not included on the TSCA Inventory or otherwise exempt for commercial purposes. Once the chemicals were identified, Swix immediately ceased importation of the products containing the PFAS substances and quarantined products in its control in the United States.

Following the 2020 settlement with Swix, in January 2022, EPA's Office of Enforcement and Compliance Assurance (OECA) issued

35. *Id.* at 15.
36. *Id.* at 19.
37. *Id.* at 22.
38. Press Release, EPA, EPA Settlement with Swix Sport USA Resolves TSCA Violations Involving PFAS (May 20, 2020), https://www.epa.gov/newsreleases/epa-settlement-swix-sport-usa-resolves-tsca-violations-involving-pfas.

an enforcement alert entitled "Violations May Put Ski Wax Users at Risk from Illegal Perfluoroalkyl Substances."[39] EPA issued the alert after identifying several high-performance ski wax consumer products containing PFAS that were not reviewed by EPA under TSCA. EPA notes that these wax products are intended for use on sports equipment to enhance the performance of the equipment's slick surfaces that are in contact with snow. The enforcement alert advises sellers of ski wax to ensure that the products they sell do not contain certain PFAS that are not on the TSCA Inventory or have prohibitions on their use in sporting goods.

7.5.2 HDPE Containers

In 2021, EPA announced that it was aware that testing found PFAS contamination of a pesticide product that was stored and transported in a fluorinated high-density polyethylene (HDPE) container.[40] Prior to the testing finding the presence of PFAS in the pesticide product, the company fluorinating the containers, the pesticide manufacturers using the containers, and EPA were all unaware that the fluorination process could cause such contamination.

In March 2022, EPA announced that it notified manufacturers (including importers), processors, distributors, users, and those that dispose of fluorinated polyolefin containers of their obligation to comply with existing TSCA requirements to ensure that unintentional PFAS contamination does not occur.[41] According to EPA's open letter to industry, the presence of PFAS formed as a byproduct in fluorinated HDPE containers may be a violation of TSCA because the PFAS do not meet the definition of a "byproduct" in the regulations regarding SNUs of chemical substances.[42] The letter reminded

39. OECA, EPA, Enforcement Alert: Violations May Put Ski Wax Users at Risk from Illegal Perfluoroalkyl Substances (2022), https://www.epa.gov/system/files/documents/2022-01/pfasskiwax.pdf.
40. Press Release, EPA, EPA Takes Action to Investigate PFAS Contamination (Jan. 14, 2024), https://www.epa.gov/newsreleases/epa-takes-action-investigate-pfas-contamination.
41. Press Release, EPA, EPA Continues to Take Actions to Address PFAS in Commerce (Mar. 16, 2022), https://www.epa.gov/newsreleases/epa-continues-take-actions-address-pfas-commerce.
42. Letter from Tala R. Henry, Ph.D., Deputy Director, Office of Pollution Prevention and Toxics, EPA, to Manufacturers, Processors, Distributors, Users, and Those That Dispose of Fluorinated Polyolefin Containers (Mar. 24, 2022), https://www.epa.gov/system/files/documents/2022-03/letter-to-fluorinated-hdpe-industry_03-16-22_signed.pdf.

industry that the LCPFAC SNUR requires notification to EPA at least 90 days before commencing the manufacture (including import) or processing of a subject chemical substance for a SNU.

EPA filed a lawsuit on December 19, 2022, in the U.S. District Court for the Eastern District of Pennsylvania, claiming that Inhance Technologies LLC generated PFAS when fluorinating HDPE containers in violation of the LCPFAC SNUR.[43] In December 2023, EPA issued TSCA section 5(f) and 5(e) orders to Inhance directing it not to produce PFAS in the production of its fluorinated HDPE containers.[44] The U.S. District Court for the Eastern District of Pennsylvania case was put on hold when Inhance challenged EPA's TSCA section 5(f) and 5(e) orders in the U.S. Court of Appeals for the Fifth Circuit.[45]

According to EPA's December 2023 announcement, in December 2022, Inhance submitted SNUNs for nine long-chain PFAS. EPA reviewed the SNUNs and, consistent with the Framework, determined that three of the PFAS "are highly toxic and present unreasonable risks that cannot be prevented other than through prohibition of manufacture."[46] EPA issued an order under TSCA section 5(f) prohibiting the continued manufacture of the three PFAS produced from the fluorination of HDPE. EPA determined that the remaining six of the nine PFAS manufactured by Inhance may present an unreasonable risk of injury to health or the environment and, under TSCA section 5(e), EPA required Inhance to cease manufacture of these chemicals and to perform additional testing if it intends to restart production.

On March 21, 2024, the U.S. Court of Appeals for the Fifth Circuit vacated EPA's December 2023 orders prohibiting Inhance from manufacturing or processing PFAS during its fluorination process. The court notes that in March 2022, EPA "charged for the first time" that Inhance's fluorination process was subject to the LCPFAC SNUR. The court rejected EPA's argument that a SNU is "any use

---

43. United States v. Inhance Techs., No. 5:22-cv-05055-JFM (E.D. Pa. dismissed May 20, 2024).
44. *EPA Orders Issued to Inhance Technologies Related to Long-Chain PFAS Significant New Use Notices*, EPA, https://www.epa.gov/reviewing-new-chemicals-under-toxic-substances-control-act-tsca/epa-orders-issued-inhance (last updated Dec. 14, 2023).
45. Inhance Techs., L.L.C. v. EPA, No. 23-60620 (5th Cir. filed Dec. 8, 2023).
46. *EPA Orders Issued to Inhance Technologies Related to Long-Chain PFAS Significant New Use Notices*, *supra* note 44.

'not previously known to the EPA.'"[47] Inhance maintained that it had no knowledge at the time of the SNUR rulemaking that its 40-year-old fluorination process generated PFAS and that any PFAS generated are subject to exemptions for impurities and articles. The court agreed that Inhance's fluorination process, which was ongoing when the LCPFAC SNUR was proposed in 2015 and issued in 2020, was not a SNU subject to TSCA section 5. Following the U.S. Court of Appeals for the Fifth Circuit's decision, EPA requested the voluntary dismissal of its case before the U.S. District Court for the Eastern District of Pennsylvania. The court dismissed the case without prejudice on May 20, 2024.

Despite the dismissal of EPA's case against Inhance, the specter of litigation remains. After the U.S. District Court for the District of Columbia dismissed a citizen suit brought in December 2022 by the Center for Environmental Health (CEH) and Public Employees for Environmental Responsibility (PEER),[48] the NGOs intervened in EPA's case in the U.S. District Court for the Eastern District of Pennsylvania. When Inhance challenged EPA's TSCA section 5(f) and 5(e) orders in the U.S. Court of Appeals for the Fifth Circuit, the NGOs intervened again. Given their persistence, it is not surprising that in May 2024, CEH and PEER filed a notice of intent (NOI) to sue EPA to stop the manufacture and distribution of fluorinated HDPE containers. The NOI claims that EPA "failed to perform its non-discretionary duty" under TSCA section 4(f) to initiate applicable action under TSCA section 5, 6, or 7 to prevent or reduce the risk posed by PFOA formed in the process of fluorinating plastic containers. CEH and PEER argue that this obligation arose within 180 days of EPA's proposed National Primary Drinking Water Regulations (NPDWR) for PFOA and five other PFAS, issued on March 29, 2023, which states: "Following a systematic review of available human epidemiological and animal toxicity studies, EPA has determined that PFOA . . . [is] likely to cause cancer (*e.g.*, kidney and liver cancer) and that there is no dose below which . . . [it] is considered safe."[49] The NOI notes that by March 29, 2023, EPA had also received data demonstrating that Inhance's fluorination process produced PFOA at levels of concern and that the fluorination was causing PFOA

47. Inhance Techs., L.L.C. v. EPA, 96 F.4th 888, 889, 893 (5th Cir. 2024).
48. CEH v. Inhance, No. 1:22-cv-03819-JEB, slip op. (D.D.C. Apr. 26, 2023).
49. PFAS National Primary Drinking Water Regulation Rulemaking, 88 Fed. Reg. 18,638, 18,639 (Mar. 29, 2023).

contamination resulting in "widespread human exposure and environmental release." CEH and PEER ask that EPA take action under TSCA sections 6 and/or 7 requiring that Inhance immediately cease all PFOA production during its fluorination process.

When the U.S. Court of Appeals for the Fifth Circuit vacated EPA's December 2023 TSCA section 5 orders prohibiting Inhance from manufacturing or processing PFAS during its fluorination process, it noted that rather than taking action under section 5, it could pursue a TSCA section 6 rulemaking. On April 11, 2024, EPA received a TSCA section 21 petition from Earthjustice on behalf of several NGOs, including CEH and PEER, requesting that EPA use its TSCA section 6 authority to issue a regulation prohibiting three PFAS formed during the fluorination of plastic containers.[50]

7.6 PFAS Reporting and Recordkeeping Requirements

On October 11, 2023, EPA issued a long-overdue final rule under TSCA section 8(a)(7) regarding reporting and recordkeeping requirements for PFAS.[51] The rule is a statutory requirement under section 7351 of the National Defense Authorization Act for Fiscal Year 2020 that amended TSCA section 8(a) to require EPA, not later than January 1, 2023, to promulgate a rule requiring each person who has manufactured a PFAS chemical in any year since January 1, 2011, to submit to EPA a report that includes, for each year since January 1, 2011, the chemical exposure and hazard information described in TSCA section 8(a)(2)(A)–(G). When EPA proposed the rule, it declined to provide exemptions offered under other TSCA rules (i.e., impurity, de minimis, small business, byproduct, and related exemptions). This invited significant pushback from industry and the small business community.

EPA determined that any TSCA chemical substance, as defined by TSCA section 3(2), that falls within the structural definition at 40 C.F.R. § 705.3 is subject to reporting if it has been manufactured

50. Kelly E. Lester et al., Citizen Petition under TSCA Section 21 to Regulate PFOA, PFNA, and PFDA Manufactured during Plastic Fluorination (Apr. 11, 2024), https://www.epa.gov/system/files/documents/2024-04/section-21-pfas-fluorination-petition-final-exhibits.pdf.

51. Toxic Substances Control Act Reporting and Recordkeeping Requirements for Perfluoroalkyl and Polyfluoroalkyl Substances, 88 Fed. Reg. 70,516 (Oct. 11, 2023).

for commercial purposes at any time since January 1, 2011. EPA concluded that a structural definition was more appropriate for this rule than a discrete list of specifically identified substances, contrary to what many requested. PFAS is defined as including at least one of the following structures:

- R-(CF_2)-CF(R')R", where both the CF_2 and CF moieties are saturated carbons (Figure 7.1)
- R-CF_2OCF_2-R', where R and R' can either be F, O, or saturated carbons (Figure 7.2)
- $CF_3C(CF_3)$R'R", where R' and R" can either be F or saturated carbons (Figure 7.3)

EPA also defined fluoropolymers, including higher molecular weight fluoropolymers, as PFAS and thus reportable under the rule. EPA "does not believe the requested data on fluoropolymers would be considered duplicative or unnecessary: this information is not reported to EPA otherwise, and any manufacturers' existing information on such fluoropolymers will inform EPA's understanding of such types of PFAS within U.S. commerce, including their downstream uses and their disposal methods."[52]

The final rule is limited to manufacturers, including importers of PFAS that are considered a "chemical substance." Even though the definition of "chemical substance" excludes mixtures, PFAS as a chemical substance may be present in a mixture. The final rule requires reporting on each chemical substance that is a PFAS, including as a component of a mixture.

The scope of "manufacturing" for the purposes of the final rule is limited to entities manufacturing for commercial purposes and includes the import, production, or manufacture of a chemical substance or mixture containing a chemical substance with the purpose of obtaining an immediate or eventual commercial advantage for the manufacturer. This includes the manufacture of chemical substances or mixtures for commercial distribution, including test marketing, or for use by the manufacturer itself as an intermediate or for product R&D.

"Manufacture for commercial purposes" also includes the coincidental manufacture of byproducts and impurities produced during

52. *Id.* at 70,519.

the manufacture, processing, use, or disposal of another chemical substance or mixture. EPA notes that "simply receiving PFAS from domestic suppliers or other domestic sources is not, in itself, considered manufacturing PFAS for commercial purposes."[53] Entities that process or use PFAS need to report only the PFAS they have manufactured/imported.

Entities that have manufactured PFAS for a commercial purpose include those that have imported PFAS, including in wastes, or those that have coincidentally produced PFAS during the manufacture, processing, use, or disposal of another chemical substance or mixture. In its proposed rule, EPA noted this may include certain waste management companies that imported PFAS in a waste or produced PFAS at their site during the disposal of another chemical substance or mixture. EPA "has determined that waste management activities involving importing municipal solid waste streams for the purpose of disposal or destruction are not within [the] scope of this rule's reporting requirements, per TSCA section 8(a)(5)(C)."[54]

The reporting standard is information "known to or reasonably ascertainable by the manufacturer." This includes "all information in a person's possession or control, plus all information that a reasonable person similarly situated might be expected to possess, control or know."[55] Reporting entities must evaluate their current level of knowledge of their manufactured products (including imports) and whether additional information exists. This standard requires submitters to conduct a reasonable inquiry within the full scope of their organization (not just the information known to managerial or supervisory employees). This may entail inquiries outside the organization to fill gaps in the submitter's knowledge. Examples of information include:

- Files maintained by the manufacturer, such as marketing studies, sales reports, or customer surveys
- Information contained in standard references showing use information or concentrations of chemical substances in mixtures, such as a safety data sheet (SDS) or a supplier notification
- Information from CAS or from Dun & Bradstreet

53. *Id.* at 70,520.
54. *Id.*
55. *Id.*

The final rule requires that PFAS manufacturers submit information for each PFAS, for each year in which that substance was manufactured since January 1, 2011, to the extent the information is known or reasonably ascertainable. For mixtures containing at least one PFAS, manufacturers must submit information for each substance in the mixture that is a PFAS. A mixture composed of PFAS A and PFAS B would result in the submission of two forms containing the information. For chemical substances of unknown or variable composition, complex reaction products, and biological materials (UVCBs), including polymers, a single form may be submitted for that UVCB. EPA "encourages submitters of mixtures and UVCBs that contain PFAS to provide additional information in the optional free text box related to the composition of that mixture or UVCB at the time of manufacture, if known."[56]

Pursuant to TSCA section 8(a)(2)(e), EPA will require the submission of "all existing information concerning the environmental and health effects" of the chemical substances covered by the final rule. EPA notes that "'[a]ll existing information concerning environmental and health effects' is defined as 'any information of any effect of a chemical substance or mixture on health or the environment or both' (to be codified at 40 CFR 705.3) and is intended to be interpreted broadly."[57] The scope of "all existing information concerning environmental and health effects" includes all health and safety studies but is not limited to formal studies.

The final rule provides a one-year information collection period following the final rule's effective date, November 13, 2023, which will then be followed by a six-month reporting period that will begin November 12, 2024, and end May 8, 2025. EPA granted an additional six months (until November 10, 2025) for reporting to small manufacturers, as defined at 40 C.F.R. § 704.3, whose reporting obligations under the final rule are exclusively from article import. "Small manufacturers" include those that meet one of two standards:

- A manufacturer (including importer) whose total annual sales, when combined with those of its parent company, are less than $120 million, and the annual production volume of a chemical substance is less than 100,000 pounds

56. *Id.* at 70,521.
57. *Id.* at 70,523.

- A manufacturer (including importer) whose total annual sales, when combined with those of its parent company, are less than $12 million

EPA "acknowledges that the scope of reporting for this rule is broader than for CDR [Chemical Data Reporting rule], and that there may be some reporting entities who have not submitted information to EPA under a TSCA section 8(a) reporting rule before (*e.g.*, some small manufacturers)."[58] Therefore, EPA agrees additional time is warranted for PFAS manufacturers to familiarize themselves with the scope of the reporting rule and reporting standard, collect the required information, and create a Central Data Exchange (CDX) account, if necessary. Reporting forms will be due May 8, 2025, except for small article importers, whose reporting forms are due November 10, 2025.

Reporters also must retain records that document any information reported to the EPA for five years, beginning on the last date of the information submission period. EPA notes that the five-year retention requirement "is consistent with the CDR rule and corresponds with the statute of limitations for violations and is necessary to preserve records to support future regulatory activities that will be informed by this information collection."[59] Although companies that do not report are not required to retain any records, it would be prudent for companies to document their due diligence and retain those records. (*See* Figure 7.6.)

EPA left the final rule largely unchanged from the proposed rule, despite many comments about the undue burden potential reporters will face to determine if they have any information to report. EPA appears to be indifferent to the due diligence burden, focusing almost entirely on the reporting burden. EPA is likely to receive tens if not hundreds of thousands of reports that the information sought is not known or reasonably ascertainable, and reporters will have spent significant effort to fill EPA's databases with nearly useless information.

Most in the business community are relieved EPA did not broaden the definition of PFAS to include substances with a single fluorinated carbon (trifluoromethyl groups). This larger universe of substances will not help EPA with the concerns it is attempting to address. On the other hand, we are surprised EPA eliminated the limitation on

58. *Id.* at 70,530.
59. *Id.*

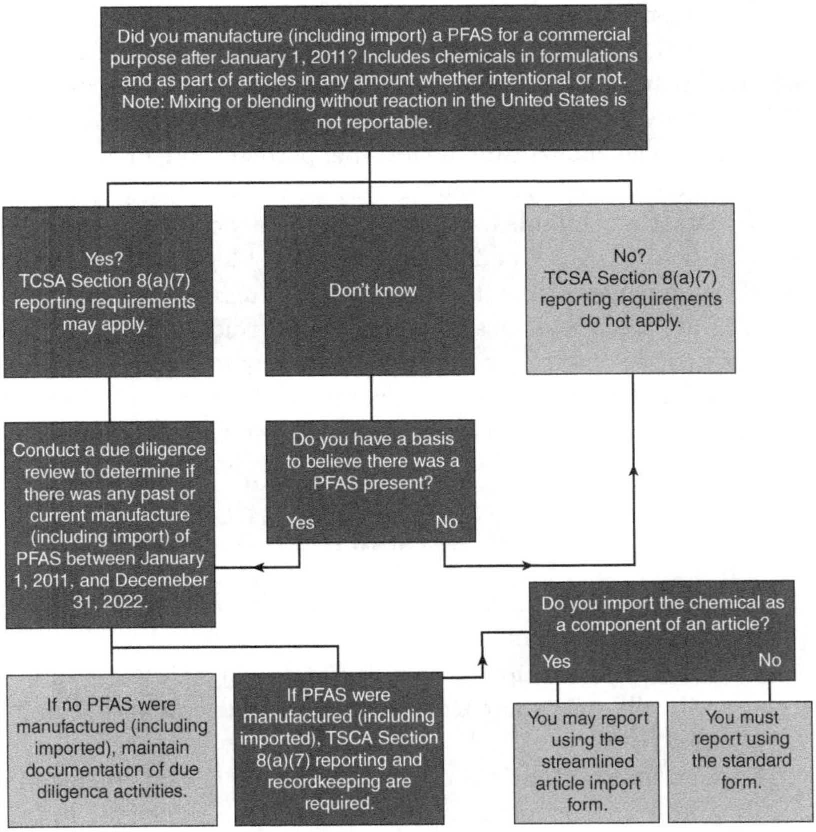

Figure 7.6. Steps for determining the applicability of the TSCA section 8(a)(7) reporting rule and requirements for conducting a due diligence review for importers of chemical substances

its structural definition wherein substances that had hydrogens adjacent to the carbons with fluorines were not considered PFAS, and we found its justification for this change lacking rigor, especially when the agency is aware that adjacent hydrogens allow for degradation via dehydrohalogenation, thereby significantly reducing the persistence concern.

Many in the business community are disappointed, however, that EPA seemingly disregarded the significant concerns identified by potential reporters in the final rule. The agency has significantly underestimated the effort required to complete the due diligence, given that the only exemption is for the import of municipal solid waste. All other importers, regardless of size, must examine every product, including articles, imported since 2011 to determine if the reporter knew or if the reporter can reasonably ascertain whether a PFAS was present in the product at any level, what PFAS is or may be present, in what quantity, and for what purpose, and, in most cases, what happens to that PFAS during processing and use.

To date, the final rule has not been judicially challenged.

This book does not address any state-level legislative or regulatory developments pertinent to PFAS. There are hundreds, and more on the way. Businesses must be vigilant and track these initiatives as most include reporting and/or disclosure requirements, and many include PFAS bans in targeted product lines. A good and free online tracking system of state legislation is maintained by Safer States.[60]

Takeaways

- PFAS is a worldwide contaminant that will pose business challenges globally.
- Knowing your supply chain and identifying all PFAS in it is critically important to avoid business disruption and minimize liability.
- Certain PFAS are essential and the burden is on commercial entities to support continued use of PFAS or prepare to exit the use and find a suitable replacement.

60. *Safer States: Bill Tracker*, Safer States, https://www.saferstates.org/bill-tracker/? (last visited Sept. 27, 2024).

8

Enforcement and the Consequences of Noncompliance

Lisa R. Burchi and Kelly N. Garson

Key Messages

- The frequency of EPA TSCA inspections is on the rise. While it may not be possible to avert TSCA inspections entirely, understanding EPA's methods and policies for determining when a company will be subject to an inspection may assist companies in avoiding, or at a minimum preparing for, such an inspection.
- Six-figure or even seven-figure penalties are possible, if not to be expected. EPA imposes penalties that are sufficiently high to telegraph a message, set a precedent, and deter others from engaging in similar noncompliant activities.
- To avoid the penalties, significant and costly business disruption, and brand damage that inevitably follow enforcement scrutiny, TSCA stakeholders are urged to develop and consistently follow operating procedures to prevent noncompliance.

8.1 Overview

It is true that the best defense against a Toxic Substances Control Act (TSCA) enforcement action is a good offense, including taking all measures to ensure compliance with applicable TSCA provisions. The preceding chapters outline the main requirements of TSCA and what companies need to know to ensure compliance. As a strict liability statute, TSCA mandates complete and precise compliance with applicable requirements regardless of a company's intent or good-faith efforts to comply. It is critical for companies to understand which TSCA provisions apply and to develop operating procedures and systems for their implementation to ensure compliance.

TSCA sections 11, 15, 16, and 17, in combination, comprise the "enforcement arm" of TSCA. Section 11 authorizes the U.S. Environmental Protection Agency (EPA) to issue administrative subpoenas. Historically, EPA seldom exercised this authority, but not anymore. EPA is routinely issuing subpoenas, and failure or refusal to comply with them exposes a recipient to possible contempt charges. EPA has broad authority to assert civil and criminal penalties for addressing TSCA noncompliance, and access to U.S. district courts to seek injunctive relief (e.g., restraining a TSCA violation or compelling compliance with a TSCA requirement) and to seize chemical substances, mixtures, products, or articles that were manufactured, processed, or distributed in commerce in violation of TSCA.

The scope of EPA enforcement actions extends to all actions required under TSCA, ranging from cases where a company did not comply with TSCA to cases where a company attempted to comply but misinterpreted an exemption or submitted a report containing inaccuracies or incomplete information. EPA is authorized to bring an enforcement action against a company that manufactured and distributed in commerce a chemical substance that was not listed on the TSCA Chemical Substance Inventory (TSCA Inventory) and for which no exemption applies. These violations are on the rise and always invite significant civil penalties. EPA's enforcement methods are more sophisticated and better calibrated to detect noncompliance, and its enforcement staff is better trained to focus on TSCA.

EPA encourages compliance in several ways, including policies and tools to help promote compliance by disseminating information and providing assistance to companies through access points, such as the TSCA Hotline,[1] as well as incentivizing voluntary internal reviews that require self-disclosures. EPA also maintains that its most important tool to promote compliance is that of deterrence—including the assessment of heroic civil penalties. In other words, EPA pursues a carrot-and-stick approach to compliance.

Commercial entities manufacturing, importing, processing, and/or using TSCA-regulated chemicals are subject to EPA's compliance inspection authority and potential enforcement. Inspections are the core of EPA's TSCA compliance monitoring program. In fiscal year (FY) 2023, EPA conducted more on-site inspections than it had since 2020.[2] The results of those inspections often end with enforcement action. For context, EPA's FY 2023 report provided statistics confirming a recent trend of increased enforcement actions.[3] Between FYs 2014 and 2023, across *all* EPA-administered statutes, EPA assessed a total of $12,072,430,386 in administrative and civil judicial penalties.[4] Civil penalties resulting from more than 1,500 TSCA enforcement actions within this time period account for nearly $71 million of the $12 billion in civil penalties.[5] Civil penalties range from the thousands to the millions. Factors impacting the outcome of an enforcement action include whether the company has any past history of violations, the number of TSCA sections covered under the enforcement action, and circumstances specific to the business, such as the size of the company and good-faith efforts to comply.

The following section and subsections offer an overview of EPA's inspection and enforcement activities, recent trends, and practical pointers on preparing for a TSCA inspection and defending against an enforcement action.

---

1. *Contact Us about Chemicals under the Toxic Substance [sic] Control Act (TSCA)*, EPA, https://www.epa.gov/chemicals-under-tsca/forms/contact-us-about-chemicals-under-toxic-substance-control-act-tsca (last updated Aug. 5, 2024).
2. Press Release, EPA, EPA's Annual Enforcement Results Shows Significant Increase in Enforcement Activity to Protect Communities from Pollution (Dec. 18, 2023), https://www.epa.gov/newsreleases/epas-annual-enforcement-results-shows-significant-increase-enforcement-activity.
3. *Id.*
4. EPA, Enforcement and Compliance Annual Results for Fiscal Year 2023, https://awsedap.epa.gov/public/extensions/FEC_AR2023/FEC_AR2023.html#IRslide.
5. *See Enforcement and Compliance History Online (ECHO): EPA Cases*, EPA, https://echo.epa.gov/ (last visited Sept. 27, 2024).

8.2 How EPA Selects Companies for Inspection and Potential Enforcement

An EPA enforcement action generally begins after a TSCA inspection or compliance review. Companies are often interested in knowing what could trigger an EPA inspection and whether a company can deter or prevent an inspection. In short, there is no way to deter or prevent an EPA inspection, but companies can seek to remain aware of activities that may increase the likelihood of an inspection.

There are several means by which EPA selects entities for a TSCA inspection. Several of these approaches are described in the Office of Enforcement and Compliance Assurance's (OECA's) TSCA Compliance Monitoring Strategy (CMS).[6] In the CMS, EPA refers to its compliance program for new and existing chemicals as its "Core TSCA" strategy. EPA states that the CMS is intended to provide "overarching, multi-year guidance for developing and implementing regional TSCA compliance monitoring programs."[7] OECA also releases every two to three years its National Program Guidance (NPG).[8] OECA states that its NPGs identify the national compliance and enforcement activities that EPA should perform to be consistent with its budget and EPA priorities. OECA also provides guidance in its TSCA Inspection Manual that is intended to offer uniform guidance to its inspectors on the conduct of its inspections, including how to select companies to be inspected.[9]

---

6. OECA, EPA, Compliance Monitoring Strategy for the Toxic Substances Control Act (TSCA) (2016) [hereinafter CMS], https://www.epa.gov/sites/default/files/2014-01/documents/tsca-cms.pdf. The CMS covers TSCA compliance issues not covered by this chapter related to polychlorinated biphenyls (PCBs); asbestos, including the Asbestos Hazard Emergency Response Act, the Worker Protection Rule, and the Model Accreditation Plan; and lead-based paint.
7. *Id.* at 4.
8. EPA, Draft Office of Enforcement and Compliance Assurance National Program Guidance, Fiscal Years 2025–2026 (2024) [hereinafter Draft FYs 2025–2026 NPG], https://www.epa.gov/system/files/documents/2024-04/fy25-26-oeca-draft-npg.pdf; EPA, Office of Enforcement and Compliance Assurance National Program Guidance, Fiscal Years 2023–2024 (2022), https://www.epa.gov/system/files/documents/2022-08/fy-2023-2024-oeca-npg.pdf; EPA, Office of Enforcement and Compliance Assurance National Program Guidance, Fiscal Years 2020–2021 (2019) [hereinafter FY 2020–2021 NPG], https://www.epa.gov/sites/default/files/2019-06/documents/fy-20-21-oeca-np-guidance.pdf.
9. OECA, EPA, Toxic Substances Control Act (TSCA) New and Existing Chemicals Inspection Manual (2022) [hereinafter TSCA Inspection Manual], https://www.epa.gov/system/files/documents/2022-04/tscanewandexistingchemicalinspectionsmanual.pdf.

These policies and practices explain the criteria by which EPA can select companies to be inspected. Indeed, these criteria and priorities are important for EPA to rely upon so that it can maintain, as it is required to do, a "neutral scheme" compliance monitoring approach in addition to inspections "for cause."[10] Based on these policies, EPA identifies the following as criteria for prioritizing targeting.

8.2.1 EPA Enforcement Priorities and Trends

The most common way for a company to be selected for inspection is because it engages in an activity that falls in one of EPA's enforcement priority categories. To optimize EPA's capacity to mitigate hazards to human health and the environment, EPA focuses its "limited" resources on "significant, potentially enforceable, and nationally important" cases.[11] Many violations do not check all the boxes to be "significant, potentially enforceable, and nationally important." Some priorities, particularly reporting and recordkeeping requirements, may seem more likely to have enforcement potential because they are "low-hanging fruit" in terms of proving a case, but not of significance or national importance. Other priorities change over time as new issues emerge, where EPA finds significant environmental risk and noncompliance patterns, or where EPA believes there may be opportunities to improve performance. (*See* Figure 8.1.)

10. *Id.* at 3-2 ("All targeting methods must meet the standard prescribed in Marshall v. Barlow's Inc., 436 U.S. 307 (1978) that requires EPA to use a Neutral Administrative Inspection Scheme (NAIS) when selecting facilities for inspection. A NAIS provides a rationale for selection of specific facilities. A neutral inspection approach allows for a non-arbitrary method of identifying inspection targets and the neutral selection of establishments for inspection.").
11. *Id.* at 3-1; CMS, *supra* note 6, app. B, at xiii.

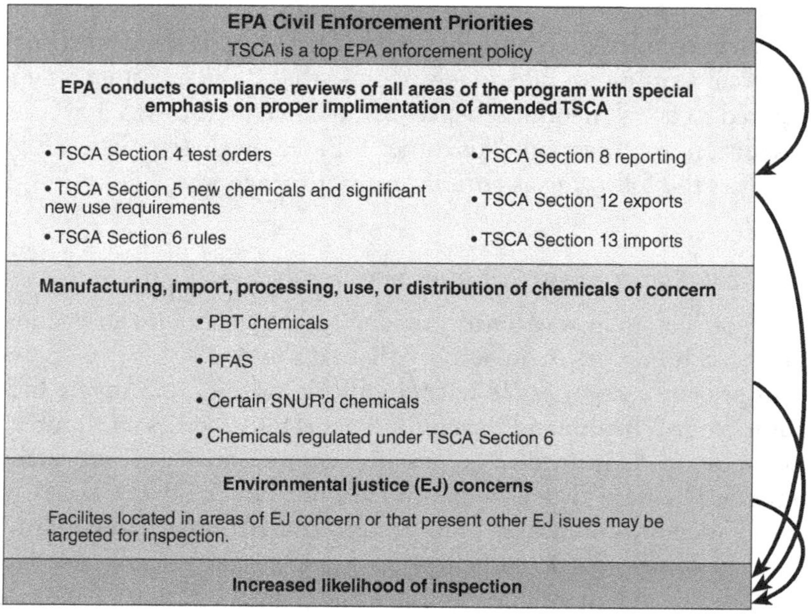

Figure 8.1. EPA civil enforcement priorities

OECA's most recent draft NPG identifies certain EPA activities within its Core TSCA compliance assurance and enforcement program activities as enforcement priorities. These priorities, combined with information in enforcement trends, provide the clearest guidance for companies in understanding how their activities can trigger inspections. These priorities include the following:

- **Companies that manufacture, process, or use chemicals regulated by section 4, 5, or 6 orders and rules**. OECA has a proposed goal for FYs 2025–2026 to conduct at least 50 percent of inspections or other off-site compliance monitoring activities at facilities manufacturing, processing, or using chemicals regulated by section 4, 5, or 6 orders and rules.[12]
  With the passage of TSCA as amended by the Frank R. Lautenberg Chemical Safety for the 21st Century Act, there are new statutory and regulatory requirements, and thereby resulting areas of emerging EPA priorities that EPA can

12. Draft FYs 2025–2026 NPG, *supra* note 8, at 42.

review to determine whether companies are complying with the new requirements set forth in amended TSCA. These priorities change over time, depending on the implementation or effective dates of new rules and regulations. That is why, for example, TSCA notification of active and inactive substances on the TSCA Inventory was a newly identified priority back in 2021 but is no longer listed as a priority.[13] In the Draft FYs 2025–2026 NPG, OECA identifies two particular TSCA amendments as priorities:

- TSCA section 4 authorizes EPA to issue orders to manufacturers and processors of certain chemical substances requiring the development of testing. EPA identifies as a priority its monitoring "for the timely and complete submission of testing in accordance with the requirements listed in section 4 test orders."
- TSCA section 6 requires EPA to issue regulations for any high-priority substances and chemicals that meet the statutory criteria for persistent, bioaccumulative, and toxic (PBT) chemicals. EPA thus prioritizes inspections at companies for which these regulations apply.[14]

- **Companies with reporting requirements**. OECA states that efforts should focus on monitoring compliance with chemical reporting and recordkeeping requirements. OECA specifically mentions two major reporting periods under TSCA section 8: the TSCA section 8(a)(7) reporting rule for per- and polyfluoroalkyl substances (PFAS) and the Chemical Data Reporting (CDR) rule requirements and substantial risk notifications under TSCA section 8(e).

  This priority has been fairly constant and can extend to any reporting or recordkeeping requirement. EPA's enforcement history demonstrates EPA's scrutiny and the imposition of substantial fines for violations such as reporting errors or omissions in CDR reporting, section 12(b) export notification, and section 13 import certification. Why? By focusing on areas where reports or other submissions are required to be submitted to EPA, plus its use of technology to make detections of violations easier, EPA may have a more

13. FY 2020–2021 NPG, *supra* note 8, at 28.
14. Draft FYs 2025–2026 NPG, *supra* note 8, at 42.

straightforward pathway to identify and demonstrate that a violation has occurred.

- **Companies that import chemical substances and articles.** EPA seeks to inspect companies that import chemical substances and articles imported into the United States for compliance with TSCA sections 5, 6, and 13.
- **Companies subject to certain TSCA section 5 orders.** OECA states its priority to focus on companies with facilities subject to section 5 orders and rules "with workplace protection requirements and chemicals used in the plastics industry."[15]
- **Companies that manufacture, import, process, use, or distribute chemicals of concern.** OECA seeks to place "special emphasis on chemicals of concern such as PFAS, [PBT] substances, and other high priority substances identified in EPA's Chemical Prioritization Process."[16]
    - PFAS deserves special attention, as EPA's focus on PFAS extends beyond TSCA. In its National Enforcement and Compliance Initiatives (NECIs), EPA identified "Addressing Exposure to PFAS" as one of the six priority areas for FYs 2024–2027.[17] Whether EPA reviews reports submitted regarding PFAS under section 8(a)(7) or identifies industry sectors that may be more likely to have manufactured or imported PFAS, it appears clear that this will be a reason for targeted inspections in upcoming years.

8.2.2 Environmental Justice

In recent years, EPA has focused on environmental justice (EJ) concerns as an enforcement priority and developed tools to identify areas that could be prioritized for compliance assurance. Based upon EPA's intent to prioritize and increase inspections in areas of potential EJ concern, a company can be selected for inspection based on nothing more than its address. For example, EPA states the following regarding its integration of EJ into its enforcement program and selecting areas for enforcement attention:

---

15. *Id.* at 43.
16. *Id. See also* CMS, *supra* note 6, app. B, at xiii.
17. *National Enforcement and Compliance Initiatives*, EPA, https://www.epa.gov/enforcement/national-enforcement-and-compliance-initiatives (last updated June 17, 2024).

> OECA recently added EJSCREEN map layers to Enforcement and Compliance History Online (ECHO) to help Regions and co-regulators (states, tribes and local government) focus compliance reviews on overburdened communities. This innovation will assist the Agency in identifying overburdened communities or locations that also appear to have facilities presenting a high likelihood of non-compliance with environmental laws. The EPA will use this mapping capability, along with on-the-ground knowledge from other EPA programs, states, tribes, and community members and groups, to help direct where we should focus our compliance efforts to make a difference to communities.[18]

Understanding these screening tools is critical. If a facility is in an EJ area, it may mean EPA may target a site for inspection, and this understanding may help companies understand the likelihood of a potential inspection. (*See* Figure 8.2.)

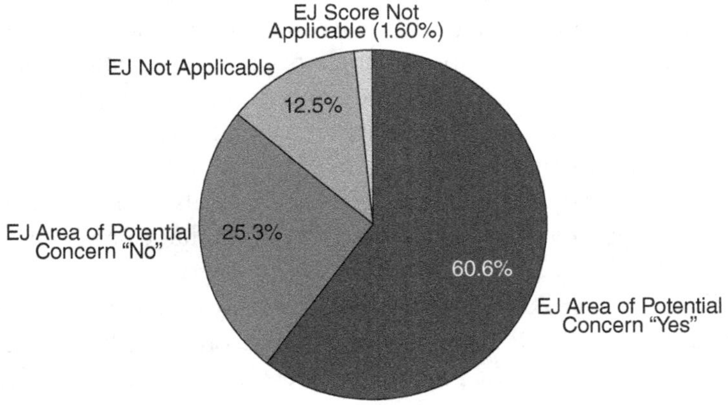

Figure 8.2. Federal inspections conducted by EPA in areas of potential EJ concern FY 2023

Source: EPA, Enforcement and Compliance Annual Results for Fiscal Year 2023, https://www.epa.gov/enforcement/enforcement-and-compliance-annual-results-fy-2023-data-and-trends.

18. FY 2020–2021 NPG, *supra* note 8, at 9. The EJScreen screening and mapping tool is at https://www.epa.gov/ejscreen (last updated Sept. 9, 2024). EPA has applied a methodology known as the Environmental Justice Strategic Enforcement Tool (EJSEAT) as a tool to take a nationally consistent screening approach in identifying priority areas with potential EJ concerns and track inspections. *See* National Environmental Justice Advisory Council (NEJAC), EPA, Nationally Consistent Environmental Justice Screening Approaches 1 (2010), https://www.epa.gov/environmentaljustice/nationally-consistent-environmental-justice-screening-approaches.

8.2.3 Third-Party Action and "for Cause" Inspections

Some inspections are not initially scheduled by EPA or selected based upon its stated priorities, but are trigged by, or in reaction to, a third party in response to a complaint, damage report, anonymous tip, whistleblower, or other source describing known or suspected non-compliance. These inspections are classified as "for cause" as opposed to the "neutral scheme" inspections, where EPA applies its criteria for compliance and enforcement focus. EPA states:

One of the many approaches the EPA uses to carry out its responsibility to assure compliance with environmental laws is to seek help from citizens by asking them to provide us with information about potentially harmful environmental activities in their communities and workplaces. Members of the public give the EPA such information through telephone hotlines, letters, the EPA's online Report Environmental Violations form, and other mechanisms. The EPA uses these tips and complaints along with its other compliance-monitoring activities to identify areas where compliance and enforcement follow-up is warranted. The EPA will track and prioritize complaints that provide a reasonable basis to believe that a violation has occurred and respond to the highest-risk violations. State, territories, tribes, and localities operating authorized programs should also consider public tips and complaints when performing their compliance and enforcement functions.[19]

TSCA section 20 includes a citizen suit provision that permits any person to file a civil lawsuit against any person, including the U.S. government to the extent permitted under the Constitution, who is alleged to be in violation of TSCA or its regulations or orders.[20] One caveat is that a citizen suit may not be initiated if the U.S. Department of Justice is already undertaking an enforcement action to compel compliance, known as the "diligent prosecution bar."[21]

Under TSCA section 21, any person may petition EPA to initiate a proceeding for the issuance, amendment, or repeal of a rule under TSCA section 4, 6, or 8, or an order under section 4, 5(e), or 5(f).[22] Though EPA has significant prosecutorial discretion as to whether to prosecute a case, citizen suit provisions and legal participation

19. FY 2020–2021 NPG, *supra* note 8, at 9.
20. TSCA § 20, 15 U.S.C. § 2619; 40 C.F.R. § 702.61 (2023).
21. TSCA § 20(b)(1)(B), 15 U.S.C. § 2619(b)(1)(B).
22. TSCA § 21, 15 U.S.C. § 2620.

in the administration and enforcement of TSCA can force EPA's engagement and in some cases add public pressure for EPA to take action on particular issues. This is another avenue by which entities outside of EPA can influence EPA policies, including but not limited to inspection and enforcement priorities.

8.2.4 Referrals from EPA Program Offices

EPA states it can also "use for-cause inspections proactively when they select inspection subjects based on EPA targeting research and analysis that indicates non-compliance."[23] OECA works closely with the Office of Chemical Safety and Pollution Prevention (OCSPP) and subsequently can select inspection targets based on information from OCSPP regarding companies, industry sectors, and/or chemical substances.[24]

EPA's ability to use available information to assess potential non-compliance has developed significantly in recent years. Electronic reporting is now required for virtually all information submitted under TSCA. From EPA's perspective, among the advantages of electronic reporting is its ability to review electronically such information and apply sophisticated algorithms to detect discrepancies and potential violations. EPA acknowledges that it, for example, analyzes CDR data to detect reporting discrepancies/violations.[25] If a company reported a chemical during one CDR reporting period but not in the next, EPA's view is that there could be a legitimate reason (e.g., the company no longer imports that chemical) or it could be an instance of nonreporting. EPA now can review data and more easily find material differences in reporting volumes, discrepancies between sites, and/or irregularities in processing and use information, all of which can trigger investigation and inspections by EPA. Under the Toxics Release Inventory (TRI) program, reporters may add an "Optional Note" explaining why reported information is different from one year to the next. While it is less clear this option is available under CDR report-

23. CMS, *supra* note 6, at 19 (emphasis removed).
24. OECA may refer to the priorities identified in the OCSPP NPG for targeting additional areas of concern. The most recent OCSPP NPG does not, however, identify any Core TSCA areas among its program priorities. EPA, Draft Office of Chemical Safety and Pollution Prevention National Program Guidance, Fiscal Years 2025–2026 (2024), https://www.epa.gov/system/files/documents/2024-04/fy25-26-ocspp-draft-npg.pdf.
25. *See, e.g.*, CMS, *supra* note 6, at 19.

ing, it is a good idea to explain meaningful differences or be prepared to do so if asked.

8.2.5 Random Selection

EPA sometimes randomly selects its enforcement targets. EPA states that random inspections should "constitute a very minor component" of its overall scheme since they typically "offer little likelihood of finding actual or significant non-compliance."[26] Even EPA's "random" inspections may have some decision-making process behind it. EPA could, for example, have a reason to focus on a company and then select other companies randomly based on nothing more than their proximity to the particular company. EPA also has noted that based on risk-based criteria it can determine the subset of companies implicated by that issue and then randomly select companies to inspect (e.g., when a new rule becomes effective, inspect companies affected by that new rule).[27]

Companies should ensure that they understand their potential liabilities under TSCA when conducting compliance checks. There are many recordkeeping obligations under TSCA, and, unsurprisingly, whether a requirement has been met and whether a record has been maintained are frequent targets of EPA's enforcement efforts. The following section and subsections explain how EPA monitors for compliance through inspections and/or information requests and how companies can prepare for these actions.

8.3 TSCA Compliance Monitoring Activities: Information Requests, Inspections, and EPA's Legal Authority

Knowing a company's operations are subject to EPA inspection and enduring one are very different propositions. TSCA section 11 authorizes EPA to conduct compliance monitoring in several ways, including "desk inspections" or information request letters (IRLs) and site inspections, by incentivizing voluntary self-audits under EPA's "Incentives for Self-Policing: Discovery, Disclosure, Correction, and Prevention of Violations," known as EPA's Audit Policy, or through

26. *Id.* at 22.
27. *Id.* at 22–23.

legal tools such as civil investigations and issuance of subpoenas. EPA's inspection authority is exceedingly *broad* and extends to any

> establishment, facility, or other premises in which chemical substances, mixtures, or products subject to title IV are manufactured, processed, stored, or held before or after their distribution in commerce and any conveyance being used to transport chemical substances, mixtures, such products, or such articles in connection with distribution in commerce.[28]

TSCA inspections, IRLs, and resulting enforcement activities are largely conducted by EPA's ten regional offices. These offices are responsible for implementing TSCA for the states within the region's jurisdiction, though EPA headquarters in Washington, D.C., may also initiate inspections and enforcement actions, and, from time to time, state agencies may assist.[29]

This section outlines what to expect when a company has been selected for compliance review by an EPA region, office, or headquarters and offers useful tips for ensuring that the review or inspection runs smoothly.

8.3.1 What Is an IRL?

EPA exercises its TSCA section 11 authority by conducting on-site inspections, often requesting information in advance of the inspection through a pre-inspection information request letter (PIIRL). EPA may also conduct a "desk inspection" of a facility by issuing IRLs.[30] In PIIRLs and IRLs, EPA may request a wide range of documents, including an overview of the company's corporate history, records that a company is required to maintain under various sections of TSCA (e.g., records demonstrating compliance with requirements under TSCA sections 5 and 8), and compilations of information relating to regulated activities, including preparing process flow diagrams

28. TSCA § 11(a), 15 U.S.C. § 2610(a).
29. *Regional and Geographic Offices*, EPA, https://www.epa.gov/aboutepa/regional-and-geographic-offices (last updated July 25, 2024).
30. EPA has issued guidance on its approach to obtaining information through formal information requests. *See* Memorandum from EPA to EPA Regional Counsel et al., Best Practices for Compliance and Enforcement-Related Information Requests (Nov. 21, 2018), https://www.epa.gov/sites/default/files/2018-11/documents/bestpracticesforcomplianceandenforcementrelatedinformation.pdf.

for each chemical substance manufactured at the facility and Excel spreadsheets detailing the chemical identity and dates of manufacture, import, export, or domestic purchase for all or certain categories of chemical substances at a site.

The scope of an IRL (that is not followed by a site inspection) may be broad and similar to the information reviewed in a TSCA site inspection. Alternatively, EPA may target its request to obtain specific records, for example, regarding a set of products, or requesting records from a specific set of dates.

As EPA is authorized to conduct inspections or issue subpoenas to collect information necessary to determine compliance, it is critically important to be responsive and provide complete and accurate records while also tailoring responses to the request. Counsel is often asked whether EPA can seek such information or whether EPA can be denied access to a facility. Yes, EPA can ask for just about anything related to a company's operations, and no, EPA cannot lawfully be denied access to a site. Any attempt to deny access will end badly.

When gathering information and records responsive to a PIIRL or a stand-alone IRL, EPA reviews the responsive documents for evidence of violations, and therefore, the response should be prepared with this in mind. It is important to ensure that responsive documents are complete, accurate, and labeled clearly to ensure that they demonstrate to EPA a company's compliance with TSCA. Documents that are business confidential should be marked accordingly. Upon receipt of the IRL, companies should note carefully the deadline for providing responsive documents. Unless it is clear from the outset that an extension will not be needed, recipients should communicate with EPA to seek more time to prepare the response. Typically, more time is needed and EPA does not unreasonably withhold extensions.

8.3.2 What Is a TSCA Inspection?

A TSCA inspection is a site visit from an EPA inspector for the purpose of gathering information to confirm TSCA compliance. Although EPA is not required to provide advance notice of an inspection, EPA generally notifies a facility in writing in a "notice of inspection" and/or by telephone that an inspection will take place and when. When EPA notifies the facility of an inspection by telephone, EPA generally provides a follow-up letter confirming in writing the date and time of the inspection, the right of authorized people at the facility to claim confidential business information (CBI), and the specific records that should be made available for review.

In FY 2023, EPA reported that it conducted 1,026 on-site TSCA inspections across each of its ten regional offices; many took place in locations identified as areas of potential EJ concerns.[31] Though certain inspections and any subsequent enforcement actions initiated in FY 2023 may remain ongoing, so far, EPA also has stated that in FY 2023, EPA settled 159 enforcement actions, with civil penalties assessed under TSCA totaling $5.6 million.

The scope of EPA's activities during an inspection may include the following: interviewing facility or site representatives; reviewing records and reports; taking photographs; collecting samples; and observing facility or site operations. As with responding to an IRL, companies must remain aware that EPA's aim is to detect instances of noncompliance, rather than to help companies identify issues of concern to promote compliance. Accordingly, companies must take time to prepare necessary documents and inform employees of what to expect during the inspection or IRL process.

8.3.3 Rights, Obligations, and Best Practices for Responding to an IRL or TSCA Inspection

Though EPA's authority to inspect a facility and/or its records for compliance is significant, the first step in preparing for an EPA compliance review (after taking a deep breath) is to be aware of several best practices and tools to help guide workers through the process. Accordingly, when preparing for an EPA inspection, PIIRL, or IRL, companies may keep in mind some of the following tenets of communication and general reminders: cooperation, completeness, clarity, candor, confidentiality, cordiality, and consultation.

Cooperation: Once EPA kicks off an inspection, companies should review closely the notice of inspection and/or IRL, ascertain the substantive information that EPA is requesting, and mark the deadlines for responding (and determine whether any extensions are needed). It is important for companies to cooperate fully with EPA's request in an IRL or during an inspection. This does not mean, however, that

31. *See FY 2023 On-Site EPA Inspections Map*, EPA, https://epa.maps.arcgis.com/apps/webappviewer/index.html?id=c522fa1e46f44d18951145cae8a0a461 (last visited Sept. 27, 2024).

companies cannot ask questions, address the scope of the audit with EPA, or request additional time to prepare, if needed.

Since there is a five-year statute of limitations for EPA to commence a civil enforcement action under TSCA, EPA often requests records dating back five years from the date of the IRL or inspection.[32] EPA can request records relating to a specific activity or the entire scope of a company's TSCA activities. Regarding the scope of the request, though EPA's inspection authority is broad, there are some limitations that EPA must follow. First, the inspection "shall be commenced and completed with reasonable promptness and shall be conducted at reasonable times, within reasonable limits, and in a reasonable manner."[33] Next, though EPA has the authority to inspect "all things within the premises or conveyance to be inspected," which includes all records, files, papers, processes, controls, and facilities, EPA's inspection authority *does not* extend to the following: (1) financial information; (2) sales information (other than shipment information); (3) pricing information; (4) personnel information; and (5) research information (other than information required under TSCA) *unless* the nature and extent of such information is described with reasonable specificity in a written notice.[34]

EPA also considers the cooperative attitude of the company during any resulting enforcement action. Though cooperation is not expressly defined, companies can generally interpret this as including communicativeness with EPA, responding in a timely manner, preparing all information and documents requested by EPA in an accessible and organized manner, and demonstrating efforts to comply with TSCA.

EPA has tools to compel compliance with IRLs and inspection notices—though companies have the right to assert that an EPA inquiry is unreasonably overbroad or unduly burdensome. For example, if a company declines to provide EPA with the requested information, EPA has the authority to compel such cooperation by issuing a subpoena for any information it deems necessary to carry out its mandate under TSCA, including requiring (1) the attendance and testimony of witnesses; (2) the production of reports, papers, documents, and answers to questions; and (3) other information that EPA

32. 28 U.S.C. § 2462.
33. TSCA § 11(a), 15 U.S.C. § 2610(a).
34. TSCA § 11(b), 15 U.S.C. § 2610(b).

"deems necessary."[35] A TSCA subpoena is enforceable in federal court unless the party that received the subpoena can demonstrate that the inquiry is unreasonably overbroad or unduly burdensome.[36]

The U.S. Constitution protects against unreasonable searches and seizures and guarantees a reasonable expectation of privacy as to private property. While EPA has the authority to conduct administrative inspections under TSCA, to conduct an inspection by gaining entry to private property, EPA must either receive *informed, voluntary* consent from the owner or a person in control of a property or obtain a warrant. EPA may obtain a warrant, if necessary, based on "probable cause," or a reasonable suspicion that a violation occurred or is occurring, or a "neutral administrative inspection scheme," wherein EPA is conducting the inspection pursuant to a neutral inspection approach (when it is not conducting a "for-cause" inspection).[37] While companies should be aware of the rights afforded when EPA selects a business for TSCA inspection, EPA has various means to commence an inspection, either by obtaining a subpoena or obtaining a warrant.

Completeness: A key goal in responding to an EPA inspection or IRL is completeness to ensure that responsive documents are accurate and available for EPA inspection. Companies should gather all pertinent records that fall under the scope of the audit or inspection and locate any misplaced documents. Companies also should interview company employees who performed the duties relevant to the subject matter of the audit or inspection in advance and determine if there are any questions, problem areas, or concerns that must be addressed well in advance of EPA engagement.

One of the best ways of ensuring all requirements are met during an inspection or in response to an IRL is to appoint a company representative who will be responsible for gathering and submitting the information to EPA and/or coordinating with EPA during and after the inspection. Companies may also develop standard operating procedures (SOPs) to help establish practices and procedures for how the company would prepare for and carry out a response to an IRL or TSCA inspection.

During an inspection, the EPA inspector should begin the inspection by holding an "opening conference." EPA should provide an

---

35. TSCA § 11(c), 15 U.S.C. § 2610(c).
36. TSCA Inspection Manual, *supra* note 9, at 2-20.
37. *Id.* at 4-3.

overview of the reason for the inspection, including the type of inspection (e.g., neutral, for cause, targeted, a follow-up on past compliance), the scope of the inspection, the expected duration of the inspection, expected inspection activities (including whether the inspector plans to review documents, conduct interviews, or tour parts of the facility), whether samples will be collected, and the procedures for claiming and handling TSCA CBI. The inspector should also note that EPA can ask for follow-up information after the inspection, including obtaining answers to questions that were not addressed during the inspection, or obtaining outstanding relevant documents (though inspection activities must be concluded in a timely manner). After the inspection is concluded, the inspector must prepare an inspection report that provides an investigation summary, the inspector's objective and accurate observations, and information on any documents, samples, photographs, reports, or other information used to determine compliance. EPA must release the inspection report to the facility.

In addition, the company representative should prepare its own internal "inspection" report of its responses to an IRL or an EPA inspection. The company should keep track of all records provided or submitted to EPA, any sampling procedures and samples taken, the areas and operations observed by the inspection, questions asked by EPA during the inspection, and verbal communications between EPA and staff before, during, and after the inspection. For example, the company representative should note any issues that require follow-up by the company and any issues that require immediate attention, as well as any plan for reviewing and addressing those issues. This step is important so that the company can access information about the inspection that one would no longer be able to recollect if not immediately captured post-inspection.

Clarity: Provide information to EPA with clarity. For example, EPA will often request that a company provide a spreadsheet with the company's production volumes for the past five years. EPA will review this "raw data" to check for compliance with various sections of TSCA and to determine whether a company's Form U submitted under CDR was complete and accurate. Any errors in a production volume record prepared and submitted in response to an IRL could lead EPA to question the accuracy of the company's CDR reporting. It is much more efficient, and less stressful for the company, to ensure that records prepared in response to inspection are clear and complete than to issue a correction of an inspection record after the fact. If a question or request made by EPA is unclear, companies should request clarification from EPA on how to respond to ensure that its responses address EPA's question and remain within the scope of the audit.

Candor: Organization and preparation for an EPA inspection or IRL response also necessarily require companies to be forthcoming. Companies should prepare employees for an inspection or IRL by discussing the scope of the request or review and noting that all questions must be answered honestly. This does not mean, however, that companies must answer all questions during an inspection if the answer is unknown or unclear. Companies should remain aware (and counsel staff accordingly) that if the company or a staff member has no knowledge, inadequate knowledge, or incomplete knowledge about a question, "I don't know" is an appropriate and accurate answer. It should be followed up with a request to find the appropriate resource or person to answer the question. Similarly, a phrase such as "I will review and circle back" in the context of an EPA inspection may help ensure that the company can prepare an accurate and complete response and avoid the need to correct an incorrect response that triggered an EPA enforcement action, which conserves both the company's and EPA's time and resources.

If a company discovers any instances of noncompliance when reviewing responsive records, it is important to determine the appropriate corrective action. Even if EPA elects to bring an enforcement action, taking measures to return to compliance and remedial actions to prevent the violation from occurring again demonstrate good faith.

Confidentiality: Companies should ensure that all CBI claims are preserved when responding to an IRL, PIIRL, or TSCA inspection. EPA generally requires the submission of information via the Central Data Exchange (CDX), which requires companies to provide both unredacted and redacted copies of all documents, and, if applicable, any substantiation (or explanation of exemption from substantiation) and apply the TSCA CBI certification statement. If the CBI claims are deemed deficient (without substantiation or the certification statement), EPA may (and likely will) invalidate the CBI claim(s) without notice to the submitter. EPA may deny requests to redact information not claimed as CBI at the time of submission if the submitter missed something.

During an inspection, companies should mark documents that contain CBI to avoid any potential confusion or inadvertent release of CBI. This may include marking each page that contains CBI with a prominent "CBI" label with a cover page stating that the document contains CBI. Companies could also segregate all CBI-containing documents into a separate folder. This file could include any document bearing the legend "Privileged and Confidential" from an attorney.

Cordiality: TSCA inspections and IRLs can be stressful. It is important to remain cordial and respectful of EPA staff. That said, it is appropriate during an inspection that the EPA inspector present appropriate credentials and a written inspection notice to the company subject to inspection and conduct the audit in a reasonable manner. The inspector also must obtain valid, informed consent for entry, meaning that EPA must gain entry to inspect a private facility based upon consent from the appropriate person (either the owner, operator, or agent in charge of the facility) that is freely and voluntarily given (and not given because of duress, misrepresentation, or coercion, either express or implied).[38] The company subject to inspection likewise has a right to request all requisite documentation and confirm that the inspection is reasonable and within the bounds of the legal requirements of TSCA section 11.

Consultation: After receiving an IRL or a PIIRL and a notice of inspection, a company may wish to prepare its responses with the help of TSCA experts. If needed, this may help the company to address any questions regarding compliance with applicable TSCA requirements in advance of EPA's review or inspection.

EPA's purpose in conducting inspections and issuing IRLs is to promote compliance. EPA policy mandates that EPA inspectors *should not* provide interpretative technical or legal assistance during compliance inspections. EPA states that companies "receiving compliance assistance are not shielded from possible enforcement actions for violations identified during the compliance inspection."[39] Companies should identify and address compliance questions *before* responding to an EPA IRL or an EPA inspection, as providing incomplete information to EPA in a compliance question could inadvertently trigger an enforcement action for additional EPA investigation. It is better to ensure that the IRL and inspection responses are complete and accu-

38. *Id.* at 4-4.
39. Memorandum from EPA to Addressees, Final National Policy: Role of the EPA Inspector in Providing Compliance Assistance during Inspections 2 (June 25, 2003), https://www.epa.gov/compliance/policy-role-epa-inspector-providing-compliance-assistance-during-inspections.

rate and demonstrate clearly the applicability of certain obligations or exemptions than to clarify or supplement information, or correct inaccuracies, during an enforcement proceeding.

8.4 EPA Enforcement Actions

Assume for present purposes that EPA has identified your facility as falling within an enforcement priority, conducted a TSCA inspection, and identified a potential instance of TSCA noncompliance. What happens next?

TSCA section 15 sets forth prohibited acts under TSCA. Specifically, it is unlawful for a person to do the following:

- Fail or refuse to comply with any requirement of TSCA itself or any rule, order, or consent agreement adopted under TSCA
- Use for commercial purposes a chemical substance or mixture that the person knew or had reason to know was manufactured, processed, or distributed in commerce in violation of section 5 or 6, or a rule or order issued under section 5, 6, or 7
- Fail or refuse to establish or maintain records; submit reports, notices, or other information; or permit access to or copying of records required under TSCA
- Fail or refuse to permit entry or inspection as required by section 11[40]

The scope of potential violations under TSCA is extensive, encompassing any failure or refusal to comply with any rule, order, or consent agreement under any section of the statute. In addition, although "use" is not defined in TSCA, the "use" of a substance for commercial purposes that was manufactured in violation of TSCA is itself a violation of TSCA.

TSCA is a strict liability statute. This means that a violator's intent to comply is not considered when determining if a violation has occurred, and there is no requirement that a violator's conduct be knowing or willful before EPA can impose civil penalties or take other enforcement action. If intent is determined to be knowing and

40. 15 U.S.C. § 2614.

willful, there is a criminal component to TSCA, and criminal penalties and/or jail time also can be imposed.

EPA enforcement actions are case-specific and the subject of significant prosecutorial discretion intended to encourage uniformity, fairness, and consistency. EPA has issued enforcement response policies (ERPs) that describe the enforcement options available to EPA and the circumstances under which EPA will decide how to proceed. For "Core TSCA" enforcement, EPA has issued three separate TSCA ERPs that address specific sections of TSCA:

- "Enforcement Response Policy for Test Rules under Section 4 of the Toxic Substances Control Act" (Section 4 ERP)[41]
- "Amended TSCA Section 5 Enforcement Response Policy" (Section 5 ERP)[42]
- "The Enforcement Response Policy for Reporting and Recordkeeping Rules and Requirements for TSCA Sections 8, 12, and 13" (Sections 8, 12, and 13 ERP)[43]

Although EPA has authority to conduct a broad range of enforcement activities, EPA does not deploy them uniformly. The type of TSCA enforcement action that EPA utilizes depends on the circumstances. Some options, such as injunctions, are used infrequently. Understanding the process by which EPA pursues enforcement and the various types of Federal Insecticide, Fungicide, and Rodenticide Act (FIFRA) enforcement actions that companies can encounter can prepare companies for what to expect and how to respond, depending on the type of action.

41. Office of Compliance Monitoring, EPA, Enforcement Response Policy for Test Rules under Section 4 of the Toxic Substances Control Act (1986) [hereinafter Section 4 ERP], https://www.epa.gov/sites/default/files/documents/tscasec4ruleserp-052886.pdf.
42. Office of Compliance Monitoring, EPA, Amended TSCA Section 5 Enforcement Response Policy (amended 1993) [hereinafter Section 5 ERP], https://www.epa.gov/sites/default/files/2016-06/documents/amendedtscasection5-erp.pdf.
43. OECA, EPA, The Enforcement Response Policy for Reporting and Recordkeeping Rules and Requirements for TSCA Sections 8, 12, and 13 (revised 1999) [hereinafter Sections 8, 12, and 13 ERP], https://www.epa.gov/sites/default/files/documents/erp8_12r.pdf.

8.4.1 Notice of Noncompliance

Once EPA identifies a violation, it has several options for notifying the company and initiating an enforcement action. The least onerous option is for EPA to issue a notice of noncompliance (NON). Under the Sections 8, 12, and 13 ERP, an NON is "appropriate for minor violations of TSCA where the impact on the Agency's regulatory and decision making process is minimal and the violator has not received a previous NON for a violation of that particular subsection."[44] The Section 4 ERP also states that EPA can issue an NON for "minor violations" that are "not considered substantive."[45] The Section 5 ERP does not include NONs as an option for any violation.

Companies can and should seek to persuade EPA that an NON is the most appropriate enforcement option for violations and should cite certain facts and circumstances (e.g., a first-time offense). Based on the examples provided in the ERPs, however, the reality is that the nature of the violation must be quite trivial for EPA to consider an NON. The Sections 8, 12, and 13 ERP, for example, states that violations of TSCA section 8 that could warrant an NON include "failure to supply required noncritical information (such as the phone number of a technical contact)" and a "[r]eport sent to an incorrect EPA address but correctly identified as a specific TSCA § 8 submission[.]"[46] The example when an NON could be appropriate under the Section 4 ERP is when a letter of intent to conduct testing is submitted timely but fails to provide all the required information.[47]

8.4.2 TSCA Section 17—Injunctive Relief and Seizures

In contrast to an NON, one of the most serious options that EPA may pursue after identifying a violation is a civil enforcement action in a U.S. district court. Under TSCA section 17(a)(1), the U.S. district courts have jurisdiction to

- restrain persons from taking actions prohibited by TSCA sections 5, 6, and 15;
- compel persons to take actions required by TSCA; and

44. *Id.* at 2.
45. Section 4 ERP, *supra* note 41, at 1.
46. Sections 8, 12, and 13 ERP, *supra* note 43, at 2.
47. Section 4 ERP, *supra* note 41, at 1.

- direct manufacturers, importers, or processors in violation of TSCA to provide notice of the violation or risk of injury to distributors in commerce and other persons in possession of such substances and replace or repurchase the product from the consumers of the violative product.[48]

Under TSCA section 17(a)(2), a civil action may be brought wherein any act, omission, or transaction constituting a violation of TSCA section 5 occurred or wherein the defendant is found or transacts business.[49] Under TSCA section 17(b), U.S. district courts may seize and condemn any chemical substance, mixture, or product manufactured, processed, or distributed in violation of TSCA.[50] TSCA section 7 gives EPA similar authority to institute an action in the district court to seize any "imminently hazardous chemical substance or mixture or any article containing such a substance or mixture."[51]

In the Section 5 ERP, EPA states that a determination to seek action under section 17 "should be limited to those instances where a civil penalty action will not mitigate a hazardous situation, is not likely to result in timely compliance, or where penalties alone do not provide a complete remedy."[52] EPA echoes this sentiment in its Sections 8, 12, and 13 ERP, while also acknowledging that action under section 17 is "more resource intensive than a civil penalty action."[53]

EPA initiates enforcement action under section 17 infrequently. A civil action was brought by EPA in 2022 pursuant to TSCA section 17(a) for declaratory and injunctive relief against Inhance Technologies LLC and reflects EPA's willingness to consider this type of action when facts warrant.[54] In the *Inhance* case, EPA initiated its enforcement action for injunctive relief in the Eastern District of Pennsylvania based on several allegations, including Inhance's refusal to comply with a notice of violation issued to it with regard to its production of certain PFAS substances. The March 21, 2024, decision of the U.S. Court of Appeals for the Fifth Circuit vacating two EPA TSCA

48. TSCA § 17(a)(1), 15 U.S.C. § 2616(a)(1).
49. TSCA § 17(a)(2), 15 U.S.C. § 2616(a)(2).
50. TSCA § 17(b), 15 U.S.C. § 2616(b).
51. TSCA § 7(a)(1)(A), 15 U.S.C. § 2606(a)(1)(A).
52. Section 5 ERP, *supra* note 42, at 4.
53. Sections 8, 12, and 13 ERP, *supra* note 43, at 3.
54. United States v. Inhance Techs. LLC, Civil Action No. 5:22-cv-05055, 2022 WL 17903769 (E.D. Pa. filed Dec. 19, 2022).

section 5 orders issued to Inhance was related to the Pennsylvania case but not dispositive of that matter.[55] EPA did, however, move to dismiss its case in the Pennsylvania court following the Fifth Circuit decision, and time will tell whether this experience will deter EPA from similar future actions, or whether particular cases and fact patterns will prompt injunctive actions. EPA's recent focus on PFAS, and the recent increase of actions under sections 5 and 6, may be just the type of violations for which EPA believes enforcement beyond civil penalties is warranted.

EPA may seek injunctive relief under TSCA section 17 in addition to seeking a civil penalty under TSCA section 16.

8.4.3 TSCA Section 16(a)—Civil Penalties

A civil penalty is EPA's preferred enforcement response for most violations. The penalties that can be assessed under TSCA are significant, and EPA enforcement is not shy in assessing those penalties. Indeed, in recent years there has been a considerable increase in EPA enforcement scrutiny under TSCA and imposition of substantial fines. It is critical for companies to understand how EPA can calculate penalties and where there may be opportunities for penalties to be reduced.

In the eight years since Congress amended TSCA in June 2016, through June 2024, EPA's regional offices and EPA headquarters have collectively levied more than 1,000 civil enforcement actions under TSCA, resulting in nearly $50 million in civil penalties.[56]

Although TSCA's statutory language refers to a specific maximum civil penalty amount,[57] that amount is not current. The Federal Civil Penalties Inflation Adjustment Act of 1990, as amended through the Federal Civil Penalties Inflation Adjustment Act Improvements Act of 2015, prescribes a formula for annually adjusting the statutory maximum (and minimum) amount of civil monetary penalties to account for inflation.[58] Previously, EPA's penalties had not been adjusted for

55. Inhance Techs., L.L.C. v. EPA, 96 F.4th 888 (5th Cir. 2024).
56. *See Enforcement and Compliance History Online* (ECHO): *EPA Cases*, *supra* note 5.
57. TSCA § 16(a)(1), 15 U.S.C. § 2615(a)(1) (a person who violates TSCA can be liable for a civil penalty in an amount not to exceed $37,500 for each such violation).
58. Memorandum from EPA to EPA Regional Administrators et al., Amendments to the EPA's Civil Penalty Policies to Account for Inflation (Effective Jan. 15, 2024) (Jan. 10, 2024), https://www.epa.gov/system/files/documents/2024-01/amendmentstotheepacivilpenaltypolicyinflation011524.pdf.

inflation. EPA's penalties now keep pace with inflation, which EPA states maintains the deterrent effect that Congress intended when it originally specified penalties. Each year, EPA issues a new rule updating the maximum (and minimum) penalties for the laws it administers. In 2024, the maximum penalty amount is $48,512 per violation.[59]

In determining the amount of any civil penalty, TSCA section 16 requires EPA to consider the following factors:

- The nature, circumstances, extent, and gravity of the violation
- The violator's ability to pay, including its ability to continue to do business
- The history of prior violations
- The violator's degree of culpability
- "[S]uch other matters as justice may require"[60]

EPA's ERPs set forth the multistep process under which EPA calculates penalties for alleged violations under TSCA. EPA first must consider certain statutory factors, including the nature, circumstance, extent, and gravity of the violation, to calculate a "gravity-based penalty," as follows:

- **Nature**. The ERPs classify the nature factor as (1) chemical control, (2) control-associated data gathering, or (3) hazard/risk assessment. Under EPA's Sections 8, 12, and 13 ERP and Section 4 ERP, the nature of all such violations is considered "hazard/risk assessment" violations.
- **Circumstance**. There are six circumstance levels from "1," which is high, to "6," which is low. The ERPs identify the circumstance level depending on the type of violation at issue. For example, a failure to report under the CDR is a Level 1 (high) one-day violation, while sending a report to an incorrect office would be a Level 6 (low) one-day violation.
- **Extent**. Extent is used to "take into consideration the degree, range, or scope of the violation."[61] There are three extent levels—major, significant, and minor. The higher the circumstance level, the more likely the extent will be major.

59. Civil Monetary Penalty Inflation Adjustment, 88 Fed. Reg. 89,309, 89,312 (Dec. 27, 2023).

60. TSCA § 16(a)(2)(B), 15 U.S.C. § 2615(a)(2)(B).

61. Section 4 ERP, *supra* note 41, at 3.

Based on these factors, there are tables in the ERPs from which EPA can calculate a gravity-based penalty for each violation at issue. As for the number of violations that can be alleged, EPA guidance sets forth those violations that are considered a one-time event and those that can be a per-day event. This distinction has critical implications since violations that are deemed to continue on a per-day basis, meaning each day that a violation occurs is a separate penalty event, can increase penalty amounts drastically. TSCA does not specify any separate statute of limitations for imposition of administrative civil penalties, so EPA must apply the general five-year statute of limitations set forth at 28 U.S.C. § 2462.[62] Although EPA cannot assess penalties for violations beyond the five-year statute of limitations, EPA can contend that this statute of limitations is reset for violations of a per-day (i.e., continuing) nature.[63]

Once a gravity-based penalty is calculated, EPA considers gravity factors and can adjust any penalty upward or downward. Factors evaluated in assessing the gravity of the violation include:

- **Degree of culpability**. If a company's action was willful, EPA can adjust the penalty upward, while if the company can demonstrate it lacked control over the alleged violations, EPA can adjust the penalty downward.
- **History of prior such violations**. If the violations noted are the company's first, this could potentially reduce penalties. If there is a history of prior noncompliance, EPA could increase the penalty.
- **Ability to pay/ability to continue in business**. EPA's 2015 memorandum providing guidance on how EPA evaluates a company's ability to pay a civil penalty provides general information regarding the data needed for a company to demonstrate its inability to pay a penalty and how EPA evaluates

62. 3M Co. v. Browner, 17 F.3d 1453 (D.C. Cir. 1994); Memorandum from EPA Office of Regulatory Enforcement to Regional Counsel and Regional Program Management Division Directors, Regions I–X, Guidance on the Application of the Federal Five-Year Statute of Limitations to Administrative and Judicial Civil Penalty Proceedings (July 13, 1994).

63. *See, e.g.*, *In re* Elementis Chromium, Inc., 16 E.A.D. 649 (EAB 2015) (Environmental Appeals Board (EAB) holding that five-year statute of limitations did not expire for failure under TSCA section 8(e) to submit a report to EPA because the "continuing violation" doctrine applied).

that information.[64] EPA uses economic models to review financial information and make determinations regarding a company's ability to pay. If this is a possibility, EPA provides additional information.[65]

- **"Such other matters as justice may require."** This phrase is stated in TSCA section 16 but does not specifically refer to any particular facts or issues. The EPA ERPs describe scenarios where this factor may impact the calculation of a penalty, including when there is an economic benefit derived from the violation that could increase a penalty amount and when a company voluntarily discloses a violation that could decrease a penalty.[66]
- **Attitude/good faith**. EPA states in its ERPs that it can consider a company's attitude, including, for example, actions to halt immediately the violative activity and steps taken to rectify the situation.[67]

While most gravity factors (e.g., degree of culpability, history of prior such violations, ability to pay, ability to continue in business, and "other such matters as justice may require") are reportedly considered when determining a penalty, EPA does not always state the percentages by which penalties can be reduced or increased based on EPA's consideration of such factors. Generally, these reductions can be in the 15–25 percent range.[68]

8.4.4 TSCA Section 16(b)—Criminal Penalties

TSCA section 16(b)(1) authorizes EPA to seek criminal penalties against any person who "knowingly or willfully" violates any provision

64. Memorandum from EPA to EPA Regional Counsel et al., Guidance on Evaluating a Violator's Ability to Pay a Civil Penalty in an Administrative Enforcement Action (June 29, 2015), https://www.epa.gov/enforcement/guidance-evaluating-ability-pay-civil-penalty-administrative-enforcement-actions.
65. *See Penalty and Financial Models*, EPA, https://www.epa.gov/enforcement/penalty-and-financial-models (last updated May 24, 2024).
66. Sections 8, 12, and 13 ERP, *supra* note 43, at 15–16; Section 5 ERP, *supra* note 42, at 17–19.
67. Sections 8, 12, and 13 ERP, *supra* note 43, at 16; Section 5 ERP, *supra* note 42, at 19.
68. Sections 8, 12, and 13 ERP, *supra* note 43, at 16 (based on a company's good-faith efforts and good attitude, EPA can reduce the penalty by a maximum of 15 percent); Section 5 ERP, *supra* note 42, at 19 (when a company can demonstrate it had no control over the violation, EPA can reduce the penalty by up to 25 percent).

of TSCA section 15. Specifically, EPA can seek criminal fines of up to $50,000 for each day the violation continues and/or imprisonment for up to one year.[69] TSCA section 16(b)(2) now includes more severe penalties that can apply if a party "knowingly and willfully" commits a violation that "places an individual in imminent danger of death or serious bodily injury." In such instances, a person can be fined up to $250,000 and/or imprisoned for up to 15 years, and an organization can be fined up to $1,000,000.[70]

Civil and criminal penalties are imposed under separate provisions of TSCA. EPA has discretion in appropriate circumstances to seek criminal penalties in lieu of, or in addition to, civil penalties. Since civil and criminal cases are not mutually exclusive, in 2024 EPA released its updated Strategic Civil-Criminal Enforcement Policy intended to increase collaboration between the civil and criminal enforcement programs, enhance case screening for what enforcement option should be utilized to address violations, improve case management through enhanced tracking of case screening, and update training programs to ensure effective partnership between civil and criminal enforcement offices.[71]

8.5 EPA Enforcement Process

When EPA engages in enforcement activities, it aims to do so in a transparent matter. There are several guidance and policy documents that set forth when and how EPA may act. The practical consequences of these policies are also well known through EPA's enforcement history. There are always outliers and exceptions, but companies that find themselves in EPA's enforcement crosshairs can have a big advantage by understanding the process and knowing not only what to expect, but what is possible.

69. TSCA § 16(b)(1), 15 U.S.C. § 2615(b)(1).
70. TSCA § 16(b)(2), 15 U.S.C. § 2615(b)(2).
71. Memorandum from EPA to EPA Regional Counsels and Deputies et al., Strategic Civil-Criminal Enforcement Policy (Apr. 17, 2024), https://www.epa.gov/system/files/documents/2024-04/strategic-civil-criminal-enforcement-policy-april-2024.pdf.

8.5.1 Prefiling Negotiations—Opportunity to Show Cause

There are a few means by which EPA can identify potential instances of noncompliance, although most are following an inspection or similar procedure (e.g., an IRL). In most cases, EPA will notify the company of the alleged violations it discovered and commence discussion or negotiation to resolve the issues. The exceptions would be when EPA files a complaint seeking a civil penalty, when taking other action not related to civil penalties (e.g., injunctive relief), or when responding to a self-confession.

When EPA discovers potential violations during an inspection, EPA generally identifies its findings in a letter providing the company with "an opportunity to show cause" as to why EPA should not take enforcement action with respect to the potential violations.[72] This is a crucial time, and a company in receipt of such a letter should review the allegations carefully and determine what arguments can be made to counter EPA's allegations. Even if a company agrees that a violation may have occurred, there are still opportunities to argue for no penalty assessment (e.g., NON) or significantly reduced penalties.

Despite these formulas and policies, TSCA section 16(a)(2)(C) states: "The Administrator may compromise, modify, or remit, with or without conditions, any civil penalty which may be imposed under this subsection."[73] This means that despite the methods set forth under its ERPs (which are policies, not laws) by which EPA calculates penalties, EPA has considerable discretion to ensure that a penalty, if any, is appropriate under the circumstances of a particular case.

EPA in most instances applies enforcement penalty calculations "by the book," thus providing companies with more limited options to seek further penalty reductions. Since most companies wish to avoid a court challenge, they should always seek opportunities to negotiate penalty amounts with EPA. Companies may wish to highlight their records of product stewardship and consistent demonstration of regulatory compliance. If the violations noted are the company's first, that should also be noted.

---

72. TSCA Inspection Manual, *supra* note 9, at 6-4.

73. 15 U.S.C. § 2615(a)(2)(C).

8.5.2 Supplemental Environmental Projects

To further EPA's goals to protect and enhance public health and the environment, certain environmentally beneficial projects, or supplemental environmental projects (SEPs), may be included in the settlement. SEPs are environmentally beneficial projects that a respondent agrees to undertake in settlement of an environmental enforcement action, but that the respondent is not otherwise legally required to perform. In return, some percentage of the cost of the SEP is considered as a factor in establishing the final penalty to be paid by the respondent.

In 2015, EPA issued an updated policy statement.[74] Importantly, EPA stated that the release of the updated SEP policy was "intended to underscore the Agency's continuing strong support for SEPs, which can be powerful tools to secure significant environmental and public health benefits beyond those achieved by compliance, and to help address the needs of communities impacted by violations of environmental laws."[75]

For companies, a SEP is a way to offset the penalty amount paid to the U.S. government and instead use those funds for an environmental project that can directly benefit the company. It may be challenging to develop an appropriate SEP since the SEP must relate to the violations at issue, and whether to include a SEP as part of a settlement of an enforcement action is within the sole discretion of EPA. Although SEPs are seldom used in conjunction with TSCA violations, companies should consider them.

8.5.3 Prefiling Negotiations—TSCA Section 16 Civil Settlements

To avoid the time and expense of adjudicating a penalty amount, there are advantages to EPA and regulated entities negotiating a settlement. If the parties can reach a settlement, the terms of that settlement will be set forth in a consent agreement and final order (CAFO).[76] There is no CAFO template per se, but there is standard language to be expected in a CAFO with regard to EPA's jurisdiction

---

74. Memorandum from EPA to EPA Regional Administrators, Issuance of the 2015 Update to the 1998 U.S. Environmental Protection Agency Supplemental Environmental Projects Policy (Mar. 10, 2015), https://www.epa.gov/sites/default/files/2015-04/documents/sepupdatedpolicy15.pdf.
75. *Id.* at 1.
76. 40 C.F.R. § 22.18(b)(2) (2023).

over the subject matter, the parties, the pertinent facts, the violations alleged, and the penalty amount and terms for payment. In addition, EPA regulations require the respondent to do the following:

- Admit that EPA has jurisdiction over the subject matter alleged in the CAFO.
- Neither admit nor deny the factual allegations set forth in the CAFO.
- Consent to the assessment of a civil penalty and the conditions specified in the CAFO.
- Waive any right to contest or appeal the alleged violations set forth in the CAFO.[77]

8.5.4 TSCA Section 16(a)—Hearing Procedure

If the parties cannot reach a settlement agreement, EPA can initiate a formal adjudicatory proceeding by issuing a complaint. The details of this procedure are set forth in regulations and guidance and require involvement of attorneys with expertise in this area.[78] EPA's Consolidated Rules of Practice for civil penalty assessments apply to all civil TSCA penalty assessments, and any hearings are before an administrative law judge (ALJ) or regional judicial officer, with an appeals process to EPA's Environmental Appeals Board (EAB).

If a case to determine an appropriate penalty is brought before an ALJ, the ALJ is required to consider any applicable civil penalty guideline, but the ALJ is not bound to apply the guidelines in a particular case. Rather, the ALJ is constrained only by the statutory penalty criteria. ALJ decisions reaffirm EPA's inherent discretion in implementing and applying ERP considerations when addressing enforcement indiscretions; in some instances, these decisions emphasize that EPA should avoid applying the penalty policy in a formulaic way if that application fails to adapt to the facts and circumstances

77. *Id.* § 22.18(b)–(c).
78. *Id.* pt. 22; Consolidated Rules of Practice Governing the Administrative Assessment of Civil Penalties, Issuance of Compliance or Corrective Action Orders, and the Revocation, Termination, or Suspension of Permits, 64 Fed. Reg. 40,138 (July 23, 1999). The Consolidated Rules of Practice have been amended several times over the years, most recently in 2017. Consolidated Rules of Practice Governing the Administrative Assessment of Civil Penalties, Issuance of Compliance or Corrective Action Orders, and the Revocation/Termination or Suspension of Permits; Procedures for Decisionmaking, 82 Fed. Reg. 2,230 (Jan. 9, 2017).

of a particular case.[79] While this may be beneficial to companies that believe the penalty proposed by EPA is well outside an amount that is appropriate to the facts and circumstances, there are downsides to pursuing ALJ review. EPA is not bound by any settlement offers it may have made during negotiations. EPA frequently informs companies that if a formal proceeding is initiated, EPA could seek the maximum penalty it can calculate under its policies.

Following an EAB order, there is a final opportunity to appeal to the U.S. Court of Appeals for the District of Columbia Circuit, or any other circuit court where that person lives or transacts business. In those cases, judicial review of TSCA penalty determinations has typically been deferential, focusing primarily on whether EPA has rationally considered the factors set forth in TSCA section 16(a)(2)(B).

Just because a formal adjudicatory process is initiated does not mean that the possibility of settlement is waived. The parties can engage in settlement discussions at any time during the course of an administrative proceeding. Indeed, EPA's procedures governing the administrative assessment of civil penalties state that EPA encourages such settlements where such an outcome is consistent with the goals of TSCA.[80]

In addition to appealing civil penalty decisions assessed under TSCA section 16, regulated entities could seek to challenge the substantive basis for an EPA enforcement action. An entity that is subject to enforcement could challenge EPA's decision to bring an enforcement action against the company. This includes administrative or civil actions that challenge EPA's interpretation or application of TSCA, its implementing regulations or orders, or any EPA policies thereunder that led to a determination of noncompliance.

---

79. *See, e.g.*, *In the Matter of* Liphatech, Inc., Docket No. FIFRA-05-2010-0016, at 105 (ALJ Mar. 12, 2014), https://yosemite.epa.gov/OA/RHC/EPAAdmin.nsf/Filings/75B55AB8E6D8F95785257CD3001BC05F/$File/FIFRA-05-2010-0016%20COVER%20LTR%20W%20ID%205-8-2014.PDF (ALJ reducing penalties when the large number of violations outweighs other factors favorable to the respondent (e.g., no impact to human health and no history of violations), resulting in a "proposed penalty [that] far exceeds the amount necessary for the purpose of deterrence, as civil penalties are meant to effectuate"); *In re* C.P. Hall Co., Docket No. TSCA-V-C-61-89, at 31 (ALJ June 9, 1992), https://yosemite.epa.gov/oarm/alj/alj_web_docket.nsf/All%20Dockets%20by%20Statute/52E0877F2CDB651385257FBC00701FA4/$File/cp_hall_co_tsca_vanderheyden_060992.pdf (ALJ acknowledged that EPA has the discretion to assess penalties per chemical, per site, but should adjust penalties to account for any unfairness).
80. 40 C.F.R. § 22.18 (2023).

8.5.5 Post-Enforcement Issues

Once a case is completed, details of the case and its resolution will be made public. EPA has a database, for example, that can be searched for companies that have settled matters where EPA has alleged violations and issued an NON or CAFO.[81] ALJ and EAB proceedings and orders also are available publicly.[82] While available, they may not receive any attention, unless EPA takes steps to bring the matter to greater public notice. EPA has the sole discretion to issue a press release regarding any settlement or case that can bring unwelcome business consequences, such as reputational damage or diminished brand trust. EPA also can highlight certain cases on its website.[83] The type of case and the amount of the penalty are significant factors for EPA when considering how to publicize a settlement or case.

Companies that have been through an enforcement action should know, or will determine, what steps are needed to ensure that any violation does not happen again. There are regulatory consequences of an enforcement action that remain even when compliance is achieved. For EPA's purposes, for example, the fact that a company has been found in violation of a particular statute (e.g., TSCA section 12(b) export notifications) means that that company would be ineligible to self-confess under EPA's Audit Policy for the same violations later.[84] A company subject to enforcement also may be more likely to be subject to follow-up inspections or related inquiries from EPA. There are commercial consequences. Depending upon materiality clauses in various commercial documents relevant in refinancing, insurance, and due diligence transactions, a prior enforcement action

81. *EPA Administrative Enforcement Dockets*, EPA, https://yosemite.epa.gov/OA/RHC/EPAAdmin.nsf (last updated Sept. 28, 2024). EPA's ECHO provides an online searchable database of various EPA enforcement actions. *Enforcement and Compliance History Online (ECHO): EPA Cases*, *supra* note 5.
82. *Administrative Law Judges: Dockets, Decisions & Orders*, EPA, https://www.epa.gov/alj/dockets-decisions-orders (last updated Sept. 25, 2024); *EAB Board Decisions*, EPA, https://yosemite.epa.gov/oa/EAB_Web_Docket.nsf/Board+Decisions?OpenPage (last updated Sept. 27, 2024).
83. *Civil and Cleanup Enforcement Cases and Settlements*, EPA, https://www.epa.gov/enforcement/civil-and-cleanup-enforcement-cases-and-settlements (last updated Sept. 17, 2024).
84. Incentives for Self-Policing: Discovery, Disclosure, Correction, and Prevention of Violations, 65 Fed. Reg. 19,618, 19,622–23 (Apr. 11, 2000) [hereinafter Audit Policy] (Audit Policy not available if same or a closely related violation occurs at the same facility within the past three years, or in a multifacility organization, if the same or a closely related violation occurs as part of a pattern of violations at one or more of these facilities within the past five years).

could affect banking, refinancing, and other commercial transactions. Those doing business with federal and state entities may also invite qualification issues.

8.6 Avoiding Enforcement by Maintaining Compliance

The clearest pathway to avoid TSCA enforcement and the possibility of major civil penalties or other EPA action is to maintain compliance. Of course, this can be easier said than done. Companies, however, can take several steps to increase the likelihood of compliance.

8.6.1 SOPs and Employee Training

There is no statutory or regulatory TSCA requirement to develop and maintain compliance policies and procedures. Companies that have clear, written procedures to address TSCA requirements have a distinct advantage in ensuring compliance. From EPA's perspective, such policies and procedures can demonstrate a company's interest and intention to ensure compliance, which also can be helpful when facing an inspection or enforcement action.

There are distinct obligations under TSCA sections 4, 5, 8, 12, and 13, so companies should first understand the scope of their activities and then determine the need for suitable operating procedures. Assignment of responsibilities and employee training go hand in hand with SOPs. This again depends on the level of a company's involvement in TSCA activities, but leaving all responsibilities to one person can undermine compliance generally. TSCA issues can at times be complex or involve sensitive corporate information. Even on more routine matters, if one person is responsible and then leaves the company, the loss of institutional knowledge can be difficult to regain.

8.6.2 Compliance Monitoring Systems to Keep Up-to-Date

TSCA requirements change rapidly, and it can be challenging to remain up-to-date with TSCA's evolving regulatory landscape. Establishing whether and how a company monitors EPA, state, and global chemical regulations for new requirements, guidance, and trends is another way to maintain compliance. There are databases, guidance, and other tools companies can use to assist in TSCA compliance. A company's needs should be tailored depending on their activities and substances, but some general resources include the following:

- **Chemical substance databases**. Companies can access the nonconfidential portion of the TSCA Inventory online for critical information regarding chemical substances (e.g., whether a chemical is on the TSCA Inventory, whether a substance has a "flag" that it is subject to a significant new use rule (SNUR)).[85] Other resources (e.g., Ariel, STN), some of which are fee-based, may provide additional information, or more user-friendly information, depending on a company's needs.
- **EPA's website, Listservs, and hotline**. EPA posts on its website multiple resources pertaining to TSCA requirements. There are fact sheets, question and answer documents, instructions to complete forms, and other guidance documents. EPA also has various email subscriptions so that anyone can sign up and receive updates from EPA on relevant issues. EPA maintains a "TSCA Hotline" that one can call or email for general TSCA inquiries.[86] On significant and uniquely vague issues, legal counsel is always a good idea.
- ***Federal Register* notices**. Monitoring the *Federal Register* is another way to stay informed about EPA developments.[87] Whether EPA seeks to implement a statutory requirement generally or to impose new regulatory requirements on a particular chemical substance, it will be set forth in a proposed rule published in the *Federal Register*. When a rule is issued in final and specific requirements and effective dates are announced, it will be set forth in a final rule published in the *Federal Register*. Even notices or announcements of availability of new guidance can be published in the *Federal Register*.

85. *How to Access the TSCA Inventory*, EPA, https://www.epa.gov/tsca-inventory/how-access-tsca-inventory (last updated Sept. 11, 2024).
86. *Contact Us about the TSCA Chemical Substance Inventory*, EPA, https://www.epa.gov/tsca-inventory/forms/contact-us-about-tsca-chemical-substance-inventory (last updated Sept. 3, 2024).
87. The *Federal Register* can be found and searched at https://www.federalregister.gov/ (last visited Sept. 27, 2024).

- **Third-party compliance assistance.** Companies also can consider outside consultants and legal experts when publicly available information does not adequately address an issue or in specialized scenarios, such as when a company is considering a new product or business line and seeks information to ensure compliance is maintained and to determine any compliance or enforcement risks. There also might be trade associations and advocacy groups that provide updates on evolving regulatory issues pertinent to a particular company or industry.

8.6.3 Internal Compliance Audits

Staying prepared and ensuring records are up-to-date and accessible are important measures for regulated entities. Internal compliance monitoring or audits for TSCA purposes could be one of many routine systems a company implements. EPA has defined "environmental audit" and "compliance management system" in the context of its audit policies. Developing an audit or system that meets EPA definitions could assist not only in identifying and correcting noncompliance but potentially avoiding civil penalties if that noncompliance is self-disclosed to EPA and meets certain conditions.

8.7 EPA's Audit Policy

It is helpful to understand options for minimizing the consequences of noncompliance once discovered, particularly EPA's Audit Policy.[88] EPA developed its Audit Policy to provide opportunities to avoid any penalties for violations that are discovered and self-confessed to EPA, provided certain conditions are satisfied. Companies that conduct periodic compliance audits to discover and correct any inadvertent

88. Audit Policy, *supra* note 84. There is a second policy to address circumstances specific to when there is a transaction and a new company takes over an existing business. This "New Owner Interim Approach" is discussed in detail in Chapter 6. The third policy, which has been in place since 2000, is specific to and provides accommodations for small businesses. In 2021, EPA issued a frequently asked questions (FAQ) document to highlight interpretations and provide clarification of EPA's self-disclosed violation policies and its e-disclosure system. *See* OECA, EPA, EPA's Audit Policy Program: Frequently Asked Questions (2021), https://www.epa.gov/compliance/epas-audit-policy-program-frequently-asked-questions.

noncompliance, or otherwise discover potential violations regarding its TSCA practices and procedures, can consider the option to self-disclose those violations to EPA.

8.7.1 Advantages and Disadvantages of the Audit Policy

There is no legal obligation for a company to self-confess. If a company chooses to do so, it generally is eligible for more lenient treatment, especially with respect to the imposition of penalties. The Audit Policy can provide 100 percent penalty mitigation when all nine conditions are satisfied, or 75 percent penalty mitigation if conditions 2–9 are satisfied.

There are other advantages to self-disclosing that may be appealing to companies. First, if there is a voluntary disclosure, there is no risk that EPA would discover these violations on its own (e.g., in the course of an inspection) and thereafter assess penalties without consideration of deductions for voluntary disclosure. EPA generally does not *recommend criminal prosecution* for entities that disclose criminal violations if all of the applicable conditions under the Audit Policy are met. EPA states it also would not generally elect to recommend criminal prosecution by the Department of Justice or any other prosecuting authority, provided the disclosing entity meets all the conditions except for the "systematic discovery" requirement, "as long as its self-policing, discovery and disclosure were conducted in good faith and the entity adopts a systematic approach to preventing recurrence of the violation."[89]

EPA also reaffirms in the Audit Policy its Environmental Auditing Policy Statement in effect since 1986, to refrain from routine requests for audit reports.[90] This means that EPA has not and will not routinely request copies of audit reports to trigger enforcement investigations.

Utilization of the Audit Policy may not be the preferred decision for everyone, however. Depending on the company and the particular facts and violations at issue, a company may need to weigh unique factors and make a business decision whether to self-disclose. Despite EPA's statements and ability to use its discretion to waive all

89. Audit Policy, *supra* note 84, at 19,622–23.

90. *Id.* at 19,620; Environmental Auditing Policy Statement, 51 Fed. Reg. 25,004 (July 9, 1986).

penalties, EPA has not, in practice, been as supportive of companies self-disclosing as industry may have hoped. Even with a self-disclosure, a company may still face penalties that are not significantly lower than it would incur without self-disclosure.

EPA also states that it will not waive or mitigate that portion of a penalty intended to deprive an entity of any economic benefits gained from the noncompliance, unless it determines such gain was insignificant. Although arguments can be made that the economic gain from noncompliance with a particular provision is not significant, EPA may disagree, resulting in additional negotiations and decisions as to how EPA calculates economic benefit and the civil penalty amount that still may be imposed.

While EPA states it will not generally recommend criminal prosecution, that advantage has its limits. EPA states that entities can remain criminally liable for "violations that result from conscious disregard of or willful blindness to their obligations under the law."[91] Individuals also can still be held liable for their criminal misconduct.

In cases where EPA agrees a company has satisfied the Audit Policy conditions, EPA may require a regulated entity to enter into a "publicly available written agreement, administrative consent order or judicial consent decree as a condition of obtaining relief under the Audit Policy, particularly where compliance or remedial measures are complex or a lengthy schedule for attaining and maintaining compliance or remediating harm is required."[92] Copies of any settlement and related documents could be released, either by EPA or following a Freedom of Information Act request, to the extent such information is not claimed as CBI. Companies that detect and report noncompliance thus must appreciate the potential for adverse publicity.

8.7.2 Satisfying the Audit Policy's Nine Conditions

EPA's Audit Policy and related guidance discuss each of nine conditions to be satisfied for the Audit Policy to be applicable. In summary, they are as follows:

- **Condition 1—Systematic Discovery.** This condition requires that the violation be discovered through (1) an environmental

91. Audit Policy, *supra* note 84, at 19,619.
92. *Id.* at 19,626.

audit, meaning a systematic, documented, periodic, and objective review by regulated entities of facility operations and practices related to meeting environmental requirements; or (2) implementation of a compliance management system, meaning some type of due diligence or systematic management plan or systematic efforts to achieve and maintain compliance.

- **Condition 2—Voluntary Discovery.** To meet this condition, the violation must not have been detected as a result of a legally required monitoring, sampling, or auditing procedure.
- **Condition 3—Prompt Disclosure.** For a disclosure to be "prompt," it must be in writing to EPA within 21 days of discovery or such shorter time as may be required by law. Discovery occurs when any officer, director, employee, or agent of the facility has an objectively reasonable basis for believing that a violation has or may have occurred.
- **Condition 4—Discovery and Disclosure Independent of Government and Third-Party Plaintiff.** To meet this condition, the violation must have been discovered before EPA or another regulator would likely have identified the violation through its own investigation or based on information provided by a third party (e.g., citizen suit, whistleblower). For entities that own or operate multiple facilities, the fact that one facility is already the subject of an investigation, inspection, information request, or third-party complaint does not preclude EPA from exercising its discretion to make the Audit Policy available for violations self-discovered at other facilities owned or operated by the same regulated entity.
- **Condition 5—Correction and Remediation.** This condition is satisfied if the violation is corrected within 60 calendar days from the date of discovery. Depending on the type of violation, EPA can order a shorter timeframe and companies can request extensions for longer timeframes.
- **Condition 6—Prevent Recurrence.** A disclosing entity must explain what steps it has taken or will be taking to prevent recurrence of the violation.
- **Condition 7—No Repeat Violations.** The disclosing entity must confirm that the specific (or closely related) violations have not occurred (1) at the same facility within the past three years; or (2) as part of a pattern at multiple facilities owned or operated by the same entity within the past five years.

- **Condition 8—Other Violations Excluded.** To meet this condition, the violation at issue did not result in serious actual harm, did not present an imminent and substantial endangerment, and/or did not violate the specific terms of an administrative or judicial order or consent agreement.
- **Condition 9—Cooperation.** A disclosing entity must commit to cooperate with EPA through the process (e.g., be prompt and responsive to EPA follow-up questions).

Takeaways

- Though knowing that your company falls within an enforcement priority may be helpful in preparing for a prospective inspection, any entity that falls under TSCA's jurisdiction, large or small, may be subject to a compliance review or an enforcement action.
- TSCA inspections follow procedures, and understanding how EPA operates can assist companies when faced with an otherwise intimidating and complex inspection.
- Knowing the law, having durable compliance SOPs, and routinely engaging in training are the best protections against noncompliance.
- If EPA determines that a violation has occurred, regardless of the type or severity of the violation at issue, EPA has the ability under TSCA section 16 to pursue enforcement and indeed does impose significant penalties.
- Taking action to ensure compliance from the outset is the best pathway for companies seeking to limit potential liabilities under TSCA. There are several resources to assist companies to ensure close, consistent, and diligent review of compliance with all applicable TSCA requirements and thus deter the significant risk of an EPA enforcement action.
- Despite their best efforts, companies that strive to and dedicate significant resources to comply with all sections of TSCA may make errors from time to time. Conducting periodic internal audits can assist in identifying such issues, and companies can try to avail themselves, as applicable, of EPA's Audit Policy and voluntary disclosure.

Appendix A

Acronym List

6:2 FTSB: 6:2 fluorotelomer sulfonamide betaine

ACE: Automated Commercial Environment

AHERA: Asbestos Hazard Emergency Response Act

ALJ: administrative law judge

AN: accession number

B&C: Bergeson & Campbell, P.C.

BFI: bona fide intent to manufacture notice

CA: Chemical Abstracts

CAA: Clean Air Act

CAFO: consent agreement and final order

CAS: Chemical Abstracts Service

CAS RN®: Chemical Abstracts Service Registry Number®

CBI: confidential business information

CBP: U.S. Customs and Border Protection

CCI: Coalition for Chemical Innovations

CDA: confidential disclosure agreement

CDR: Chemical Data Reporting

CDX: Central Data Exchange

CEH: Center for Environmental Health

CEQ: Council on Environmental Quality

C.F.R.: *Code of Federal Regulations*

China REACH: Measures for the Environmental Management Registration of New Chemical Substances

CMS: compliance monitoring strategy

CoC: concentration of concern

COU: condition of use

CPSC: U.S. Consumer Product Safety Commission

CRS: Congressional Research Service

CWA: Clean Water Act

decaBDE: decabromodiphenyl ether

DTSC: California Department of Toxic Substances Control

EAB: Environmental Appeals Board

ECA: enforceable consent agreement

ECEL: existing chemical exposure limit

ECHO: Enforcement and Compliance History Online

EJ: environmental justice

EJSEAT: Environmental Justice Strategic Enforcement Assessment Tool

EPA: U.S. Environmental Protection Agency

ERP: enforcement response policy

EU: European Union

EWG: Environmental Working Group

FACA: Federal Advisory Committee Act

FAQ: frequently asked question

FDA: U.S. Food and Drug Administration

FFDCA: Federal Food, Drug, and Cosmetic Act

FIFRA: Federal Insecticide, Fungicide, and Rodenticide Act

FOIA: Freedom of Information Act

FY: fiscal year

GAO: U.S. Government Accountability Office

HDPE: high-density polyethylene

HFPO: trifluoro(trifluoromethyl)oxirane

HPS: high-priority substance

IARC: International Agency for Research on Cancer

India REACH: Chemical Management and Safety Rules, 20xx

Inventory: TSCA Chemical Substance Inventory or TSCA Inventory

IRL: information request letter

KKDIK: Kimyasalların Kaydı, Değerlendirilmesi, İzni ve Kısıtlanması, known as Turkey REACH

K-REACH: Act on the Registration and Evaluation of Chemicals

Lautenberg: Frank R. Lautenberg Chemical Safety for the 21st Century Act

LBP: lead-based paint

LCPFAC: long-chain perfluoroalkyl carboxylate

LOD: limit of detection

LOQ: limit of quantification

LoREX: low release and low exposure exemption

LPS: low-priority substance

LVE: low volume exemption

MAP: Model Accreditation Plan

MCAN: microbial commercial activity notice

MOA: mode of action

MOE: margin of exposure

MRRE: manufacturer-requested risk evaluation

NAIS: Neutral Administrative Inspection Scheme

NDA: nondisclosure agreement

NDAA: National Defense Authorization Act

NECI: National Enforcement and Compliance Initiative

NEJAC: National Environmental Justice Advisory Council

NGO: nongovernmental organization

NIOSH: U.S. National Institute for Occupational Safety and Health

NMP: *N*-methyl pyrrolidone

NOA: notice of activity

NOAEL: no-observed-adverse-effect level

NOC: notice of commencement

NOI: notice of intent

NON: notice of noncompliance

NPDES: National Pollutant Discharge Elimination System

NPDWR: National Primary Drinking Water Regulations

NPG: National Program Guidance

NRC: U.S. National Research Council

NTP: National Toxicology Program

OCSPP: Office of Chemical Safety and Pollution Prevention

OECA: Office of Enforcement and Compliance Assurance

OECD: Organisation for Economic Co-operation and Development

OSHA: Occupational Safety and Health Administration

PAIR: Preliminary Assessment Information Rule

PBT: persistent, bioaccumulative, and toxic

PCB: polychlorinated biphenyl

PEER: Public Employees for Environmental Responsibility

PEL: permissible exposure limit

PESS: potentially exposed or susceptible subpopulation

PFAS: per- and polyfluoroalkyl substances

PFOA: perfluorooctanoic acid

PFOS: perfluorooctane sulfonate

PIIRL: pre-inspection information request letter

PIP (3:1): phenol, isopropylated phosphate (3:1)

PMN: premanufacture notice

POD: point of departure

PPE: personal protective equipment

ppm: parts per million

Prop 65: Proposition 65

Q&A: question and answer

R&D: research and development

RCRA: Resource Conservation and Recovery Act

REACH: Registration, Evaluation, Authorisation and Restriction of Chemicals

RQ: risk quotient

SACC: Science Advisory Committee on Chemicals

SDS: safety data sheet

SEP: supplemental environmental project

SNU: significant new use

SNUN: significant new use notice

SNUR: significant new use rule

SOP: standard operating procedure

STEL: short-term exposure limit

TCE: trichloroethylene

TERA: TSCA experimental release application

TME: test marketing exemption

TRI: Toxics Release Inventory

TSCA: Toxic Substances Control Act

TSCA Inventory: TSCA Chemical Substance Inventory

Turkey REACH: *see* KKDIK

TWA: time-weighted average

U.S.C.: U.S. Code

USDA: U.S. Department of Agriculture

UVCB: chemical substance of unknown or variable composition, complex reaction products, and biological materials

WCPP: Workplace Chemical Protection Program

WPR: Worker Protection Rule

Appendix B

Glossary

Article: A manufactured item (1) that is formed to a specific shape or design during manufacture, (2) that has end use function(s) dependent in whole or in part upon its shape or design during end use, and (3) that has either no change of chemical composition during its end use or only those changes of composition that have no commercial purpose separate from that of the article, and that result from a chemical reaction that occurs upon end use of other chemical substances, mixtures, or articles; except that fluids and particles are not considered articles regardless of shape or design.[1]

Blanket certification: A certification that all chemical substances in all shipments of listed products imported from listed suppliers are either in compliance with the Toxic Substances Control Act (TSCA) or not subject to TSCA. Blanket certification can be used in lieu of separate import certifications for each individual shipment. The blanket certification is made on an annual basis, subject to renewal. The certification must be made on the letterhead of the certifying firm, signed by an authorized person, and submitted to the District Director of the U.S. Customs and Border Protection (CBP). The commercial invoice or entry document for each shipment covered by the blanket

1. 40 C.F.R. §§ 704.3, 710.3(d), 720.3(c) (2023). *See also* 19 C.F.R. § 12.120(a) (2024).

certification must include a statement incorporating the blanket certification by reference.[2]

Bona fide intent (BFI) to manufacture notice: A request by a manufacturer or importer that the U.S. Environmental Protection Agency (EPA) search its TSCA Confidential Inventory if the identity of a particular chemical substance has been claimed a trade secret, or if the chemical substance is not listed on the public version of the TSCA Chemical Substance Inventory and a manufacturer or importer has reason to believe that the chemical substance may be listed on the TSCA Confidential Inventory.

Byproduct: A substance produced without a separate commercial intent during the manufacture, processing, use, or disposal of another chemical substance(s) or mixture(s).[3]

Chemical Abstracts Service Registry Number (CAS RN): A unique number assigned by the Chemical Abstracts Service to a specific chemical substance.

Chemical substance: Any organic or inorganic substance of a particular molecular identity, including (1) any combination of such substances occurring in whole or in part as a result of a chemical reaction or occurring in nature, and (2) any element or uncombined radical.[4]

***Code of Federal Regulations* (C.F.R.):** The codification of the general and permanent rules published in the *Federal Register* by the departments and agencies of the federal government, available at https://www.govinfo.gov/app/collection/cfr/.

Conditions of use (COUs): The circumstances, as determined by the Administrator, under which a chemical substance is intended, known, or reasonably foreseen to be manufactured, processed, distributed in commerce, used, or disposed of.[5]

Confidential business information (CBI): Pursuant to 5 U.S.C. § 552(b)(4), CBI is considered "trade secrets and commercial or financial information obtained from a person and privileged or confidential."

---

2. *See* TSCA § 13, 15 U.S.C. § 2612; 19 C.F.R. §§ 12.118–.127 (2024); 40 C.F.R. § 707.20 (2023).
3. 40 C.F.R. § 710.3(d) (2023).
4. TSCA § 3(2)(A), 15 U.S.C. § 2602(2)(A); 40 C.F.R. § 710.3(d) (2023).
5. TSCA § 3(4), 15 U.S.C. § 2602(4).

Dose-response assessment: The determination of the relation between the magnitude of exposure and the probability of occurrence of the health effects in question.[6]

Due diligence: The process of investigation carried on usually by a disinterested third party (as an accounting or law firm) on behalf of a party contemplating a business transaction (as a corporate acquisition or merger, loan of finances, or especially purchase of securities) for the purpose of providing information with which to evaluate the advantages and risks involved.[7]

Entered for warehouse: Defined as meaning that a warehouse entry summary, or documentation or electronic submission of data necessary for CBP to assess duties, collects statistics on imported merchandise and determines compliance with applicable laws or regulations. The summary has been filed with CBP in proper form through the Automated Commercial Environment (ACE) or any other CBP-authorized electronic data interchange system.[8]

Existing chemical substance: A chemical substance that is listed on the TSCA Inventory.

Export notification: Notice to EPA that the notifier has exported, or intends to export, a chemical substance or mixture subject to TSCA section 12(b) export notification requirements. Chemical substances subject to export notification requirements are those for which data have been required under TSCA section 4 or TSCA section 5(b), an order has been issued under TSCA section 5, a rule has been proposed or promulgated under TSCA section 5 or 6, or an action is pending or relief has been granted under TSCA section 5 or 7. EPA maintains a list of chemical substances for which export notification is required. No notice is required for articles unless EPA requires otherwise.[9]

Exporter: The principal party in interest in the export who has the power and responsibility for controlling the shipment of the chemical substance or mixture outside of the customs territory of the United States.[10]

---

6. National Research Council, Risk Assessment in the Federal Government: Managing the Process (1983), https://doi.org/10.17226/366.
7. *Due Diligence*, Merriam-Webster Dictionary, https://www.merriam-webster.com/dictionary/due%20diligence (last visited Sept. 27, 2024).
8. 19 C.F.R. § 141.0a (2024).
9. *See* TSCA § 12(b), 15 U.S.C. § 2611(b); 40 C.F.R. pt. 707, subpt. D (2023).
10. 40 C.F.R. § 707.63 (2023).

Exposure assessment: The determination of the extent of human exposure before or after application of regulatory controls.[11]

***Federal Register* (Fed. Reg.)**: Published by the Office of the Federal Register, National Archives and Records Administration (NARA), the *Federal Register* is the official daily publication for rules, proposed rules, and notices of federal agencies and organizations, as well as executive orders and other presidential documents, available at https://www.govinfo.gov/app/collection/FR/.

Hazard identification: The determination of whether a particular chemical is or is not causally linked to particular health effects.[12]

High-priority substance (HPS): A chemical substance that EPA "concludes, without consideration of costs or other nonrisk factors, may present an unreasonable risk of injury to health or the environment because of a potential hazard and a potential route of exposure under the conditions of use, including an unreasonable risk to a potentially exposed or susceptible subpopulation identified as relevant by the Administrator."[13]

Import certification: Certification to CBP either that all chemical substances and mixtures in an import shipment comply with all applicable rules and orders under TSCA and are not offered for entry in violation of TSCA (positive certification) or that all chemicals in the shipment are not subject to TSCA (negative certification). Under TSCA section 13, the Secretary of the Treasury shall refuse entry into the customs territory of the United States any chemical substance or mixture or any article containing a chemical substance or mixture if it fails to comply with TSCA. Under CBP regulations, chemical substances or mixtures that are imported as part of an article are subject to the certification requirements only if required by a TSCA rule or order.[14]

Importer: Any person who imports any chemical substance, including a chemical substance as part of a mixture or article, into the customs territory of the United States. "Importer" includes the person primarily liable for the payment of any duties on the merchandise, or

11. National Research Council, *supra* note 6.
12. *Id.*
13. TSCA § 6(b)(1)(B)(i), 15 U.S.C. § 2605(b)(1)(B)(i).
14. *See* TSCA § 13, 15 U.S.C. § 2612; 19 C.F.R. §§ 12.118–.127 (2024); 40 C.F.R. § 707.20 (2023).

an authorized agent acting on his or her behalf. The importer may be (1) the consignee; (2) the importer of record; (3) the actual owner of the merchandise, if an actual owner's declaration and superseding bond has been filed in accordance with 19 C.F.R. § 141.20; or (4) the transferee of the merchandise, if the right to withdraw merchandise in a bonded warehouse has been transferred in accordance with 19 C.F.R. Part 144, Subpart C.[15]

Impurity: A substance unintentionally present with another chemical substance.[16]

Low-priority substance (LPS): A chemical substance that EPA "concludes, based on information sufficient to establish, without consideration of costs or other non-risk factors, that such substance does not meet the standard identified in [section 6(b)(1)(B)(i)] for designating a chemical substance a high-priority substance."[17]

Low releases and low exposures exemption (LoREX): An exemption from premanufacture notice (PMN) requirements for a chemical substance that satisfies certain criteria for low environmental releases and low human exposure. The presumptive criteria are as follows: for consumers and the general population, there will be no dermal and inhalation exposure and no exposure in drinking water greater than one milligram per year; for workers, adequate controls will ensure there will be no dermal or inhalation exposure; there will be no releases to ambient surface water resulting in concentrations exceeding one part per billion; there will be no releases to ambient air from incineration in excess of one microgram per cubic meter (annual average); and there will be no releases to groundwater, land, or a landfill. Higher quantities of releases may be allowed if EPA is satisfied such quantities will not pose a hazard to human health or the environment. Persons wishing to manufacture or import a new chemical substance under the LoREX exemption must submit a notice to EPA at least 30 days prior to such manufacture or import, demonstrating the criteria will be met. If EPA takes no action within 30 days, the submitter may begin manufacture or import of the chemical substance.[18]

15. 40 C.F.R. § 710.3(d) (2023); 19 C.F.R. § 101.1 (2024).
16. 40 C.F.R. § 710.3(d) (2023).
17. TSCA § 6(b)(1)(B)(ii), 15 U.S.C. § 2605(b)(1)(B)(ii).
18. *See* 40 C.F.R. pt. 723, subpt. B (2023).

Low volume exemption (LVE): An exemption from PMN requirements for a chemical substance to be manufactured or imported in quantities of 10,000 kilograms per year or less. A person who wishes to manufacture or import a new chemical substance under the LVE must submit a notification to EPA at least 30 days before such manufacture or import. If EPA takes no action within 30 days, the submitter may begin manufacture or import of the chemical substance. EPA will permit more than one person to use the LVE for a given substance, as long as EPA determines the total quantity manufactured or imported will not pose a hazard to health or the environment.[19]

Manufacture: To import into the customs territory of the United States (as defined in general note 2 of the Harmonized Tariff Schedule of the United States), produce, or manufacture.[20] Under TSCA, "manufacture" is also defined to mean "manufacture . . . for commercial purposes."[21]

Manufacture for commercial purposes: To import, produce, or manufacture with the purpose of obtaining an immediate or eventual commercial advantage for the manufacturer.[22]

Manufacturer: A person who imports, produces, or manufactures a chemical substance.[23]

Mixture: Any combination of two or more chemical substances if the combination does not occur in nature and is not, in whole or in part, the result of a chemical reaction; except that such term does include any combination that occurs, in whole or in part, as a result of a chemical reaction if none of the chemical substances comprising the combination is a new chemical substance and if the combination could have been manufactured for commercial purposes without a chemical reaction at the time the chemical substances comprising the combination were combined.[24]

Naturally occurring substance: Any chemical substance that is naturally occurring and (1) that is (i) unprocessed or (ii) processed only by manual, mechanical, or gravitational means; by dissolution in

---

19. *See id.*
20. TSCA § 3(9), 15 U.S.C. § 2602(9). *See, e.g.*, 40 C.F.R. § 710.3(d) (2023) ("Manufacture means to manufacture, produce, or import for commercial purposes.").
21. TSCA §§ 5(i)(1), 8(f), 15 U.S.C. §§ 2604(i)(1), 2607(f).
22. 40 C.F.R. §§ 704.3, 710.3(d), 716.3, 717.3(e), 720.3(r) (2023).
23. *Id.* §§ 704.3, 716.3, 720.3(t).
24. TSCA § 3(10), 15 U.S.C. § 2602(10). *See also* 40 C.F.R. § 720.3(u) (2023).

water; by flotation; or by heating solely to remove water; or (2) that is extracted from air by any means.[25]

Negative import certificate: A negative import certificate is a signed statement submitted to CBP, certifying that the chemical substances contained in a shipment offered for entry into the United States customs territory are not subject to TSCA. TSCA section 13 requires the Secretary of the Treasury to refuse entry of any chemical substance, mixture, or article containing a chemical substance, if the chemical substance fails to comply with any TSCA rule or is offered in violation of an order under TSCA section 5, 6, or 7. CBP has promulgated regulations that require any importer of a shipment containing a chemical substance to submit either a positive certification that all chemical substances in the shipment comply with TSCA or a negative certification that all chemicals in the shipment are not subject to TSCA.[26]

New chemical substance: Any chemical substance that is not included in the TSCA Inventory compiled and published under TSCA section 8(b).[27]

New chemicals bias: This refers to a "bias" against a new chemical that is subject to a protective measure when compared to an existing substance of equal or greater hazard that is not (or not yet) subject to such measures. The "new chemicals bias" is a critical consideration for a company as it plans innovation cycles and market entries. If a business is to develop new chemical substances, it must account for the new chemicals bias if the company intends to supply TSCA markets. Avoiding or diminishing the effect of the new chemicals bias occurs only if the chemical supplies uses not covered by TSCA (e.g., food, drugs, cosmetics) or supplies markets outside of the United States.

Nonisolated intermediate: A substance formed during a chemical reaction that is reacted further without being isolated from the reaction vessel or ancillary equipment, including continuous flow reactors.[28]

Notice of commencement (NOC) of manufacture or import: A notice submitted to EPA that manufacture or import of a new chemical substance has commenced. Persons who intend to manufacture

---

25. 40 C.F.R. § 710.4(b).
26. TSCA § 13, 15 U.S.C. § 2612; 19 C.F.R. § 12.121 (2024); 40 C.F.R. § 707.20 (2023).
27. TSCA § 3(11), 15 U.S.C. § 2602(11); 40 C.F.R. § 720.3(v) (2023).
28. 40 C.F.R. § 704.3 (2023).

or import a new chemical substance for a nonexempt commercial purpose must submit a PMN to EPA at least 90 days prior to such manufacture or import. Subsequently, within 30 days of the date of manufacture of the first nonexempt amount of the chemical substance or import of the first nonexempt shipment of the chemical substance into U.S. customs territory, the manufacturer or importer must submit a NOC to EPA, using a form provided by EPA. Upon receipt of the NOC, EPA adds the chemical substance to the TSCA Inventory. The NOC must identify the specific chemical identity of the substance; a generic chemical name, if the specific name is claimed confidential; the date of commencement of manufacture or import for a nonexempt purpose; name, address, and telephone information for the submitter and a technical contact; the address of the site where commencement of manufacture occurred; and indications of whether information is being claimed as CBI. Submitters who claimed the chemical identity as CBI on the PMN, and who wish to maintain that confidentiality, must reassert and provide substantiation for the claim.[29]

Persistent, bioaccumulative, and toxic (PBT) chemicals: Chemicals identified in the 2014 update of the TSCA Work Plan for Chemical Assessments "(A) that the Administrator has a reasonable basis to conclude are toxic and that with respect to persistence and bioaccumulation score high for one and either high or moderate for the other, pursuant to the TSCA Work Plan Chemicals Methods Document published by the Administrator in February 2012 (or a successor scoring system), and are not a metal or metal compound, and for which the Administrator has not completed a Work Plan Problem Formulation, initiated a review under section 5, or entered into a consent agreement under [section 4], prior to June 22, 2016 [the date of enactment of the Frank R. Lautenberg Chemical Safety for the 21st Century Act]; and (B) exposure to which under the conditions of use is likely to the general population or to a potentially exposed or susceptible subpopulation identified by the Administrator, or the environment, on the basis of an exposure and use assessment conducted by the Administrator."[30]

Person: Any individual, firm, company, corporation, joint venture, partnership, sole proprietorship, association, or any other business entity; any state or political subdivision thereof; any municipality;

29. *Id.* § 720.102.
30. TSCA § 6(h)(1), 15 U.S.C. § 2605(h)(1).

any interstate body; and any department, agency, or instrumentality of the federal government.[31]

Positive import certificate: A signed statement submitted to CBP, certifying that the chemical substances contained in a shipment offered for entry into the U.S. customs territory comply with TSCA. TSCA section 13 requires the Secretary of the Treasury to refuse entry of any chemical substance, mixture, or article containing a chemical substance, if the chemical substance fails to comply with any TSCA rule or is offered in violation of an order under TSCA section 5, 6, or 7. CBP has promulgated regulations that require any importer of a shipment containing a chemical substance to submit either a positive certification that all chemical substances in the shipment comply with TSCA or a negative certification that all chemicals in the shipment are not subject to TSCA.[32]

Potentially exposed or susceptible subpopulation (PESS): A group of individuals within the general population identified by the Administrator who, due to either greater susceptibility or greater exposure, may be at greater risk than the general population of adverse health effects from exposure to a chemical substance or mixture, such as infants, children, pregnant women, workers, or the elderly.[33]

Premanufacture notice (PMN): A notice submitted to EPA that the submitter intends to manufacture or import a new chemical substance.[34]

Process: The preparation of a chemical substance or mixture, after its manufacture, for distribution in commerce "(A) in the same form or physical state as, or in a different form or physical state from, that in which it was received by the person so preparing such substance or mixture, or (B) as part of an article containing the chemical substance or mixture."[35]

Process for commercial purposes: Processing "with the purpose of obtaining an immediate or eventual commercial advantage" and "[p]rocessing of any amount of a chemical substance or mixture . . . ."[36]

31. 40 C.F.R. §§ 704.3, 710.3(d), 716.3, 717.3(f), 720.3(x) (2023).
32. TSCA § 13, 15 U.S.C. § 2612; 19 C.F.R. § 12.121 (2024); 40 C.F.R. § 707.20 (2023).
33. TSCA § 3(12), 15 U.S.C. § 2602(12).
34. TSCA § 5, 15 U.S.C. § 2604; 40 C.F.R. pt. 720 (2023).
35. TSCA § 3(13), 15 U.S.C. § 2602(13); 40 C.F.R. § 720.3(aa) (2023). *See also* EPA, Question and Answer Summary: EPA Seminar on Industry Obligations under TSCA 1–2 (1986).
36. 40 C.F.R. § 704.3 (2023).

Processor: Any person who processes a chemical substance or mixture.[37]

Risk characterization: The description of the nature and often the magnitude of human risk, including attendant uncertainty.[38]

Risk evaluation: An evaluation "to determine whether a chemical substance presents an unreasonable risk of injury to health or the environment, without consideration of costs or other nonrisk factors, including an unreasonable risk to a potentially exposed or susceptible subpopulation identified as relevant to the risk evaluation by [EPA], under the conditions of use." Under section 6 of TSCA, EPA is directed to establish, by rule, a process to conduct risk evaluations in accordance with the above-listed definition.[39]

Science Advisory Committee on Chemicals (SACC): Per TSCA section 26(o), not later than one year after the date of enactment, EPA shall establish the SACC with the purpose to "provide independent advice and expert consultation, at the request of [EPA], with respect to the scientific and technical aspects of issues relating to the implementation of this title." The SACC shall be composed of "representatives of such science, government, labor, public health, public interest, animal protection, industry, and other groups as the Administrator determines to be advisable, including representatives that have specific scientific expertise in the relationship of chemical exposures to women, children, and other potentially exposed or susceptible subpopulations."[40]

Self-executing exemptions: Exemptions from PMN requirements that do not require EPA approval.

Significant new use (SNU): A use of a chemical substance that EPA has designated under TSCA section 5(a)(2) as requiring notice prior to manufacture or processing for that use. In determining that a use is a SNU, EPA is to consider "all relevant factors," including "(A) the projected volume of manufacturing and processing of the substance, (B) the extent to which a use changes the type or form of exposure of human beings or the environment to a chemical substance, (C) the extent to which a use increases the magnitude and duration of exposure of human beings or the environment to a chemical substance,

---

37. TSCA § 3(14), 15 U.S.C. § 2602(14); 40 C.F.R. § 720.3(bb) (2023).
38. National Research Council, *supra* note 6.
39. TSCA § 6(b)(4)(A)–(B), 15 U.S.C. § 2605(b)(4)(A)–(B).
40. TSCA § 26(o), 15 U.S.C. § 2625(o).

and (D) the reasonably anticipated manner and methods of manufacturing, processing, distribution in commerce, and disposal of a chemical substance."[41]

Significant new use notice (SNUN): A notice that a manufacturer or processor wishing to engage in a designated SNU must submit at least 90 days before engaging in the new use, if EPA promulgates a SNUR. EPA states that this notification provides it with the opportunity to evaluate the new use and, if necessary, take action to prohibit or limit the activity.

Significant new use rule (SNUR): A rule limiting the manufacture and processing of a chemical substance for a use that EPA has determined to be a SNU.[42]

Test marketing exemption (TME): An exemption from PMN requirements for a manufacturer or importer to distribute a predetermined amount of a chemical substance or mixture, or an article containing that chemical substance or mixture, "to no more than a defined number of potential customers to explore market capability in a competitive situation during a predetermined testing period."[43]

Tiered testing: "[A] tiered screening and testing process, under which the results of screening-level tests or assessments of available information inform the decision as to whether 1 or more additional tests are necessary, unless information available to [EPA] justifies more advanced testing of potential health or environmental effects or potential exposure without first conducting screening-level testing." Tiered testing will be employed by EPA when the development of new information under TSCA section 4(a)(4) is required.[44]

TSCA chemical substance imported as part of a mixture: A chemical substance as set forth in TSCA section 3(2) (15 U.S.C. § 2602(2)) that is part of a combination of two or more chemical substances as set forth in TSCA section 3(10).[45]

TSCA chemical substance imported in bulk form: A chemical substance as set forth in TSCA section 3(2) (15 U.S.C. § 2602(2))

41. TSCA § 5(a)(2), 15 U.S.C. § 2604(a)(2).
42. TSCA § 5(a)(2), 15 U.S.C. § 2604(a)(2); 40 C.F.R. pt. 721 (2023).
43. TSCA § 5(a), (h)(1), 15 U.S.C. § 2604(a), (h)(1); 40 C.F.R. § 720.3(gg) (2023); *id.* § 720.38.
44. TSCA § 4(a)(4), 15 U.S.C. § 2603(a)(4).
45. 19 C.F.R. § 12.120(c) (2024).

(other than as part of an article) in containers used for purposes of transportation or containment, provided that the chemical substance is intended to be removed from the container and has an end use or commercial purpose separate from the container.[46]

TSCA Confidential Inventory: A portion of the TSCA Chemical Substance Inventory of chemical substances manufactured or processed in the United States that consists of chemical substances whose identities are confidential and only accessible to EPA.[47]

TSCA Inventory: A list of each chemical substance that is manufactured or processed in the United States. The Inventory consists of two subsets—the Public Inventory and the Confidential Inventory.[48]

TSCA Public Inventory: A portion of the TSCA Inventory of chemical substances manufactured or processed in the United States that consists of chemical substances whose identities are not confidential. The Public Inventory is accessible to everyone.[49]

United States Code (U.S.C.): The codification by subject matter of the general and permanent laws of the United States. It is divided by broad subjects into 53 titles and published by the Office of the Law Revision Counsel of the U.S. House of Representatives.[50]

Unreasonable risk of injury to health or the environment: A standard to be applied by EPA in determining whether to promulgate a rule or issue an order concerning a chemical substance or mixture. The unreasonable risk standard appears throughout TSCA. For example, EPA is to promulgate section 4 test rules to develop data necessary to determine whether a chemical substance or mixture presents an unreasonable risk of injury to health or the environment. Similarly, EPA is to promulgate a section 6 limitation or ban upon a finding that activities involving a chemical substance or mixture present or will present an unreasonable risk of injury to health or the environment.[51]

46. *Id.* § 12.120(b).
47. *See* TSCA § 8(b), 15 U.S.C. § 2607(b).
48. TSCA § 8(b)(1), 15 U.S.C. § 2607(b)(1).
49. *See* TSCA § 8(b), 15 U.S.C. § 2607(b).
50. References to TSCA in this book are based on the U.S.C. version of TSCA, http://uscode.house.gov/view.xhtml?path=/prelim@title15/chapter53&edition=prelim (last visited Sept. 27, 2024).
51. *See* TSCA §§ 2(a), 2(b), 4(a), 4(e), 4(f), 5(b), 5(e), 5(f), 5(h), 6, 9(a), 12(a)(2), 21(b)(4)(B), 15 U.S.C. §§ 2601(a), 2601(b), 2603(a), 2603(e), 2603(f), 2604(b), 2604(e), 2604(f), 2604(h), 2605, 2608(a), 2611(a)(2), 2620(b)(4)(B).

Appendix C

Checklists, Flowcharts, and Decision Trees

Chapter 2: In a Nutshell: TSCA Overview

"Putting it all together," from TSCA Tutor® T101—An Overview of TSCA, https://training.lawbc.com/courses/t101-an-overview-of-tsca-2023. (*See* Appendix D, Resources, for a coupon for *free access* to T101.)

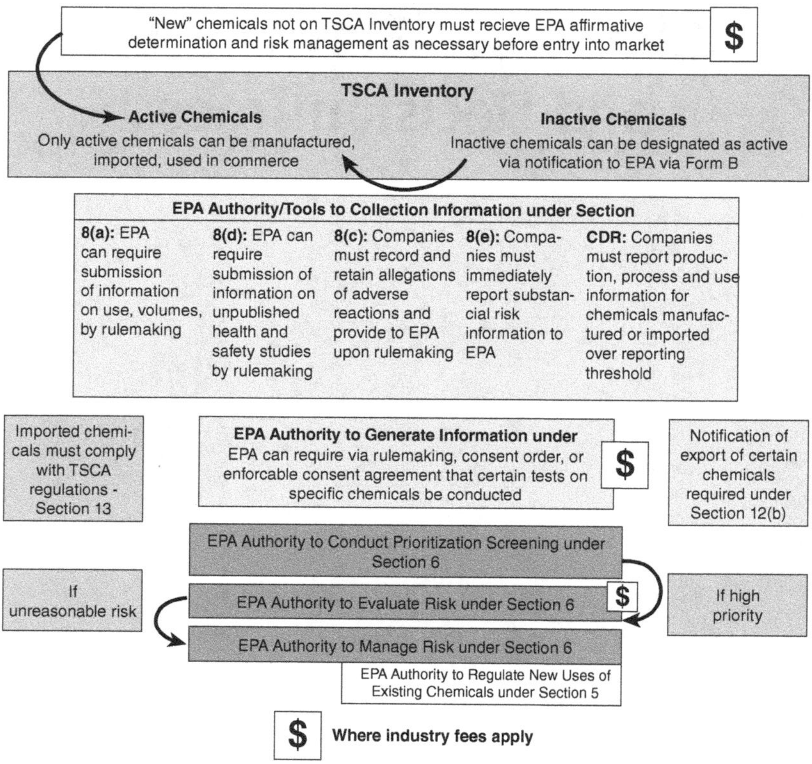

Chapter 3: Importing Chemicals and Other Goods into the United States

EPA, TSCA Section 13 Import Compliance Checklist (2008), https://www.epa.gov/sites/default/files/2015-03/documents/checklist.pdf.

Chart summarizing requirements for the TSCA import certification process:

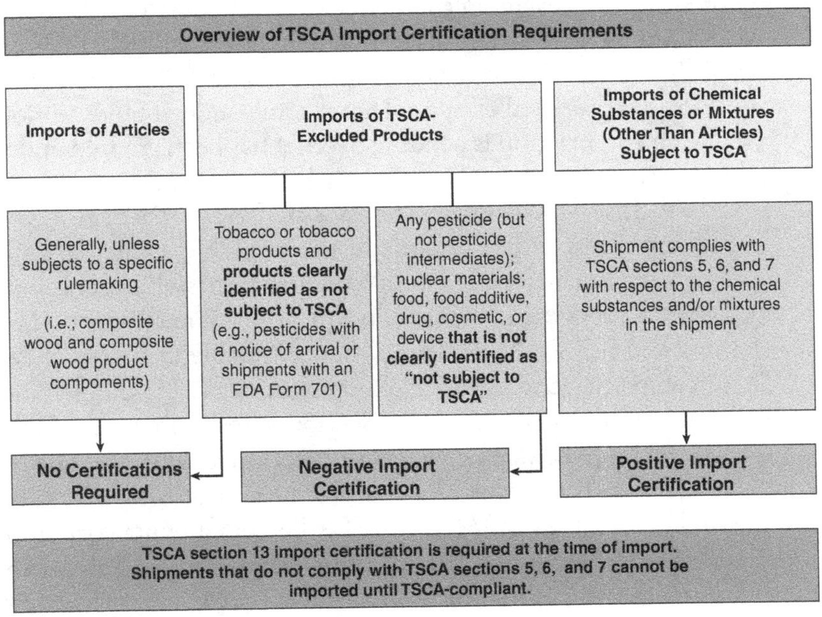

Chapter 5: What Exporters Need to Know

Section 12(a) Export-Only Requirements

- Is the chemical substance or article manufactured, processed, or distributed in commerce only for export?
- If the answer is yes, has the U.S. Environmental Protection Agency (EPA) found that the chemical substance or mixture presents an unreasonable risk of injury to health within the United States or to the environment of the United States?

If the answer to the first question is yes and the answer to the second question is no, the substance qualifies for the "export-only" exemption under section 12(a) of the Toxic Substances Control Act (TSCA). The substance must be labeled in accordance with TSCA section 12(a)(1)(B). Companies must ensure that the substance and any container in which it is enclosed is stamped or labeled "For Export Only." The recordkeeping and reporting requirements of TSCA section 8 still apply.

Section 12(b) Export Notification Requirements

- Search the *Federal Register* (https://www.federalregister.gov/) to determine whether data are required under TSCA section 4 or 5(b); EPA has issued an order under TSCA section 5; EPA has proposed or promulgated a rule under TSCA section 5 or 6; or an action is pending or relief has been granted under TSCA section 5 or 7. Although EPA offers other resources (EPA List of Chemicals Subject to TSCA Section 12(b) Export Notification Requirements, available at https://www.epa.gov/tsca-import-export-requirements/chemicals-subject-tsca-section-12b-export-notification-requirements (last updated July 2, 2024); ChemView, available at https://chemview.epa.gov/chemview/ (last updated Sept. 28, 2024); and List of Chemicals Subject to Section 4 Test Orders, available at https://www.epa.gov/assessing-and-managing-chemicals-under-tsca/list-chemicals-subject-section-4-test-orders (last updated Mar. 25, 2024)), the EPA List of Chemicals Subject to TSCA Section 12(b) Export Notification Requirements states that exporters "have an affirmative obligation to review the *Federal Register* for future publication of actions that may trigger section 12(b) reporting obligations."
- For chemicals subject to a final TSCA section 4 rule, determine if the rule has sunset. If it has, and there are no other export notification triggers, then notification is not required.
- If a chemical substance is subject to TSCA section 12(b) notification based on the *Federal Register* search, it may be present in de minimis quantities such that section 12(b) export notification is not required. Notification is not required for a chemical substance being exported at a concentration of less than 1 percent (by weight or volume), unless that chemical is
  - listed as a "known to be human carcinogen" or "reasonably anticipated to be human carcinogen" in the

National Toxicology Program's (NTP's) *Report on Carcinogens* (https://ntp.niehs.nih.gov/whatwestudy/assessments/cancer/roc);

- classified as a Group 1, Group 2A, or Group 2B carcinogen by the International Agency for Research on Cancer (IARC) in the list of IARC Monographs on the Evaluation of Carcinogenic Risks to Humans and their Supplements (https://monographs.iarc.who.int/); or
- alpha-naphthylamine (Chemical Abstracts Service Registry Number® (CAS RN®) 134-32-7) or 4-nitrobiphenyl (CAS RN 92-93-3).

For chemicals falling into one of the above categories, a de minimis concentration level of less than 0.1 percent (by weight or volume) applies. For exports of polychlorinated biphenyls (PCBs), notification is not required if the chemical is being exported at a concentration of less than or equal to 50 parts per million (ppm) (by weight or volume).

- There also are specific export requirements and restrictions under TSCA section 6 for certain chemicals, including but not limited to PCBs and elemental mercury and mercury compounds.
- For chemical substances subject to section 12(b) export notification, there are either annual or one-time reporting requirements.
    - **Annual reporting**: For chemical substances or mixtures subject to orders or regulations under TSCA section 5(f), 6, or 7, TSCA section 12(b) export notices must be submitted to EPA for the first export of the chemical substance or mixture to each country to which it will be shipped within each calendar year that TSCA section 12(b) requirements apply.
    - **One-time reporting**: For chemical substances or mixtures subject to a TSCA section 4 test rule or enforceable consent agreement (ECA), a section 5(a)(2) rule, a section 5(e) order, or a section 5(b) rule, only a one-time TSCA section 12(b) export notice must be submitted for the first export of that chemical substance or mixture to each country.
- Export notices must be submitted through EPA's Central Data Exchange (CDX) (https://cdx.epa.gov/) within seven days of forming the intent to export or on the date of export, whichever is earlier. A notice of intent to export must be based on a definite contractual obligation, or an equivalent intracompany agreement, to export the regulated chemical.

If the EPA action prompting the notice is a proposed rule, the requirement to submit export notices begins 30 days after publication of the action in the *Federal Register*.

Chapter 6: TSCA and Commercial Transactions: What to Look For

Office of Enforcement and Compliance Assurance (OECA), EPA, Toxic Substances Control Act (TSCA) New and Existing Chemicals Inspection Manual app. E (2022), https://www.epa.gov/system/files/documents/2022-04/tscanewandexistingchemicalinspectionsmanual.pdf.

OECA, EPA, The Enforcement Response Policy for Reporting and Recordkeeping Rules and Requirements for TSCA Sections 8, 12, and 13, at 42 (1999) (Penalty Calculation Worksheet), https://www.epa.gov/sites/default/files/documents/erp8_12r.pdf.

TSCA Due Diligence Review

The following is a representation of some of the major questions to be asked to determine the nature and extent of a company's compliance with requirements under TSCA:

Section 4:

- Has the facility manufactured, imported, or processed a chemical substance for which EPA has issued a final TSCA section 4 test rule that has not sunset? A list of chemical substances subject to a final test rule that have not sunset can be found on EPA's website at https://www.epa.gov/assessing-and-managing-chemicals-under-tsca/sunset-dates-chemicals-subject-final-tsca-section-4-test (last updated Aug. 15, 2024).

Section 5:

- Has the company/facility filed a premanufacture notification (PMN) or a significant new use notice (SNUN)?
- Has the company/facility filed a low volume exemption (LVE), low releases and low exposures exemption (LoREX), an LVE modification, or a LoREX modification?
- Has the company/facility manufactured or imported any chemical substances that qualify for the test market exemption

application (TMEA) or research and development (R&D) exemption from listing on the TSCA Chemical Substance Inventory?

- Does the polymer exemption apply for any chemical substance manufactured or imported by the company/facility?
- Are there any chemical substances manufactured, imported, or domestically purchased that are subject to a significant new use rule (SNUR) under TSCA section 5(a)?

Section 8:

- TSCA section 8(a)—Chemical Data Reporting (CDR)
    - Were any chemical substances manufactured or imported subject to the 2016 or 2020 CDR rule requirements? If you respond "yes," name the chemical substance(s) for which CDR reports were submitted.
    - If a chemical substance was exempt from the 2016 or 2020 CDR requirements (e.g., no manufacture/import, production quantities fewer than 25,000 pounds), describe the nature of the exemption and any documentation the facility has retained demonstrating that exemption criteria are met.
- TSCA section 8(a)— Preliminary Assessment Information Rule (PAIR)
    - Has the company/facility manufactured or imported any chemical substance that has been subject to a PAIR? If you respond "yes," name the chemical substance(s) for which PAIR forms were submitted.
    - If a chemical substance was exempt from PAIR reporting requirements (i.e., production quantities fewer than 500 kilograms per site), describe the nature of the exemption and any documentation the company/facility has retained demonstrating that exemption criteria are met.
- TSCA section 8(c)
    - Is there a TSCA section 8(c) file system in place? If you respond "yes," where are the files maintained?
    - When was the last time the company/facility trained its employees regarding TSCA section 8(c) and the procedures in place to report significant adverse effects?
- TSCA section 8(d)
    - Within ten years of a TSCA section 8(d) health and safety data rule being issued, has the company/facility

manufactured, imported, or distributed any chemical substance that has been subject to a section 8(d) rule (*See* 40 C.F.R. § 716.120 for the list of chemical substances subject to section 8(d) rules.)? If you respond "yes," name the chemical substance(s) for which section 8(d) reports were submitted.
  - If a chemical substance was exempt from section 8(d) reporting requirements (i.e., studies previously submitted to EPA's Office of Pollution Prevention and Toxics), describe the nature of the exemption and any documentation the facility has retained demonstrating that exemption criteria are met.
- TSCA section 8(e)
  - Has a TSCA Section 8(e) Committee been established? If so, when was the last time the committee met?
  - Have any TSCA section 8(e) reports been submitted to EPA? If so, explain the circumstances.
  - Have any "For Your Information," or FYI, reports been submitted to EPA? If so, explain the circumstances and the reason(s) the company/facility did not identify the information as substantial risk information under TSCA section 8(e).

Section 12(b):

- Has the company/facility exported products with chemical substances? If you respond "yes," provide the name of the chemical substance(s) and the product in which it was exported, if applicable.

Section 13:

- Has the company/facility imported chemical substances (including chemical substances that are components of mixtures and chemical substances or mixtures contained in articles that are designed to be used or released from the articles)?
- If you respond "yes," does the company/facility prepare all necessary import certificates or does the company/facility use a broker? If the company/facility uses a broker, please name that company.
- Does the company/facility ever receive unsolicited samples of chemical substances for which import certificates have not

been prepared? If you respond "yes," describe the company/facility's procedures for addressing such circumstances.

- Has the company/facility's import shipments ever been detained by U.S. Customs and Border Protection? If you respond "yes," describe the circumstances and resolution.

Chapter 7: PFAS and TSCA

Steps for determining the applicability of the TSCA section 8(a)(7) reporting rule and requirements for conducting a due diligence review for importers of chemical substances:

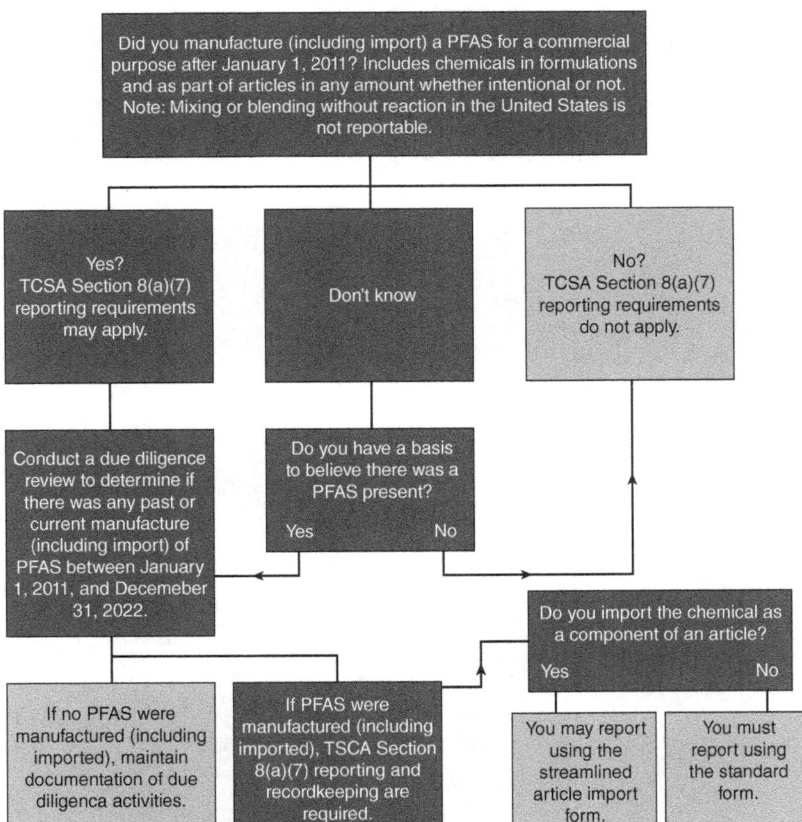

Chapter 8: Enforcement and the Consequences of Noncompliance

OECA, EPA, The Enforcement Response Policy for Reporting and Recordkeeping Rules and Requirements for TSCA Sections 8, 12, and 13, at 42 (1999) (Penalty Calculation Worksheet), https://www.epa.gov/sites/default/files/documents/erp8_12r.pdf.

OECA, EPA, Toxic Substances Control Act (TSCA) New and Existing Chemicals Inspection Manual app. E (2022), https://www.epa.gov/system/files/documents/2022-04/tscanewandexistingchemicalinspectionsmanual.pdf.

Appendix D

Resources[1]

General Resources

Environmental Protection Agency (EPA)

Central Data Exchange (CDX), https://cdx.epa.gov/.

Summary of the Toxic Substances Control Act (TSCA), https://www.epa.gov/laws-regulations/summary-toxic-substances-control-act.

The Frank R. Lautenberg Chemical Safety for the 21st Century Act, https://www.epa.gov/assessing-and-managing-chemicals-under-tsca/frank-r-lautenberg-chemical-safety-21st-century-act.

National Archives

eCFR (Electronic Code of Federal Regulations), http://www.ecfr.gov.

Sample searches: If you are searching for a specific section, search for, for example: 40 cfr 720.30; if you are searching for a specific part, search for, for example: 40 cfr 720; if you are searching for regulations that apply to premanufacture notice (PMN), or premanufacture notification, enter those search terms. You can filter the search by choosing Title 40.

Federal Register, https://www.federalregister.gov/.

Sample searches: If you are searching for a specific *Federal Register* notice, search for, for example: 67 FR 11108; if you are searching for notices addressing significant new use rules, enter significant new use rule, or SNUR. You can organize your search results by relevant, newest, or oldest.

1. All websites last visited September 27, 2024.

Bergeson & Campbell, P.C. (B&C®)

TSCAblog®, https://www.lawbc.com/brand/tscablog/.

News and analysis from B&C's TSCA team regarding TSCA reform implementation and related legal and administrative developments.

TSCA FAQs, https://www.lawbc.com/news/knowledge-resources-faq-tsca/.

TSCA Tutor®, https://training.lawbc.com/collections/tscatutor.

B&C is pleased to offer our suite of online, on-demand regulatory training courses. Professionals seeking expert, efficient, essential training can enroll in on-demand classes to complete at their own pace and timing. Online courses are offered at $100 for one-hour modules and $200 for two-hour modules. Course bundles are available at a reduced cost per course.

The full TSCA Tutor curriculum is listed at the end of this appendix, with a coupon for *free access* to the "T101—Overview of TSCA" course.

Chapter 1: Old TSCA and the Forces That Led to Its Revitalization

Lynn L. Bergeson, *Do It Now, or It May Never Be Done*, Env't F., May/June 2014, at 46, https://www.lawbc.com/lynn-l-bergeson-tsca-reform-do-it-now-or-it-may-never-be-done-eli-forum-may-june-2014/.

Lynn L. Bergeson, *TSCA Reform: The New State of Play*, Env't Quality Mgmt., Winter 2013, https://www.lawbc.com/lynn-l-bergeson-tsca-reform-the-new-state-of-play-environmental-quality-management-winter-2013/.

Chapter 2: In a Nutshell: TSCA Overview

FDA, Federal Food, Drug, and Cosmetic Act (FD&C Act), https://www.fda.gov/regulatory-information/laws-enforced-fda/federal-food-drug-and-cosmetic-act-fdc-act.

EPA, Federal Insecticide, Fungicide, and Rodenticide Act (FIFRA), https://www.epa.gov/enforcement/federal-insecticide-fungicide-and-rodenticide-act-fifra-and-federal-facilities.

EPA, TSCA Chemical Substance Inventory, https://www.epa.gov/tsca-inventory.

Lynn L. Bergeson, *Toxics Regulation: A Brave New World Catching Many Off Guard*, 6 PLI CURRENT (2022), https://www.lawbc.com/uploads/docs/Bergeson_PLI_Current_Vol6_2022.pdf.

CHAPTER 3: IMPORTING CHEMICALS AND OTHER GOODS INTO THE UNITED STATES

OECA, EPA, COMPLIANCE GUIDE FOR THE CHEMICAL IMPORT REQUIREMENTS OF THE TOXIC SUBSTANCES CONTROL ACT (2008) https://www.epa.gov/compliance/compliance-guide-chemical-import-requirements-toxic-substances-control-act.

U.S. CUSTOMS AND BORDER PROTECTION (CBP), CBP AND TRADE AUTOMATED INTERFACE REQUIREMENTS: TIPS FOR TRADE WHEN FILING AN EPA TSCA CERTIFICATION IN ACE (2019), https://www.cbp.gov/document/publications/ace-tips-filing-epa-tsca.

CBP, CBP AND TRADE AUTOMATED INTERFACE REQUIREMENTS: EPA SUPPLEMENTAL GUIDELINES (2024), https://www.cbp.gov/document/forms/epa-supplemental-catair-guidelines.

EPA, OCTOBER 2022 REFRESHER FOR NCBFAA ON EPA IMPORT PROGRAMS: RESPONSE TO WEBINAR QUESTIONS (updated 2023), https://www.epa.gov/system/files/documents/2023-10/updated-_final-epa-import-programs-refresher-q-and-a_october-2023-ptd_0.pdf.

EPA issued a "*statement* of policy" for TSCA imports in December 1983 found at 40 C.F.R. § 707.20.

Chapter 4: New and Existing Chemicals: How EPA Evaluates and Manages Risk

Chemical Abstracts Service (CAS), https://www.cas.org/.

EPA

Reviewing New Chemicals under the Toxic Substances Control Act (TSCA), https://www.epa.gov/reviewing-new-chemicals-under-toxic-substances-control-act-tsca.

TSCA Chemical Substance Inventory, https://www.epa.gov/tsca-inventory.

Filing a Pre-manufacture Notice with EPA, https://www.epa.gov/reviewing-new-chemicals-under-toxic-substances-control-act-tsca/filing-pre-manufacture-notice-epa.

Sample PMN Form, https://www.epa.gov/reviewing-new-chemicals-under-toxic-substances-control-act-tsca/sample-premanufacture-notification.

Identifying Existing Chemicals for Prioritization under TSCA, https://www.epa.gov/assessing-and-managing-chemicals-under-tsca/identifying-existing-chemicals-prioritization-under.

Chapter 5: What Exporters Need to Know

TSCA

TSCA section 12, 15 U.S.C. § 2611, https://www.govinfo.gov/content/pkg/USCODE-2022-title15/html/USCODE-2022-title15-chap53-subchapI-sec2611.htm.

C.F.R.

40 C.F.R. Part 707, Subpart D, Notices of Export under Section 12(b), https://www.ecfr.gov/current/title-40/chapter-I/subchapter-R/part-707/subpart-D.

40 C.F.R. § 720.3, Definitions, https://www.ecfr.gov/current/title-40/chapter-I/subchapter-R/part-720#720.3.

40 C.F.R. § 721.3, Definitions, https://www.ecfr.gov/current/title-40/chapter-I/subchapter-R/part-721/subpart-A/section-721.3.

EPA

Chemicals Subject to TSCA Section 12(b) Export Notification Requirements, https://www.epa.gov/tsca-import-export-requirements/chemicals-subject-tsca-section-12b-export-notification-requirements.

The list includes a disclaimer that it is intended simply as an information resource and that exporters "have an affirmative obligation to review the Federal Register for future publication of actions that may trigger section 12(b) reporting obligations."

ChemView, https://chemview.epa.gov/chemview/.

ChemView includes an option to search for a list of chemicals subject to TSCA section 12(b) export notification. The text of consent orders can also be found on ChemView by searching for a PMN number.

List of Chemicals Subject to Section 4 Test Orders, https://www.epa.gov/assessing-and-managing-chemicals-under-tsca/list-chemicals-subject-section-4-test-orders.

Chapter 6: TSCA and Commercial Transactions: What to Look For

Lynn L. Bergeson, *Due Diligence in Mergers and Acquisitions Involving Chemical Products*, Financier Worldwide (2022), https://www.lawbc.com/lynn-l-bergeson-due-diligence-in-mergers-and-acquisitions-involving-chemical-products-financier-worldwide-october-2022/.

Incentives for Self-Policing: Discovery, Disclosure, Correction, and Prevention of Violations, 65 Fed. Reg. 19,618 (Apr. 11, 2000) (Audit Policy), https://www.govinfo.gov/content/pkg/FR-2000-04-11/pdf/00-8954.pdf.

Interim Approach to Applying the Audit Policy to New Owners, 73 Fed. Reg. 44,991 (Aug. 1, 2008) (New Owners Interim Approach), https://www.govinfo.gov/content/pkg/FR-2008-08-01/pdf/E8-17715.pdf.

Civil Monetary Penalty Inflation Adjustment, 88 Fed. Reg. 89,309, 89,312 (Dec. 27, 2023), https://www.govinfo.gov/content/pkg/FR-2023-12-27/pdf/2023-28555.pdf.

EPA

OECA, EPA's Audit Policy Program: Frequently Asked Questions (2021), https://www.epa.gov/sites/default/files/2021-02/documents/epaauditpolicyprogramfaqs2021.pdf.

Press Release, EPA Announces Renewed Emphasis on Self-Disclosed Violation Policies (May 15, 2018), https://www.epa.gov/sites/default/files/2018-05/documents/refreshannouncementfordisclosures.pdf.

OECA, Toxic Substances Control Act (TSCA) New and Existing Chemicals Inspection Manual (2022), https://www.epa.gov/system/files/documents/2022-04/tscanewandexistingchemicalinspectionsmanual.pdf.

Protocol for Conducting Environmental Compliance Audits of Facilities with PCBs, Asbestos, and Lead-Based Paint Regulated under TSCA (2000), https://www.epa.gov/sites/production/files/documents/apcol-tsca.pdf.

OECA, Compliance Monitoring Strategy for the Toxic Substances Control Act (TSCA) (2016), https://www.epa.gov/sites/default/files/2014-01/documents/tsca-cms.pdf.

Enforcement Response Policy for Test Rules under Section 4 of the Toxic Substances Control Act (1986) (Section 4 ERP), https://www.epa.gov/enforcement/enforcement-response-policy-tsca-section-4-test-rules.

Amended TSCA Section 5 Enforcement Response Policy (1993) (Section 5 ERP), https://www.epa.gov/sites/default/files/2016-06/documents/amendedtscasection5-erp.pdf.

The Enforcement Response Policy for Reporting and Recordkeeping Rules and Requirements for TSCA Sections 8, 12, and 13 (1999) (Sections 8, 12, and 13 ERP), https://www.epa.gov/enforcement/issuance-revised-enforcement-response-policy-tsca-sections-812-13.

EPA Administrative Enforcement Dockets, https://yosemite.epa.gov/OA/RHC/EPAAdmin.nsf.

EPA's Enforcement and Compliance History Online (ECHO) database, https://echo.epa.gov/.

Filing a Pre-Manufacture Notice with EPA ("Transfer notice" requirement), https://www.epa.gov/reviewing-new-chemicals-under-toxic-substances-control-act-tsca/filing-pre-manufacture-notice-epa#tab-3&#transfer.

Successor Transfer Forms under TSCA Section 5, https://www.epa.gov/reviewing-new-chemicals-under-toxic-substances-control-act-tsca/successor-transfer-forms-under-tsca.

"Transfer Notice" Form for Section 5(e) Consent Orders, https://www.epa.gov/sites/default/files/2016-09/documents/sucesr5e.pdf.

Fact Sheet: Reporting after Changes to Company Ownership or Legal Identity (2020), https://www.epa.gov/chemical-data-reporting/fact-sheet-reporting-after-changes-company-ownership-or-legal-identity-2020.

Maintenance of CBI Contact/Ownership Questions, https://www.epa.gov/tsca-cbi/final-rule-requirements-confidential-business-information-claims-under-tsca#Maintenance%20of%20CBI%20contact/ownership%20questions.

Chapter 7: PFAS and TSCA

TSCA

TSCA section 8(a)(7), 15 U.S.C. § 2607(a)(7), https://www.govinfo.gov/content/pkg/USCODE-2022-title15/html/USCODE-2022-title15-chap53-subchapI-sec2607.htm.

C.F.R.

40 C.F.R. § 721.9582, SNUR for certain perfluoroalkyl sulfonates, https://www.ecfr.gov/current/title-40/chapter-I/subchapter-R/part-721/subpart-E/section-721.9582.

40 C.F.R. § 721.10536, SNUR for long-chain perfluoroalkyl carboxylate chemical (LCPFAC) substances, https://www.ecfr.gov/current/title-40/chapter-I/subchapter-R/part-721/subpart-E/section-721.10536.

40 C.F.R. § 721.11777, SNUR for PFAS designated as inactive on the TSCA Inventory, https://www.ecfr.gov/current/title-40/chapter-I/subchapter-R/part-721/subpart-E/section-721.11777.

40 C.F.R. Part 705, Reporting and Recordkeeping Requirements for Certain PFAS, https://www.ecfr.gov/current/title-40/chapter-I/subchapter-R/part-705.

EPA

Enforcement Alert: Violations May Put Ski Wax Users at Risk from Illegal Perfluoroalkyl Substances (Jan. 2022), https://www.epa.gov/system/files/documents/2022-01/pfasskiwax.pdf.

Framework for TSCA New Chemicals Review of PFAS Premanufacture Notices (PMNs) and Significant New Use Notices (SNUNs) (2023), https://www.epa.gov/system/files/documents/2023-06/PFAS%20Framework_Public%20Release_6-28-23_Final_508c.pdf.

Letter from Tala R. Henry, Ph.D., Deputy Director, Office of Pollution Prevention and Toxics, EPA, to Manufacturers, Processors, Distributors, Users, and Those That Dispose of Fluorinated Polyolefin Containers (Mar. 24, 2022), https://www.epa.gov/system/files/documents/2022-03/letter-to-fluorinated-hdpe-industry_03-16-22_signed.pdf.

National PFAS Testing Strategy: Identification of Candidate Per- and Polyfluoroalkyl Substances (PFAS) for Testing (2021), https://www.epa.gov/system/files/documents/2021-10/pfas-natl-test-strategy.pdf.

PFAS Low Volume Exemption Stewardship Program, https://www.epa.gov/reviewing-new-chemicals-under-toxic-substances-control-act-tsca/pfas-low-volume-exemption.

PFAS Strategic Roadmap: EPA's Commitments to Action 2021–2024 (2021), https://www.epa.gov/system/files/documents/2021-10/pfas-roadmap_final-508.pdf.

Risk Management for Per- and Polyfluoroalkyl Substances (PFAS) under TSCA, https://www.epa.gov/assessing-and-managing-chemicals-under-tsca/risk-management-and-polyfluoroalkyl-substances-pfas.

TSCA Section 8(a)(7) Reporting and Recordkeeping Requirements for Perfluoroalkyl and Polyfluoroalkyl Substances, https://www.epa.gov/assessing-and-managing-chemicals-under-tsca/tsca-section-8a7-reporting-and-recordkeeping.

B&C

Per- and Polyfluoroalkyl Substances (PFAS) News and Information, https://www.lawbc.com/per-and-polyfluoroalkyl-substances-pfas-news-and-information/.

PFAS: Bans, Restrictions, Reporting, and Minimizing Liability (2024), https://www.lawbc.com/wp-content/uploads/PFAS_Summary.pdf?version=1.1.

Lynn L. Bergeson, *Reporting PFAS: Reporting Burden Is the Least of Businesses' Worries*, Financier Worldwide (2023), https://www.lawbc.com/lynn-l-bergeson-reporting-pfas-reporting-burden-is-the-least-of-businesses-worries-financier-worldwide-july-2023/.

Nongovernmental Organization (NGO)

Safer States, Safer States: Bill Tracker, https://www.saferstates.org/bill-tracker/?.

Chapter 8: Enforcement and the Consequences of Noncompliance

Toxic Substances Control Act, https://www.govinfo.gov/app/details/COMPS-895/.

40 C.F.R. § 372.5, Persons subject to this part, https://www.ecfr.gov/current/title-40/section-372.5.

Federal Register, https://www.federalregister.gov/.

Regulations.gov, https://www.regulations.gov/.

EPA

Substance Registry Services, https://cdxapps.epa.gov/oms-substance-registry-services/search.

EPA Compliance Resources

Compliance, https://www.epa.gov/compliance#resources.

National Compliance Assistance Centers, https://www.compliance assistance.net/.

Toxic Substances Control Act (TSCA) Hotline, https://www.ep a.gov/aboutepa/epa-hotlines#tscah.

Welcome to EPA FAQs, https://usepa.servicenowservices.com/ecss /en?id=ecss_kb_home&kb_id=98a9e8ce1b4858104614ddb6bc4 bcb03.

Compliance: Toxic Substances Control Act (TSCA) Compliance Monitoring, https://www.epa.gov/compliance/toxic-substances -control-act-tsca-compliance-monitoring.

OECA, Compliance Monitoring Strategy for the Toxic Substances Control Act (TSCA) (2016), https://www.epa.gov/com pliance/compliance-monitoring-strategy-toxic-substances-control -act-tsca.

Compliance: Resources and Guidance Documents for Compliance Assistance: Toxic Substances, https://www.epa.gov/compliance/reso urces-and-guidance-documents-compliance-assistance#toxic.

OECA, Compliance Guide for the Chemical Import Requirements of the Toxic Substances Control Act (2008), https://www.epa .gov/compliance/compliance-guide-chemical-import-requirements -toxic-substances-control-act.

EPA Audit Policies

Compliance: EPA's Audit Policy, https://www.epa.gov/compliance /epas-audit-policy.

Compliance: Small Business Compliance, https://www.epa.gov/com pliance/small-business-compliance.

EPA Inspection Resources

Compliance: Resources and Guidance Documents for Compliance Monitoring, https://www.epa.gov/compliance/resources-and-guidance -documents-compliance-monitoring.

OECA, Toxic Substances Control Act (TSCA) New and Existing Chemicals Inspection Manual (2022), https://www.epa.gov/system/files/documents/2022-04/tscanewandexistingchemicalinspectionsmanual.pdf.

PCB Inspection Manual (2004), https://www.epa.gov/sites/default/files/2013-09/documents/pcbinspectmanual.pdf.

National Policy: The Role of the EPA Inspector in Providing Compliance Assistance during Inspections (2003), https://www.epa.gov/compliance/policy-role-epa-inspector-providing-compliance-assistance-during-inspections.

EPA Enforcement Goals and Initiatives

Enforcement, https://www.epa.gov/enforcement.

Planning Budget Results: EPA Strategic Plan, https://www.epa.gov/planandbudget/strategicplan.

Planning Budget Results: National Program Guidances (NPGs), https://www.epa.gov/planandbudget/national-program-guidances-npgs.

Enforcement: National Enforcement and Compliance Initiatives, https://www.epa.gov/enforcement/national-enforcement-and-compliance-initiatives.

Enforcement: Compliance Advisories and Enforcement Alerts, https://www.epa.gov/enforcement/compliance-advisories-and-enforcement-alerts.

Enforcement: Environmental Justice in Enforcement and Compliance Assurance, https://www.epa.gov/enforcement/environmental-justice-enforcement-and-compliance-assurance.

EJScreen: Environmental Justice Screening and Mapping Tool, https://www.epa.gov/ejscreen.

EPA Enforcement Actions and Penalty Policies

Enforcement: Basic Information on Enforcement, https://www.epa.gov/enforcement/basic-information-enforcement.

Enforcement: Enforcement Policy, Guidance & Publications, https://www.epa.gov/enforcement/enforcement-policy-guidance-publications.

Enforcement: Enforcement Policy, Guidance & Publications: General Civil Enforcement Penalty Policies, https://www.epa.gov/enforcement/enforcement-policy-guidance-publications#general.

Enforcement: Enforcement Policy, Guidance & Publications: Penalty Inflation Rules and Penalty Policy Amendments, https://www.epa.gov/enforcement/enforcement-policy-guidance-publications#penalty.

Enforcement: Enforcement Policy, Guidance & Publications: Additional Cross-Program Policies and Guidance, https://www.epa.gov/enforcement/enforcement-policy-guidance-publications#additional.

Enforcement: Small Businesses and Enforcement, https://www.epa.gov/enforcement/small-businesses-and-enforcement.

Enforcement: Waste, Chemical and Cleanup Enforcement Policy, Guidance, and Publications, https://www.epa.gov/enforcement/waste-chemical-and-cleanup-enforcement-policy-guidance-and-publications.

EPA Enforcement Cases and Related Data

Enforcement and Compliance History Online (ECHO), https://echo.epa.gov/.

Enforcement: Civil and Cleanup Enforcement Cases and Settlements, https://www.epa.gov/enforcement/civil-and-cleanup-enforcement-cases-and-settlements.

Enforcement: Summary of Criminal Prosecutions, https://www.epa.gov/enforcement/summary-criminal-prosecutions.

EPA Administrative Enforcement Dockets, https://yosemite.epa.gov/OA/RHC/EPAAdmin.nsf.

Filings, Procedures, Orders, and Decisions of EPA's Administrative Law Judges, https://www.epa.gov/alj.

Environmental Appeals Board, https://yosemite.epa.gov/oa/EAB_Web_Docket.nsf/.

EPA Cited Documents

Press Release, EPA's Annual Enforcement Results Shows Significant Increase in Enforcement Activity to Protect Communities from Pollution (Dec. 18, 2023), https://www.epa.gov/newsreleases/epas-annual-enforcement-results-shows-significant-increase-enforcement-activity#:~:text=Additional%20highlights%20of%20our%20accomplishments,of%2070%25%20over%20FY%202022.

Enforcement and Compliance Annual Results for Fiscal Year 2023, https://awsedap.epa.gov/public/extensions/FEC_AR2023/FEC_AR2023.html#IRslide.

Enforcement and Compliance History Online (ECHO): EPA Cases, https://echo.epa.gov/.

EPA Administrative Enforcement Dockets, https://yosemite.epa.gov/OA/RHC/EPAAdmin.nsf.

Administrative Law Judges: Dockets, Decisions & Orders, https://www.epa.gov/alj/dockets-decisions-orders.

Environmental Appeals Board: Board Decisions, https://yosemite.epa.gov/oa/EAB_Web_Docket.nsf/Board+Decisions?OpenPage.

Enforcement: Civil and Cleanup Enforcement Cases and Settlements, https://www.epa.gov/enforcement/civil-and-cleanup-enforcement-cases-and-settlements.

Draft Office of Enforcement and Compliance Assurance National Program Guidance, Fiscal Years 2025–2026 (2024), https://www.epa.gov/system/files/documents/2024-04/fy25-26-oeca-draft-npg.pdf.

Office of Enforcement and Compliance Assurance National Program Guidance, Fiscal Years 2023–2024 (2022), https://www.epa.gov/system/files/documents/2022-08/fy-2023-2024-oeca-npg.pdf.

Office of Enforcement and Compliance Assurance National Program Guidance, Fiscal Years 2020–2021 (2019), https://www epa.gov/planandbudget/final-fy-2020-2021-office-enforcement-and-compliance-assurance-oeca-national-program.

National Policy: The Role of the EPA Inspector in Providing Compliance Assistance during Inspections (2003), https://www.epa.gov/compliance/policy-role-epa-inspector-providing-compliance-assistance-during-inspections.

Enforcement Response Policy for Test Rules under Section 4 of the Toxic Substances Control Act (1986) (Section 4 ERP), https://www.epa.gov/sites/default/files/documents/tscasec4ruleserp-052886.pdf.

Amended TSCA Section 5 Enforcement Response Policy (1993) (Section 5 ERP), https://www.epa.gov/sites/default/files/2016-06/documents/amendedtscasection5-erp.pdf.

The Enforcement Response Policy for Reporting and Recordkeeping Rules and Requirements for TSCA Sections 8, 12, and 13 (1999) (Sections 8, 12, and 13 ERP), https://www.epa.gov/sites/default/files/documents/erp8_12r.pdf.

Memorandum from EPA to EPA Regional Administrators et al., Amendments to the EPA's Civil Penalty Policies to Account for Inflation (Effective Jan. 15, 2024) (Jan. 10, 2024), https://www.epa.gov/system/files/documents/2024-01/amendmentstotheepacivilpenaltypolicyinflation011524.pdf.

Memorandum from EPA to EPA Regional Counsels and Deputies et al., Strategic Civil-Criminal Enforcement Policy (Apr. 17, 2024), https://www.epa.gov/system/files/documents/2024-04/strategic-civil-criminal-enforcement-policy-april-2024.pdf.

Memorandum from EPA to EPA Regional Administrators, Issuance of the 2015 Update to the 1998 U.S. Environmental Protection Agency Supplemental Environmental Projects Policy (Mar. 10, 2015), https://www.epa.gov/sites/default/files/2015-04/documents/sepupdatedpolicy15.pdf.

Memorandum from EPA Office of Regulatory Enforcement to Regional Counsel and Regional Program Management Division Directors, Regions I–X, Guidance on the Application of the Federal Five-Year Statute of Limitations to Administrative and Judicial Civil Penalty Proceedings (July 13, 1994).

Memorandum from EPA to EPA Regional Counsel et al., Guidance on Evaluating a Violator's Ability to Pay a Civil Penalty in an Administrative Enforcement Action (June 29, 2015), https://www.epa.gov/enforcement/guidance-evaluating-ability-pay-civil-penalty-administrative-enforcement-actions.

Enforcement: Penalty and Financial Models, https://www.epa.gov/enforcement/penalty-and-financial-models.

Other Cited Documents

3M Co. v. Browner, 17 F.3d 1453 (D.C. Cir. 1994).

40 C.F.R. Part 22, Consolidated Rules of Practice Governing the Administrative Assessment of Civil Penalties and the Revocation/ Termination or Suspension of Permits.

Consolidated Rules of Practice Governing the Administrative Assessment of Civil Penalties, Issuance of Compliance or Corrective Action Orders, and the Revocation, Termination, or Suspension of Permits, 64 Fed. Reg. 40,138 (July 23, 1999).

Consolidated Rules of Practice Governing the Administrative Assessment of Civil Penalties, Issuance of Compliance or Corrective Action Orders, and the Revocation/Termination or Suspension of Permits: Procedures for Decisionmaking, 82 Fed. Reg. 2,230 (Jan. 9, 2017).

Incentives for Self-Policing: Discovery, Disclosure, Correction, and Prevention of Violations, 65 Fed. Reg. 19,618 (Apr. 11, 2000) (Audit Policy).

TSCA Tutor® Curriculum

B&C is pleased to present our suite of regulatory training courses online and on demand at https://training.lawbc.com/. Professionals seeking expert, efficient, essential training can enroll in on-demand classes to complete at their own pace and timing. The courses were developed and are presented by members of B&C's renowned TSCA practice group. Online courses are offered at $100 for one-hour modules and $200 for two-hour modules. Course bundles are available at a reduced cost per course. Enrollment is valid for one full year.

B&C is pleased to offer readers of this book a *complimentary enrollment* in "T101—An Overview of TSCA." Use the coupon code ABAT101 at checkout to receive a 100% discount on enrollment.

One-Hour Courses

T101—An Overview of TSCA: This module provides a general overview of TSCA—its legislative intent, key components, and role in the management of industrial chemicals. This module is especially useful for anyone who is engaged in commercial activities, any component of which is regulated by TSCA—chemical manufacturers, processors, distributors, importers, and end users of chemical substances.

T103—Import Requirements, TSCA Section 13: This module focuses on TSCA import requirements, including discussions on how to work with foreign suppliers in preparing joint submissions to EPA.

T104—Export Requirements, TSCA Section 12: This module focuses on TSCA export requirements, including timelines associated with reporting sunset provisions and the application of the de minimis concentration exemption.

T105—Confidential Business Information (CBI): Protecting a company's confidential and proprietary ingredients and/or processes and related confidential information is commercially critical. The rules of the game have changed dramatically, however, and the stakes have never been higher in understanding what is presumptively CBI, what is not, how the process works, for how long, and what your rights are when challenged. This module focuses on all these important aspects of TSCA.

T106—Reporting and Retention of Information, TSCA Section 8: TSCA, especially the Frank R. Lautenberg Chemical Safety for the 21st Century Act ("new TSCA"), is data- and information-driven, and stakeholders are required to generate and maintain copious amounts of information, some of which must be shared with EPA and the public through a much-reviewed EPA electronic database. Curating this information is critically important both for compliance purposes and in terms of managing a narrative for your commercial partners, neighbors, competitors, and shareholders. This module reviews these critically important requirements. It also covers adverse effects identification and reporting. Being able to pick an adverse effect out of the TSCA lineup is crucially important at several levels. Violations of this "TSCA 8(e)" provision have proven to attract record-setting EPA penalties in the multiple million-dollar range, as EPA considers it one of the most important obligations under TSCA. Failure to identify an adverse effect can invite commercially devastating consequences in terms of product and toxic tort liability. This module instructs on how to identify an adverse effect and how to develop a TSCA section 8(e) reporting process that is legally sufficient and effective.

Two-Hour Courses

T201—Inspections and Audits:

Preparing for a TSCA audit. Any commercial entity engaged in the manufacture, import, process, and/or use of chemicals regulated under TSCA is subject to EPA enforcement and compliance inspection authority. When EPA elects to conduct such inspections, it does not typically give facility operators much time to prepare. Knowing what EPA will ask for before it sends a formal letter is critically important in determining how well a company will fare under the audit.

TSCA penalties/overview of self-confession policy. The penalties that can be assessed under TSCA are not trivial—up to $37,500 per violation, per day. While no one intends to be found in noncompliance with TSCA, it is possible that it could occur; knowing how EPA calculates potential penalties is important in negotiating with EPA. This module covers these areas and EPA penalty policies related to those circumstances in which a company finds noncompliance during internal review processes and elects to self-report to EPA.

T202—TSCA Section 5 (Part 1) Chemical Inventory, Exemptions:

Definitions. Understanding the language of TSCA is critical, as key terms and new concepts added by new TSCA are heavily nuanced and in some cases evolving. "Conditions of use," "potentially exposed and susceptible subpopulations," and "significant new use" are but three of the many terms unique to TSCA and upon which the complex regulation of industrial chemicals rests.

TSCA Inventory. The TSCA Chemical Substance Inventory (TSCA Inventory) is a component that is critically important in understanding the great divide between new chemicals, for which EPA pre-market approval is required; active existing chemicals, for which commercialization is permitted, unless a TSCA Inventory flag tells us otherwise; and inactive existing chemicals. What is a TSCA Inventory flag, what is listed on the TSCA Inventory and why, and most importantly what is not listed on the TSCA Inventory are concepts critical to TSCA compliance. This module includes an overview as to how a company can determine if chemical(s) of interest are included on the TSCA Inventory. It also covers aspects of new TSCA of which chemical stakeholders should be aware.

Exemptions. There are a number of self-executing exemptions that permit companies to manufacture or import substances that are not listed on the TSCA Inventory without notifying EPA in advance. This module examines the various exemptions and provides insight into how to ensure compliance with some of the most frequently used exemptions, including the polymer, research and development (R&D), nonisolated intermediate, export-only, and "h(7)" exemptions.

T203—TSCA Section 5 (Part 2) New Chemicals/New Use:

New chemicals/new use. If a chemical is not listed on the TSCA Inventory and not otherwise exempt from section 5 notification, EPA must review the "new" chemical and make a judgment as to whether it is likely to pose unreasonable risk. If EPA is unable to make the determination or decides that it is likely to pose unreasonable risk, the new chemical's commercialization prospects are diminished or destroyed—a devastating commercial consequence. This module carefully reviews the how, what, and why of EPA's new chemical review process, how to develop a smart premanufacture notice, or a "smart PMN," and how to manage efficiently the EPA review process.

SNURs. SNURs are the new normal under TSCA, and a significant number of new chemical reviews result in these regulations. What SNURs are, how to decipher the rule language, why their issuance is sometimes inevitable, and how they can be averted are the focuses of this module. This module also covers required downstream communication requirements for SNURs that potentially affect all entities along the value chain—manufacturers, importers, distributors, formulators, repackagers, and users.

T204—Chemical Data Reporting (CDR):

CDR overview. Every four years, chemical manufacturers and importers are required to provide EPA with information on the chemicals they produce. The information is often not straightforward, and missteps in reporting can invite enforcement and commercial liability. This module focuses on discharging these reporting obligations and successfully reporting the information electronically in EPA's Chemical Data Exchange (CDX) system.

Byproduct reporting under the CDR rule. Companies today are working toward more sustainable manufacturing processes that include opportunities to reuse or reprocess byproduct chemicals that might otherwise be disposed of as waste. Under current EPA policies, these recycled, reused, and/or reprocessed byproducts could be viewed as manufactured chemicals and, thus, subject to reporting under the CDR rule. This module provides an overview of the EPA byproducts policies and which byproduct substances are subject to reporting.

T205—Chemical Testing (Regulatory)/Animal Welfare:

Chemical testing. New TSCA provides new authority to EPA to compel chemical testing. This module focuses on what chemical stakeholders must do when confronted with a chemical testing order and considers strategies to address chemical testing smartly and efficiently.

How to prepare/engage if a chemical of interest is listed under TSCA section 4. EPA has indicated its view that it expects companies to develop a coordinated response in addressing testing needs under section 4. The creation of industry testing consortia is, thus, anticipated. Such coordination must include cost sharing for data required under the testing order, cost sharing of EPA fees, and the cost of identifying and administering needed consortia management work. Understanding EPA's expectations, coupled with today's business realities on establishing and participating in these types of groups, is essential.

T206—Prioritization and Risk Evaluation:

Overview of section 6 risk framework—prioritization, evaluation, and management. Amended TSCA includes a rigid process and timeframe for the evaluation of chemicals under TSCA section 6. This module reviews the steps that EPA will take to identify high-priority chemicals, the evaluation process applied to high-priority chemicals, and risk management approaches that are applied to chemicals found by EPA to pose unreasonable risk.

How to prepare/engage if a chemical of interest is listed under section 6. EPA has indicated its view that it expects companies to develop a coordinated response in information gathering under section 6. The creation of industry testing consortia is, thus, anticipated. Such coordination must include cost sharing for data submitted, cost sharing of EPA fees, and the cost of identifying and administering needed consortia management work. Understanding EPA's expectations, coupled with today's business realities on establishing and participating in these types of groups, is essential.

Index

D